Routledge Revivals

Politics, Foreign Trade and Economic Development

Politics, Foreign Trade and Economic Development (1986) discusses politics, foreign trade and economic development in the Dominican Republic in order to show why the country is so poor and to put forward suggestions concerning how the position might be improved. It argues that a major reason for poor economic performance is the fact that successive regimes have been more committed to increasing personal wealth of the rulers than to fostering the economic development of the country.

Politics, Foreign Trade and Economic Development

A Study of the Dominican Republic

Claudio Vedovato

Routledge
Taylor & Francis Group

First published in 1986
by Croom Helm Ltd

This edition first published in 2026 by Routledge
4 Park Square, Milton Park, Abingdon, Oxon, OX14 4RN

and by Routledge
605 Third Avenue, New York, NY 10017

Routledge is an imprint of the Taylor & Francis Group, an informa business

A Library of Congress record exists under LCCN: 86003825

ISBN: 978-1-041-29435-1 (hbk)
ISBN: 978-1-003-76948-4 (ebk)
ISBN: 978-1-041-29436-8 (pbk)

Book DOI 10.4324/9781003769484

POLITICS, FOREIGN TRADE & ECONOMIC DEVELOPMENT

A Study of the Dominican Republic

Claudio Vedovato

CROOM HELM
London & Sydney

Croom Helm Ltd, Provident House, Burrell Row
Beckenham, Kent BR3 1AT
Croom Helm Australia Pty Ltd
64–76 Kippax Street, Surry Hills, NSW 2010, Australia

British Library Cataloguing in Publication Data
Vedovato, Claudio
Politics, foreign trade and economic development:
a study of the Dominican Republic.
1. Dominican Republic——Economic policy
I. Title
330.97293'05 HC153.5
ISBN 0-7099-2621-9

Printed and bound in Great Britain by
Biddles Ltd, Guildford and King's Lynn

CONTENTS

for my parents

ACKNOWLEDGEMENTS

The present book is a slightly revised version of my doctoral thesis presented at the University of Lund in February 1985. During my work I have been able to draw on the valuable comments made by numerous participants during the regular seminars in international economics at the Department of Economics.

Yves Bourdet, Anders Danielsson, Björn Hansson, Göte Hansson, Lennart Petersson, Carl Hampus Lyttkens, Tore Sjökvist and Åsa Weibull all read earlier drafts and their scrutiny and helpful suggestions have undoubtedly helped to improve the quality of the study. Erling Petersson also provided invaluable assistance when trying to solve the arcane mysteries of the word processor.

I am particularly grateful to my supervisor Mats Lundahl who has combined profound learning with a sincere engagement in my work. His help and support have been invaluable.

Professor Hans Illy improved the quality of the work by a number of constructive criticisms. Arne Bigsten read the manuscript at an early stage and provided valuable comments.

I also owe a special thanks to Jan and Rosemary Lundius who suggested various improvements. Moreover, this study would never have been completed without their encouragement and hospitality during my stay in Santo Domingo.

I also wish to thank Alan Harkess who undertook the difficult task of converting my 'English' into English. The financial assistance from the Swedish Agency for Research and Cooperation with Developing Countries (SAREC), without which this book could not have been published, is also gratefully acknowledged. The Institute of Latin American Studies, Stockholm, has also provided financial support for which I wish to express my gratitude.

1 INTRODUCTION

This book is about the long-run economic development of a small open economy, the Dominican Republic. The main thread of this study is the important role played by political and institutional factors in the Dominican economy. The behaviour of the state deserves particular consideration. It will thus be shown how the state has influenced both the pattern of development (sectoral composition of output, structure of foreign trade, etc.) and the distribution of income. The behaviour of the state has had a strong impact on the formation of property rights in land and hence on the consequent organization and utilization of agricultural resources. The state has not mainly been interested in generating overall development, as has often, at least implicitly, been assumed in studies on development. In the present case the state can rather be viewed as an instrument by which certain individuals or groups have been able to alter the distribution of income in their favour. The behaviour of different governments thus accounts for many of the economic difficulties confronting the Dominican Republic.

In the study much concern will be given to the development of international trade and its impact on the Dominican economy. Our focus on foreign trade is motivated by the importance of this sector in the Dominican Republic. An indicator of the importance of foreign trade for the Dominican economy is the fairly high ratio (0.46) of exports plus imports to gross domestic product.[1]

The mere size of the foreign sector makes trade and trade policy a central issue for the Dominican Republic as well as for many developing countries. Much of the development debate during the last decades has also circled around the trade strategy on which developing countries should embark. Comparative studies on trade strategies are among the most comprehensive and discussed works on development.[2]

The focus on foreign trade in the present study will also highlight the importance of the state in economic development since different Dominican governments have had a particular concern for foreign trade. The behaviour of the state has been important for the shaping of the structure of the country's foreign trade and for the distribution of the gains from trade.

The Role of the State

In general, economic theory has been concerned with the allocation of resources via 'impersonal' market forces. In models where individual producers and consumers are too small to decide over anything but quantities to produce and consume, the resource base, technology and demand determine the level and structure of output, and income distribution. Little has normally been said about the ownership of production factors or about political factors. This also applies to studies on development. In his widely used reader *Leading Issues in Economic Development*, where the mainstream of the subject is presented, Gerald Meier expresses some dissatisfaction with the present state of arts, stressing that economists should try to '. . . evaluate more thoroughly the non economic factors in the development process'.[3]

The structure of land ownership is often taken as given in development studies. However, the formation of property rights in land will have a profound impact on agricultural organization and income distribution and thereby represent a major factor in the process of economic development. In a study of the long-run development of the Dominican economy we must therefore include an analysis of the formation of property rights in land. It will be shown that these have largely been an outcome of non-market forces. The use of violence or threats of violence have been very important for the formation of property rights in land.

The argument presented in this book is that without consideration of non-market factors, the production and trade structures of the Dominican Republic cannot be fully understood. There are individuals and groups which, through for instance their access to violence, have had an extensive impact upon how Dominican resources have been used and how income has been distributed.

Both the use or potential use of violence and the formation of property rights is intimately connected with the nature and behaviour of the state.

The rationale for state intervention has in economic theory mainly been based on the presence of market failures; public goods, externalities, etc., and the need for stabilization policy. In the literature on development the government is often given a more ample sphere of activity as the launching of ambitious development plans. The government is also generally assumed to be impartial in the sense that in the choice between different policy options its only concern is for the public interest.

Discussing the rationale for government policies Benjamin Higgins argues that the economist or development planner '. . . will accept the objectives laid down by government, with the belief — or at least the hope — that the government will be responsible to the people and responsive to their wishes.'[4]

A similar spirit permeates Meier's book where government implicitly is assumed to selflessly select policies among available options. In *Leading Issues* there is a large section on planning and policy making where several more or less sophisticated planning models are presented. Nothing is however said about the aims of governments, and very little is said about weak administrations or about extensive corruption, making the implementation of such plans, even if they should be desired by government, illusory.

The approach used in this book is another. In many developing countries, governing may be seen primarily as a way of increasing the rulers' share of the national wealth. To increase personal wealth may even in some cases be seen as the only motive for gaining political power.[5] Hence the notion of a 'predatory state'.[6] If we assume that the primary motive for the ruler is to enhance his own wealth we may expect overall economic inefficiency to be the consequence. There will normally be a conflict between the property rights which maximize the wealth of those in power and those which lead to overall economic efficiency/growth. Overall inefficiency may thus be the *rule* rather than exception.

It will be argued that government power in the Dominican Republic has traditionally been used to increase the rulers' personal wealth and to favour certain groups or individuals. This has created a situation where the conditions facing different economic actors have been extremely disparate. These government-induced distortions are thus not a result of lack of knowledge or competence but mainly a consequence of deliberate action consistent with government preferences. The point that we would wish to make is that different governments and persons connected with government have been able, often by the use of force, to change 'the rules of the game' in order to improve their own position, and this has not been conducive to development.

In our analysis of the causes of the difficulties confronting the Dominican economy, distortions and inefficiences induced by different governments will play a central role. We will give attention to such policies and to the relation between policies and different interest groups. The behaviour of the state can be considered, it will be argued, to account for a considerable part of the country's economic problems.

Before presenting in more detail the plan of the study, it is necessary to outline some of the economic and social problems of the Dominican Republic.

Some Aspects of Dominican Underdevelopment

The Dominican Republic discloses most features instrinsic to underdevelopment: low average income, a very skewed distribution of income and property, massive unemployment, widespread malnutrition, etc. The following figures should give a picture of the kinds of problems with which our study is ultimately concerned.

The *per capita* income in the Dominican Republic amounted to US$ 1,237 in 1980.[7] This figure is below the average of US$ 2,320 for the Caribbean and Latin America, but comparable to that of countries such as Colombia (1,237), Guatemala (1,082) and Ecuador (1,361).[8] However, the Dominican Republic is relatively well off in comparison with its extremely poor neighbour Haiti, which has an average income of US$ 283 (1980). Income is very unequally distributed. Fifty per cent of the population receive only 13 per cent of total income, while the richest 6 per cent receive 43 per cent.[9]

One reason for this inequality in income is the extremely skewed distribution of land. The structure of land ownership is an issue on which we will have much to say in later chapters. It is sufficient here to note that 2.7 per cent of the farms own 54 per cent of total land, while 72 per cent of the farms control less that 13 per cent.[10] This concentration of land strongly contributes to deplorable living conditions in rural areas. The average daily intake of calories and protein is far below the level recommended by the Dominican authorities. Moreover, 64 per cent of rural families have an average income below or near the rural poverty line.[11] In the capital, Santo Domingo, open unemployment amounts to about 20 per cent while about 60 per cent of those who hold jobs are underemployed.[12]

Growth rates have, despite this gloomy picture, been fairly satisfactory during the last two decades. The growth of GDP *per capita* averaged 3.5 per cent per year between 1960 and 1979, a figure which is in line with the average for the Caribbean and Latin America and for the developing market economies as a whole (3.3 and 3.6 per cent, respectively).[13] Two alarming trends are however manifest. First, the agricultural sector has lagged behind. The production of food for internal consumption, was lower, in *per capita* terms, in 1980 than in 1960.[14] Second, overall growth has decreased after the mid-1970s and the decline has been conspicuous during the last few years. *Per capita* GDP increased by only 0.6 per cent in 1981 and fell by 1.3 per cent in 1982.[15] According to preliminary figures, a small recovery took place in 1983.[16]

Dominican Foreign Trade

Dominican exports are concentrated on a few primary commodities. This is a characteristic which the country shares with many Third World countries. Table 1.1 gives the composition of Dominican exports in 1970 and 1981.

Table 1.1: Structure of Dominican Exports, Percentage Composition

	1970	1981
Traditional Exports	87.9	64.1
Raw sugar and sugar by-products	51.7	47.1
Coffee	13.5	6.4
Cocoa beans	9.0	3.8
Leaf tobacco	6.6	5.5
Bauxite	7.1	1.3
Non-traditional Exports	12.1	35.2
Gold and silver	—	17.5
Ferronickel	—	9.3
Chemical fertilizers	—	1.2
Leather manufactures	—	0.5
Other manufactured products	—	4.6
Other agricultural products	2.9	2.1

— nil or insignificant

Source: ECLA (1983b), p. 701.

Four agricultural products: sugar, coffee, cocoa and tobacco, have traditionally made up the bulk of Dominican exports. The most important product, sugar, has traditionally accounted for 50 to 60 per cent of exports. The increased exploitation of gold and silver deposits has implied that the share of traditional agricultural exports has decreased during the past decade. However, exports remain highly concentrated and this high dependence on a few products makes the economy very susceptible to fluctuations in world market prices. The economy is of course particularly vulnerable to changes in sugar prices. Table 1.2 portrays the development of both world market prices for sugar and the value of Dominican sugar exports.

Table 1.2: World Market Prices and Value of Dominican Exports of Sugar

Current prices	1974	1975	1976	1977	1978	1979	1980	1981	1982	1983	1984
Price: USc/pound[a]	29.7	20.4	11.5	8.1	7.8	9.6	28.9	16.9	8.4	7.1	5.2
Exports: Million Dominican pesos	340	577	269	231	181	200	309	533	281	263	275

Note: a. Not all sales are made at these average annual prices. Price received will depend on the timing of sales. A variable proportion of exports are made at preferential prices to the United States.

Source: Banco Central, *Boletín Mensual*, various issues.

Table 1.2 shows that price fluctuations have been quite pronounced. After the peak years 1974 and 1975, prices declined considerably during the late seventies. A rise in 1980 was followed by a sharp drop in 1981 and 1982. The decline, which continued in 1983 and 1984, would be more manifest if account was taken of inflation.

Table 1.3 shows the development of the price of coffee and cocoa during recent years at nominal prices. To some extent the price decline between 1977–8 and the early 1980s magnified the difficulties caused by the drop in the price of sugar. The net effect of price changes during recent years has been a terms of trade deterioration of 15 per cent between 1979 and 1983.[17]

Table 1.3: Prices for Dominican Coffee and Cocoa (US$/100 pounds)

Current prices	1976	1977	1978	1979	1980	1981	1982	1983	1984
Coffee	134	223	153	168	119	105	120	129	135
Cocoa	97	176	154	132	98	74	61	90	107

Source: Banco Central, *Boletín Mensual*, various issues.

The deficits in the balance of payments have been considerable. The current account in 1982 showed a deficit of 442 million pesos which, compared to total exports of 767 million, gives an indication of the magnitude of the difficulties.[18] In 1983 the *trade* deficit was 448 million while exports amounted to 782 million.[19]

It can be argued that the picture given in Tables 1.2 and 1.3 exaggerates the difficulties caused by external factors since sugar prices were unusually high in 1974, as were prices of coffee and cocoa in 1977. In fact, in terms of a longer view there does not appear to be any downward trend in the Dominican terms of trade. With 1970=100, the terms of trade index was 73.6 and 82.3 in 1960 and 1965, respectively, compared to 86.6 in 1979 and 103.2 in 1980.[20] This also shows that the present difficulties are not simply of a cyclical nature. For instance, after 1963 the country has actually faced a constant current account deficit, even during the years when export prices have been high.[21]

World market prices were no less volatile during the 1950s and early 1960s than today, but at that time the current account mainly exhibited surpluses. The fact that the terms of trade do not appear to show any long-run downward trend also indicates that mainly internal factors account for the problems generated.

In this study, we will thus be concerned with internal factors, and although we have indicated the recent development of some macroeconomic variables, such as the balance of payments, our interest will be focused on issues of a long-run nature. We have pointed to the fact that *per capita* production of agricultural products has stagnated over a long period and that the distribution of income and land is very unequal. These are issues which we will give considerable consideration. Stagnating rural incomes combined with a fast rate of population growth, about 3 per cent per year, create a strong necessity to provide employment off the land. Industrialization policies have, however, not served to foster an efficient industry able to absorb the increase in urban labour force and to provide foreign exchange. The shortcomings of industrialization policies will be discussed.

The Dominican Republic: A Plantation Economy

The cornerstone of the Dominican economy and society is sugar. Sugar is much more than an important export product. A good deal of Dominican hopes for development are connected to sugar.

So are much of its factual failures. Sugar is a crop that concerns the whole nation. The weekly participation of the Dominican president in the board meeting of the huge state sugar council is well covered in mass media. Every night the telecast news report the daily price quotation of raw sugar on the New York market.

The fact that price quotations on a distant commodity exchange mean so much for the Dominican economy, creates a particular way of thinking. It creates a notion of 'dependence', i.e. a view that Dominican development, or lack of development, depends on forces beyond the country's own control. This is a common phenomenon in the Third World, since many developing countries are in a situation comparable to that of the Dominican Republic. For about half of the developing countries, one export product makes up between 50 and 75 per cent of total exports.[22]

The fact that so much depends on fluctuating world market prices makes Dominican scholars and policy makers give much consideration to issues beyond Dominican reach. They repeatedly complain about low export prices, which are sometimes said to be unfair.[23] They constantly stress the need to make international efforts to improve the terms of trade.[24]

We do not want to belittle the problems caused by fluctuating world market prices. These fluctuations are of course troublesome. But there is not much Dominican policy makers can do about world market prices, and prices are not unfair just because they are too low to make Dominican sugar exports profitable.

The roots of the Dominican problems are very much internal and related to how Dominican resources are used. These are issues on which policy makers have had, and continue to have, an influence. Both scholars and policy makers complain on the 'unfair' international division of labour as if the Dominican specialization on sugar exports was something forced upon them by rich nations.[25] Although during the United States occupation (1916–24) force was used in order to expand American sugar estates, the expansion of sugar production is mainly a consequence of internal decisions and actions. In fact two-thirds of Dominican sugar production is today supplied by a hugh state producer.

The enormous expansion of the sugar industry during this century has transformed the Dominican Republic into what many observers have called a 'monoculture', since such a large share of the country's arable land is dedicated to sugar cane production.

George Beckford has also used the term 'plantation economy' to characterize the Dominican Republic.[26] Since such a large share of the Republic's resources are used for sugar production, policies concerning the sugar sector have an important impact not only on the sugar sector *per se*, but of course on the whole Dominican economy.

The losses of the state sugar council have for several years constituted a drain on resources. Despite low sugar prices and continued losses for the state sugar producer, decision makers have not taken any real steps towards diversification of production, although the word diversification is constantly used in official publications. Since the economy's susceptibility to wide price fluctuations is repeatedly deplored, one could imagine that diversification would be a highly desirable target for economic policies. However, the policies pursued have rendered diversification more difficult.

We will give much consideration to the development of the sugar plantation sector. It will be shown that the behaviour of the state has been a determinant factor for the expansion of this sector. It has been in the interest of different Dominican rulers, primarily interested in political survival and wealth, to promote the development of sugar plantation production. The discussion on the expansion of the plantation sector will also serve to illustrate the discrimination by the state of the peasant sector.

Plan of the Study

The Dominican State and Economic Development

A factor that will be emphasized in our analysis is the crucial role of the state in the economic life of the Dominican Republic. In Chapter 2 we will discuss the role of the state in the country in a historical context. We will start by reviewing some of the views presented by different observers: political scientists, sociologists, etc., on the role of the state in developing countries in general. These scholars point to the extensive abuse of power, which may take the form of, for instance, private use of the public treasury, illicit taxation or seizing of property from others, in poor countries. Terms such as 'parasitism' and 'kleptocracy' are employed to describe this form of exercising political power. A notion that will be much used in the present work is that of a 'predatory state' according to which the state is an instrument for the ruler or ruling class to increase the ruler's/ruling class' share of the national income. Such a state will normally enforce property rights that reduce overall efficiency.

It will then be argued that Dominican governments conform with the predatory view of the state. Persons in power have mainly used the state apparatus for their personal benefit. The promulgation of different laws, the use of the treasury, etc., has primarily served the interests of those in power. The state sets the 'rules of the game' for the economic actors but our discussion suggests that 'economic development' has not been the aim of the country's rulers. Rulers may very well have implemented policies which, while increasing the wealth and security of the rulers themselves, have led to lower national income. Consequently, the behaviour of the state can be considered to account for a significant part of Dominican underdevelopment.

The Predatory State and International Trade

A conspicuous feature of Dominican trade is the concentration on a few primary exports, particularly sugar. This high reliance on sugar exports has, as we have suggested, important repercussions for the Dominican economy and society. An important task for trade theory is, of course, to explain the structure of trade. Trade theory also discusses the static welfare gains from trade and the relation between trade and development. In Chapter 3 we will very briefly consider how these issues are treated in the literature. The traditional (neoclassical) comparative advantage version of trade will be contrasted with some approaches that emphasize institutional factors in explaining production and trade structures. Our ambition is not to make a survey of trade theory, but rather to present some notions to which the subsequent discussion of Dominican trade will be referred. The analysis in subsequent chapters will for instance show that the well-known Hecksher-Ohlin theory cannot provide a satisfactory explanation of why the Dominican economy today is so heavily specialized on sugar production. The trade structure of the Dominican Republic cannot be understood without consideration to institutional factors.

A framework will then be outlined which will help, in this context, to explain the concentration of substantial economic resources in the production of a single export plantation crop. The combination of, on the one hand, a strong state, which through its activities exerts a major influence on the trade structure, and which is primarily interested in collecting taxes and gaining control of foreign exchange, and on the other, the presence of transaction and monitoring costs, may lead to an allocation of resources (and trade structure) quite different from that which would obtain in the decentralized world with zero transaction costs of traditional trade theory.

The Development of the Export Economy: Sugar

The framework developed in Chapter 3 will be employed in Chapter 4 where we set out to discuss the reasons for the Dominican economy's heavy dependence on sugar exports. Large-scale sugar production started in the late nineteenth century and has expanded during the present, very much due to special institutional arrangements. During the United States occupation of the Dominican Republic, land legislation was changed to the convenience of American sugar companies. The dictator Rafael Trujillo used his army and the state treasury to expand sugar production during the 1950s, and the institutional arrangement under which sugar has been produced since the death of Trujillo has maintained the pro-plantation bias. We will thus try to show that it has been in the interest of Dominican rulers, which have aimed at increasing their personal security and wealth, to promote plantation production. This outcome could not have been predicted by traditional theory.

The other side of pro-plantation policies is an anti-peasant bias. While sugar plantations in the late nineteenth century could expand partly on uncultivated land, measures were soon taken in order that plantations could establish control over peasant land. The new land legislation, promulgated during the American occupation, was certainly not undertaken for the benefit of peasants. In fact many peasants were dispossessed of their land under the auspices of the new law. Even today, peasants claim the right to land controlled by sugar estates. Trujillo continued to alienate land from the peasants. It will thus be evident that the present structure of land ownership is not an outcome of the smooth working of the price system.

While the state has provided infrastructure for the sugar estates and *latifundios*, the lack of roads, electricity, irrigation, etc., is conspicuous in peasant areas. These policies reflect both the weak link between peasant production and the income of the rulers, and the lack of political influence by the peasants.

Plantation Exports and Development

Gottfried Haberler has stated: 'My overall conclusion is that international trade has made a tremendous contribution to development of less developed countries in the nineteenth and twentieth centuries . . .'[27] Our analysis in Chapter 5 will cast some doubts on the validity of such an assertion for the Dominican Republic. Despite secular involvement in large-scale sugar exports, with a large share of production resources devoted to export production, living conditions for a majority of the Dominican population are still deplorable and conditions for the workers in the sugar industry have been compared to slavery. This is not because there is something intrinsically wrong with foreign trade. Rather, the argument is that the trade pattern reflects the interests of the state and influential plantation owners and *latifundistas* and that these thus have been able to reap the lion's share of the profits from international trade.

Those institutional factors which have favoured the plantation sector have had detrimental effects on other economic variables. The concentration of land in a few hands has for instance had very negative effects. Apart from the obvious effect on income distribution, the concentration of land ownership has led to a low overall utilization of land, which has contributed to lagging agricultural production and poor nutritional levels.

Profits generated in the sugar industry by foreign estates have mainly been repatriated and Trujillo placed substantial amounts of dollars in foreign banks. Since wages in the sugar industry have been kept very low through extensive labour imports, there have been few incentives to improve production techniques. The contribution to capital accumulation and technical progress by large-scale sugar exports does accordingly appear to have been limited.

The Political Economy of Import Substitution

The anti-peasant bias implied by policies favouring the plantation sector and *latifundios* has been reinforced by industrialization policies pursued during the past two decades. These policies will be discussed in Chapter 6. Import substitution had started during the Trujillo era. Trujillo had raised tariffs to protect his own industry. In the mid-1960s the industrial sector was still quite small. The administration of Joaquín Balaguer stimulated production of industrial products for the home market. This was done by increasing tariffs and giving special privileges to industries that were classified according to an 'incentive law' promulgated in 1968. This gave classified firms access to inputs that were exempt from tariffs, and they received extensive tax exemptions. Cheap credit have been geared towards classified firms. The Dominican peso has been maintained at par with the US dollar, while the price of the dollar on the parallel market has increased. Price regulations have been introduced for most agricultural goods in order to keep food prices low.

The consequence of these policies for the Dominican economy is similar to the experience of other countries pursuing similar policies. Lack of competition has created an inefficient industry, with most firms operating at very low levels of capacity utilization. Dependence on imported inputs has increased. Exports have stagnated and the agricultural sector has lagged behind.

The distortions created are largely a reflection of the fact that different interest groups have had influence on government decisions. The influence of 'large business' on government policy accounts for much of the inefficiency generated.

Import Substitution vs Export Promotion? Industrial and Agricultural Policies for Development

Economists within the neoclassical tradition almost unanimously condemn import substitution strategies. The comparative OECD and NBER studies provide evidence, from different countries, of the negative consequences of such strategies. The experience of the Dominican Republic, discussed in Chapter 6, suggested that the industrialization policies pursued in this country have not been very successful either. However, we should be very careful not to blame everything that has gone wrong on 'import substitution'. In Chapter 7, which includes a discussion of the experience of some other developing countries which appear to have pursued rather successful policies, it will be suggested that unequal distribution of income, lagging agricultural production, etc. in the Dominican Republic is probably more the result of a general discrimination of the peasants through the very skewed distribution of land, distortion in the credit market, lack of rural extension service, etc. than a consequence of tariffs and import prohibitions on industrial goods. The importance of trade policies for explaining differences in economic performance among countries should thus not be exaggerated. We however side with the mainstream view on the role given to the exchange rate. The exchange rate should, it will be argued, be allowed to reflect more closely the scarcity of foreign exchange.

Conclusion

In Chapter 8 we will first sum up some of the main arguments concerning the relation between the Dominican state and economic development presented in the book. Finally we will briefly discuss whether continued democratic rule of the Dominican Republic can be expected to lead to policies that improve overall economic performance. Reference will be made to recent policies and some possible constraints on the behaviour of the government will be mentioned. This discussion does not allow us to be particularly optimistic about the course of future events.

Appendix: Studies on the Dominican Economy

Many Dominican economists publish books containing newspaper articles which have been written over a period of years. Recent examples of such publications are Hugo Guiliani's *Reflexiones acerca de la economía Dominicana*,[28] Bernardo Vega's *Comentarios sabatinos*[29] and Lucas Vicens' *Crisis Economica 1978–1982*.[30]

Of more analytical interest are PhD theses on Dominican issues published in US universities. The following represent the most interesting from the point of view of the present study.

Rural poverty and the slow growth of agriculture is discussed in a thesis by Eric Graber: *Strategy, Policies and Programs for Economic Growth and Social Progress: with Reference to Rural Development*.[31]

Evaluating an FAO programme, the possibility of increasing yields within the existing agrarian structure, is analysed by George Munguia in *A Transitional Stage in the Agricultural Sector: The Case of the Dominican Republic*.[32] Farmers who had access to technical assistance and credit attained higher yields than farmers in the same areas who did not receive such assistance.

Different policies affecting the rural sector are discussed by Norberto Quezada in *Endogeneous Agricultural Price and Trade Policy in the Dominican Republic*.[33]

With regards to studies on the country's foreign trade the early formation of the Dominican export base is discussed in an economic history thesis by Paul Muto *The Illusory Promise: the Dominican Republic and the Process of Economic Development, 1900–1930*.[34] Muto describes some aspects of how the modern Dominican economy was built on the production and exports of sugar. However the study is not very analytical.

The most voluminous work on the Republic's foreign trade is Gustavo Volmar's thesis *Impact of the Foreign Sector on the Domestic Economic Activity of the Dominican Republic 1950–1967*.[35] The study is an agglomeration of regression equations on aggregate economic variables. Imports are regressed on exports, for yearly data, without lags and with exports lagged one and two periods, and for quarterly data, without lags and with exports lagged one and two periods. In addition, imports are disaggregated to imports of foodstuffs, machinery, cars, etc., and each variable correlated with different domestic price indices, with and without lags. Exports are regressed on investment and gross domestic product. All this is done twice, first for the period 1950 to 1958, and then for 1959 to 1967. However, Segundo does not try to give a sound analytical underpinning of the equations he is estimating. On the contrary, the regressions are usually supplemented with a host of *ad hoc* explanations of why, for example, the correlation coefficient for an equation where the independent variable is lagged two periods is larger than when it is lagged one period. Despite its size, 476 pages, and its ambition to present a 'broad analysis' this work is of very limited interest when it comes to explaining the role of foreign trade in the Dominican Republic.

Bernardo Vega,[36] Fabio Rafael[37] and Alieto Aldo[38] discuss some aspects of import substitution policies. The works of Ramon Tamames[39] and Bernardo Vega[40] discuss the opportunities for regional co-operation.

Statistics are generally in short supply. The development of the economy before 1950 is mostly undocumented except for data on foreign trade.[41] But also for the most recent period there is a shortage of information of various kinds.

Notes

1. International Monetary Fund (1983), p. 243.
2. Cf. the OECD study summarized in Little, Scitovsky and Scott (1970) and the NBER study summarized in Bhagwati (1978) and Krueger (1978). See Chapter 6 for additional references.

3. Meier (1976), p. 851. The writings of Gunnar Myrdal do give much consideration to institutional factors. See Myrdal (1957), (1968) and (1977).
4. Higgins (1959), p. 370.
5. Haiti seems to come close to such a case. See Lundahl (1985).
6. See Chapter 2.
7. United Nations (1983), p. 7.
8. Ibid. As observed by for instance Boserup (1978) GDP figures from developing countries are usually impaired by serious shortcomings.
9. Wiarda and Kryzanek (1982), p. 52.
10. See Chapter 4.
11. The rural poverty line was drawn, in 1978, at 35 pesos per month, see World Bank (1978a), p. 13. Actual intake (in 1982) of calories by 50 per cent of the population, is half of what is recommended by the authorities. See Moya Pons (1982c), p. 120.
12. See Chapter 6.
13. United Nations (1982).
14. ECLA (1983a), pp. 578–9. See Chapter 5 for details.
15. ECLA figures in Rubí (1984), p. 250.
16. ECLA (1984).
17. Ibid.
18. International Monetary Fund (1985), p. 176. The external debt amounted to US$ 1,916 million at the end of 1982. Debt servicing amounted to 50 per cent of the value of exports the same year. Rubí (1984).
19. International Monetary Fund (1985), p. 176.
20. ECLA (1983a).
21. See for instance IMF (1983), pp. 242–3.
22. See Hansson (1984).
23. Vega (1982), p. 80. See also Vicens (1982).
24. See for instance speech by José Francisco Peña Gomez in Del Villar (1979). Peña Gomez is party secretary of the party in government, *Partido Revolucionario Dominicano*.
25. See for instance Vicens (1982), p. 32.
26. Beckford (1972), p. 244.
27. Haberler (1959), p. 5.
28. Guiliani (1980).
29. Vega (1982).
30. Vicens (1982).
31. Graber (1978).
32. Munguia (1975).
33. Quezada (1981).
34. Muto (1976).
35. Volmar (1971).
36. Vega (1973).
37. Rafael (1973).
38. Aldo (1975).
39. Tamames (1968).
40. Vega (1966) and (1978).
41. Quezada (1981), p. 12.

2 THE DOMINICAN STATE AND ECONOMIC DEVELOPMENT

A central theme throughout this book is that a study of economic development should include an analysis of the behaviour of the state. The discussion in the following chapters will show that government-induced distortions, in the land market, credit market, etc., are important elements in explaining many of the economic difficulties that confront the Dominican Republic today. The secular discrimination against the peasant sector is particularly marked.

Accordingly this chapter will deal with the role of government/state in Dominican development. It will be argued that the main motivation of Dominican rulers has been to increase their personal security and wealth. The state has accordingly enforced property rights and rules that govern the economic actions which have served these objectives. The consequence for overall 'efficiency' has clearly been detrimental.

First we will consider a number of studies which discuss politics and the role of the state in developing countries in general. We will start our review of the Dominican experience by discussing the pre-Trujillo period before 1930. This period was mainly characterized by the fight between different *caudillos* who used state power for personal enrichment. Attention will then be paid to the 1930–61 period when the country was ruled by Rafael Trujillo. This is the period when the conflict between the interests of the ruler and the Dominican society perhaps stands out most clearly. Finally, the post-Trujillo period will briefly be discussed. We will have more to say about the most recent period in the final chapter in the book, Chapter 8.

The Predatory State

Economists have often assumed that the state is a benevolent actor, correcting market failures as in the welfare theory tradition, or, generally, providing a general, disinterested commitment to an improvement of 'society's' welfare. More recently, however, the state has received an increasing amount of attention by the economic profession. The approach crystallized in the so-called public choice school is that government and the bureaucracy have their own utility functions. The relation between government decisions and different interest groups has been discussed. Yet this increasing interest in the behaviour of the state, and institutions in general, has failed to make any profound impression on the literature on development. There are of course excellent exceptions, such as the writings of Gunnar Myrdal whose interest for institutional factors is of early origin.[1] But on the whole development economists continue to pay scant consideration to the state in their analysis of developing countries.

This is a serious lacuna. The state is omnipresent in the economic life of developing countries and governing may often be seen primarily as a way of increasing the ruler's share of the national wealth. This also implies that government may implement policies which while they increase the wealth of the ruler may even lead to a decrease of national income.

The economic historian Douglass North argues that despite the fact that the behaviour of the state is essential for there being or not being economic growth, economists have traditionally paid little attention to the issue. According to North the study of economic history requires an analysis of the state: '. . . models of the state should be an explicit part of any analysis of secular changes'.[2] Development economics is typically concerned with long-run issues, such as the conditions for structural change and sustained growth, and the state should thus be given a more important role in studies on development.

Before looking at North's model of the state, which to some extent will act as guide in this study, we will briefly consider some views on the state in developing countries put forth by some non-economists.

The link between economic development and politics in Latin America is discussed by the sociologist Stanislaw Andreski who observes that graft is an important aspect of politics in this region as well as in other underdeveloped areas. Andreski argues that the poorer a society the greater the likelihood that politics will take the form of graft or parasitism since there are less opportunities to become wealthy outside the political arena: 'The greater and more general the poverty the more important the stakes of political contests.'[3] He also affirms that '. . . throughout Latin America political power has always been the surest and quickest way to wealth and more often than not it was the only way'.[4]

Thus poverty stimulates parasitism. But extensive parasitism will in turn maintain a country poor. Parasitism means that there are people who succeed in obtaining a large share of wealth without contributing to its production. Andreski argues that by destroying the link between effort and reward parasitism constitutes a powerful brake on economic progress.

Andreski chooses to term 'kleptocracy' a system where public office is used for illegal acquisition of wealth. Kleptocracy has many facets and may operate at all levels of the administrative and political system. Thus the police may themselves pocket the proceeds from fictitious fines and clerks may expect to be compensated for complying with formalities. As an individual's influence over society increases there is a concomitant increase in the opportunity for accumulating wealth. The Latin American dictators have thus been the greatest kleptocrats. Dictators have made use of the treasury, public land, seizure of property from others, taxation, etc., to reward supporting groups and increasing their personal wealth.

Violence or threat of violence is according to Andreski a vital aspect of parasititsm and of Latin American politics:

> Even when there is no open fighting the government rests entirely or partly on naked force: everywhere there are important sections of the population which would disobey or even overthrow the government if they were not forcibly restrained.[5]

The political scientists Harold Lasswell and Abraham Kaplan use the term 'predatory state' for a society where brigandage is the predominant form of power. In such a society those who are specialists in violence will constitute the ruling clique.[6]

Samuel Huntington, also a political scientist, terms 'oligarchical praetorianism' the political system which dominated nineteenth century Latin America and which has persisted in the twentieth century in the Caribbean. A praetorian society lacks, according to Huntington, political institutions which are recognized as legitimate intermediaries to moderate group conflict. Group interest thus faces group interest in a rather direct way. The dominant groups in oligarchical praetorianism are the great landowners, the leading clergy and the 'wielders of the sword'. 'Families, cliques, and tribes struggle unremittingly with each other for power, wealth and status.'[7]

The importance of violence is also stressed by North who states that '. . . the key to understanding the state, involves the potential use of violence to gain control over resources'.[8] Since the state enforces property rights and the 'rules of the game' which condition economic performance, violence is also an important element in economic development/underdevelopment. Our discussion, below and in subsequent chapters, shows that violence has been an integral part of the exercising of political power in the Dominican Republic and has thus had important effects on economic development.

Two general explanations for the state exist according to North: a contract theory and a predatory or exploitation theory. Contract theories explain the development of efficient[9] property rights and the state thus plays the role of wealth maximizer for society. These models can be seen as logical extensions of the theorems of exchange and are held by many neoclassical economists. According to the predatory view, the state is instead an '. . . agency for a group or class; its function, to extract income from the rest of the constituents in the interest of that group or class.'[10] Such a state '. . . would specify a set of property rights that maximize the revenue of the group in power regardless of its impact on the wealth of the society as a whole'.[11] The distribution of 'violence potential' is crucial for the nature of the ensuing state. In contrast to the contract theory which assumes an equal distribution of violence potential the predatory theory assumes an unequal distribution. Groups who are able to control the state by military superiority can extract income from the rest of the constituents.

The tendency of states to produce inefficient property rights can be explained by the presence of two constraints on the ruler: a competitive constraint and a transaction cost constraint. The former refers to the fact that the ruler will avoid offending powerful groups. If powerful groups have access to alternative rulers, the ruler will be threatened, and will thus agree to a property rights structure favourable to these groups, regardless of its effect on efficiency. The latter constraint hinges on the presence of transaction costs in connection with taxation (costs for monitoring, metering and collecting such taxes). Efficient property rights may thus lead to higher income in the state but lower the ruler's tax revenue. He may thus find it in his interest to grant a monopoly rather than promote property rights which would lead to competitive conditions.

According to North these two constraints then, account for the wide spread of inefficient property rights. 'In effect, the property rights structure that will maximize rents to the ruler (or ruling class) is in conflict with that that would produce economic growth.'[12] Even a casual observation from history and the contemporary world makes clear, North argues, that 'inefficient' property rights are the rule not the exception.

According to Gordon Tullock several Third World governments, for example South American and African dictatorships, come fairly close to an exploitative model of the state.[13] Mats Lundahl argues that Haiti can be described as a predatory state, which is an important factor in explaining the country's underdevelopment.[14]

We will argue that the Dominican state during long periods could also be described as a predatory state. The unequal distribution of violence potential has led to the enforcement of property rights in land and to the implementation of other policies, for instance government spending, which have had as their primary motive the enrichment or protection of those in power.

Caudillo Fighting in the Dominican Republic

From the gaining of independence from Haiti in 1844 up until Trujillo's seizure of power in 1930, the presidency changed hands 50 times and 30 revolutions took place, according to Daniel Spitzer.[15] The presidency was usually taken by some regional *caudillo* who, while in power, would use the state to increase his personal wealth and security. However, these presidents did not have a monopoly on violence. Such a monopoly took form first under Trujillo, which explains the frequent and violent changes of rulers. The fight over political power was a fight for a share of the treasury, or as Paul Muto expresses it: 'The battle was one of individual advantage.'[16] As the Dominican historian Frank Moya Pons puts it, the state was at the time, with the exception of sugar and tobacco production, the only 'industry' of the country.[17] This implied that politicians and militaries expected to be economically supported by the president in power. The ruler then had to provide resources for this group independent of the effect that this would have on national wealth.

Using North's terminology we could say that these *caudillos* faced both a competitive and a transaction cost constraint. There were always groups who would be prepared to support a competing ruler for the existing state if this offered him higher income, thereof the competitive constraint. The *caudillo* in power was thus forced to agree to a property rights structure favourable to important groups. As will be shown rulers agreed to property rights in land which favoured important groups such as sugar estate owners (see particularly Chapter 4) and thus promoted the concentration of land in few hands. The transaction cost constraint is manifest in a primitive economy based on peasant production which did often not reach a market but was consumed by the peasants themselves. To extract taxes on rural production would thus have entailed formidable transaction costs. Rulers thus mainly relied on taxes on foreign trade which is easier to tax (we will expand on this in Chapters 3 and 4), on taking up foreign and domestic loans and on the printing of unsecured money and sometimes on direct theft.

One of the *caudillos* constantly fighting for power around the middle of the nineteenth century was Buenaventura Báez. Báez was forced to leave the country on various occasions, usually bringing the treasury with him.[18] After some time he used to return and manoeuvre himself back into the presidency. He held the presidency no less than five times. When in power he accumulated wealth as quickly as possible, knowing that he was soon likely to be overthrown again. Under Báez the Dominican state took up large foreign loans, most of which ended up in the pockets of Báez and his supporters. He monopolized the trade in tobacco, one of the most important products at the time.[19]

The rule of *caudillo* Ulises Heureaux, between 1882 and 1899, is another case in point. Heureaux lived an extravagant life but the Dominicans had to pay for it. Heureaux secured political support by for instance enforcing property rights suitable to his personal interests. He did this by creating and supporting a class of *latifundistas* whom he hoped would offer some kind of political stability to his regime. Friends of Heureaux could thus turn themselves into *latifundistas*. These could take hold of the best land in various parts of the country. Heureaux personally took control over vast tracts of land.[20] Heureaux badly needed money to finance both the expansion of the repressive apparatus, i.e. the military and the espionage service, and his extravagant way of life. As a result he was forced to take up large loans. A sugar magnate,

Juán Batista Vicini, provided Heureaux with large loans. In return, Vicini received special government favours, obtaining exemption from import duties, land concessions, etc. This kind of 'barter' has generally been more the rule than the exception throughout Dominican history.

Heureaux also accumulated a huge foreign debt, knowing that he was not the one who would have to pay it back. In 1893 the government's indebtedness was US$ 17 million, many times the total government budget.[21] The situation deteriorated further and in 1897 Heureaux was so desperate that he printed five million dollars worth of unsecured paper money which no one was prepared to accept. Heureaux's extravagant economic affairs finally led to the taking over by United States authorities of the Dominican customs. Under the US Customs Receivership the Dominican government received 45 per cent of the revenue while the remaining 55 per cent was distributed among foreign creditors.[22]

Between the assassination of Heureaux in 1899 and the American occupation in 1916 there was a continuing struggle among different *caudillos*.

The experience of the Dominican Republic conforms with that of its neighbour, Haiti. Between 1843 and 1915 Haitian politics was characterized by constant turmoil and struggle for power.[23] The extraordinary amount of revolutionary activity that took place during this period can, according to Lundahl, be classified as a series of 'distributional conflicts'.[24] State power was definitely used for personal enrichment. There are several factors in such a context that, according to Lundahl, reduce the economy's capacity to produce goods and services. First, budget funds which could be used for productive purposes have been transferred to the pockets of the rulers. Second, an unstable political situation is not conducive to investment, since an investor has no guarantee that he will be able to reap the profits of his investment. Third, resources are used up in revolutionary activity, both by those wanting to gain power and by those already in power. The former have to expend resources in order to become rulers, while the latter must invest in a counter-revolutionary machinery if they want to remain in a position that enables them to appropriate government resources. In both cases we are dealing with what Jagdish Bhagwati has classified as 'directly unproductive, profit seeking activities'.[25] Such activities are profitable to the individuals undertaking them, if they succeed, but do not lead to an increase of real output. These arguments are equally valid for the Dominican experience.

US Military Occupation

Whether the primary motive behind the US occupation (1916–24) was strategic (to prevent influence of other foreign powers) or to protect American economic interests is not clear, and this issue does not have to occupy us here.[26] However, two consequences of the occupation are crucial: the change in property rights in land and the creation of a national constabulary which in the hands of Trujillo obtained a virtual monopoly of violence potential.

We will discuss the 'clarification' of land titles carried out by the US military government in Chapter 4 and we can be very brief here. The US policy in this area meant the enforcement of clear property rights for US sugar and lumber companies and domestic *latifundistas* where previously a system of communal lands had been in force. It is reasonable to assume that the predominance of communal lands, *terrenos comuneros*, and unclear titles was not the most suitable for an efficient use of resources. The change carried out by the US occupants does however not appear to have been motivated by the desire to improve 'efficiency' in general, but by a concern with the interests of particular groups. We know that in order to enforce clear property rights for the sugar companies, the US Marines were used in order to evict peasants from their lands.

The US Marines created a constabulary which was to replace the various regional armies that had fought for power. Trujillo's rise to power began in the ranks of this constabulary. The combination of a US trained constabulary and Trujillo's determination and shrewdness were to lead to a long dictatorship with devastating effects on the Dominican community.

From the above discussion it may be inferred that up to 1930 Dominican rulers were fully occupied fighting each other. They had no concern whatsoever for the welfare of the majority of the population, that is, the peasantry. State power was used for personal enrichment; special concession of for instance land was made to important persons in return for political support and financial advantages. This was not a climate suitable for general development. The US occupation meant temporary political stability but it also implied an accentuation of *caudillo* policies in the enforcement of property rights in land favouring a small group of *latifundistas* and plantation owners.

The Dictatorship of Rafael Trujillo

The term 'predatory state' provides a perfect description of the rule of Trujillo (1930–61). Trujillo used all conceivable means to increase his own wealth independently of the effects on the welfare of the Dominican population. The key to the understanding of the protractedness of his rule is Trujillo's virtual monopoly of violence potential. The constabulary created by the US occupants was centralized, well organized and efficient. During his regime Trujillo increased the importance of this apparatus of violence potential over which he maintained absolute personal control. The control by Trujillo of the army gave him absolute power over Dominican society. There was no group or sector of the Dominican society which could have had an influence on Trujillo's political decisions. Howard Wiarda argues: 'Trujillo did not share power with anyone but maintained all authority in his own hands.'[27] We can thus confine our discussion to Trujillo and need not take interest groups into account in our analysis of the policies that prevailed during the time span of Trujillo's dictatorship.

This implied that, in terms of North's model, Trujillo did not face a competitive constraint. He did not need to fear competitors to his rule and did accordingly not need to make concessions to important groups in the Dominican society. He did, however, face a transaction cost constraint. During his rule the Dominican economy was overwhelmingly rural and it would have been very costly to tax peasants directly. The option Trujillo chose was instead to take direct control over vast economic resources and run production activities himself. By owning large segments of the Dominican economy he or his family directly controlled the income these could generate. The most evident economic result of Trujillo's long rule was thus the extreme concentration of Dominican property and income in the hands of Trujillo and his family.

We will review three main spheres of Trujillo's economic activities: 1) the effect on land ownership and agricultural production; 2) Trujillo's virtual monopoly of industrial and commercial activities; and 3) government spending heavily biased in favour of military expenditure.

Agrarian Structure

The impact on land ownership of Trujillo's activities will be discussed at length in Chapters 4 and 5, so our comments can be brief at this stage. By different methods, for instance by forcing landowners to sell at ridiculous prices or by simply dispossessing peasants of their lands, Trujillo and his family came to control as much as 50 to 60 per cent of Dominican land. One use that Trujillo made of his lands was to grow sugar cane. As will be discussed in Chapter 4, in addition to the search for profits there appear to be other motives for Trujillo's engagement in sugar production, not least the aim of controlling the most important source of foreign exchange.

The effect of the concentration of land in a few hands and the resultant proliferation of *minifundios*, may very well have implied a lower overall agricultural output.[28] This would be consistent with North's description of the predatory state:

> The predatory state would specify a set of property rights that maximized the revenue of the group in power, regardless of its impact on the wealth of the society as a whole.[29]

But would it not be better for the ruler to enforce property rights which maximized national income and to use taxes to extract a surplus? Here we must consider the importance of transaction costs. If the alternative to plantations is smallholder production, the difference in costs for collecting revenue between these two activities may lead the ruler to opt for a set of property rights which favour plantations although this means lower overall output. If peasant production is taking place on small widely scattered plots, subject to poor communication, the costs for collecting a tax on peasant production may be very high. The same kind of problem applies if government opts for smallholder production for exports. The cost of creating an incentive system which would gear peasant production to export crops would be very high.[30] Thus a concentration of land, and hence of sugar production, in a few hands may very well be a means of maximizing the ruler's, in this case Trujillo's, revenue and access to foreign exchange, even if it lowers overall output.[31]

Industrial Monopolies

An industrial promotion law was promulgated in 1950 giving additional tariff protection to the incipient Dominican industry. Behind tariffs and with government subsidies this incipient industry could make ample profits. The industry mainly belonged to

Trujillo and his family. According to one estimate the Trujillo family owned 119 enterprises accounting for some 80 per cent of the volume of business in Ciudad Trujillo.[32] The legislation, the tax system, government spending, everything served the interests of Trujillo's business. 'Special concessions' gave Trujillo a monopoly over several activities. He controlled the distribution of milk, the slaughterhouse business, he had a monopoly on salt, animal fats, meat exportation, etc. The banking system served, in Wiarda's words, '. . . as a clearing house for his private transactions'.[33] The state bank Banco Agricola mainly worked to finance Trujillo's sugar activities. The near-monopoly which the dictator had over most sectors of the Dominican economy did not create incentives or a 'climate' favourable for general industrial development.

Unproductive Government Spending

The treasury was of course used for the personal benefit of Trujillo. Since the basis for his power was the armed forces, spending for military purposes had a very high priority for Trujillo. In 1931, 11.5 per cent of the national budget went to the military.[34] In 1957 the share had risen to 25 per cent and by 1961 it had reached 36 per cent, according to official figures.[35] However, these figures, even if they appear to be large, probably underestimate the contribution to the military since a considerable amount of money budgeted to other ministries was actually channelled to the armed forces and to the paramilitary or police forces, which all served as Trujillo's instruments to firmly supervise and control the Dominicans. Pope Atkins estimates that in 1959 as much as 50 per cent of the budget was military related.[36]

Including irregulars Trujillo could probably muster a force of 75,000 to 80,000 during the 1950s. He created a large naval force which, according to Wiarda, could have overpowered any other navy in the Caribbean and Central America with the possible exception of Venezuela.[37] According to for instance Germán Ornes the huge Dominican army could hardly be related to any danger from outside. Its major function was internal.[38]

Most non-military government spending also served the interests of Trujillo: '. . . few, if any, projects were instigated which did not materially benefit the regime or its reigning family.'[39] Public works (roads, irrigation and so forth) were directed to Trujillo's properties.

While the military obtained the most modern weaponry, the health service and the educational system were in a disastrous state. The share of national income devoted to education in the Dominican Republic was one of the lowest in Latin America.[40] The rate of illiteracy was one of the highest. The few schools that existed were situated in towns while in rural areas, education facilities were extremely few. It is worth noting that in a predominantly agrarian country there was *one* graduate per million inhabitants with higher education in agriculture.[41] This was the lowest figure in Latin America. This clearly reveals the lack of concern shown by the Dominican state for agricultural development.

The educational system was used to glorify Trujillo rather than to teach children to read and write. 'The official cult of Trujillo was the most important subject taught in the schools.'[42] On the whole Trujillo made substantial efforts to indoctrinate the Dominican population. School system, church, mass media everything served the purpose of glorifying the father of the nation, *el Benefactor*. As argued by North, rulers will generally develop ideologies which legitimize the existing structure of property rights and consequent income distribution.[43] This is a less costly way of controlling the population than by simple use of force, espionage and so forth. Trujillo appears in this respect to have been rather successful. According to Ian Bell, after his death Trujillo was more often remembered by the *campesinos* as 'the father of the country' than as a ruthless dictator.[44] For instance Trujillo distributed worthless land to dispossessed peasants accompanied by widespread propaganda praising the dictator for his 'land reform'.

The above shows that for a period of 30 years, government policies served *one* purpose, to enrich Trujillo and his relatives/friends. The enforcement of property rights, the implementation of tariffs, taxes, government spending, etc., was designed to accomplish this aim. It should be evident that these 'rules of the game' were not implemented to promote development. If this was actually achieved it was a pure coincidence. Some overall growth took place, particularly during the 1950s, but was mainly confined to manufacturing and, of course, sugar. Since these activities were controlled by Trujillo and a small group around him the majority of the population did apparently not gain from the increase in gross domestic product. The majority of the population lived in rural areas, and the figures presented in Chapter 4 indicate that agricultural production (except sugar) *per capita* decreased. Such important factors for rural development as education, access to credit, transports, irrigation, drainage, storage facilities, etc. were completely neglected. The *minifundio-latifundio* problem was accentuated during the period.

Trujillo could, however, accumulate a fortune, which, according to Trujillo's principal bankers amounted to some US$ 800 million.[45] This can be compared with the gross domestic product of US$ 634 million in the final year of Trujillo's dictatorship, 1961.[46]

The Post-Trujillo Period[47]

'Despotism . . . cannot ensure peace for periods exceeding the length of one reign unless it is based on an undisputed rule of inheritance.'[48] Such an undisputed rule was not established by Trujillo in the Dominican Republic and his death in 1961 gave rise to a period of political instability which culminated in civil unrest in 1965. We will not provide a detailed account of what happened during these turbulent years, but we must linger on the presidency of Juan Bosch which ended with a military takeover. The dismal experience of Bosch's democratic regime shows the difficulty (impossibility?) of carrying out policies which threaten the interests of groups which have access to a large violence potential. Subsequently, we will discuss the rule of Joaquín Balaguer. It will be shown that Balaguer, while maintaining several of the facets of the Trujillo regime, had to try to satisfy demands of several interest groups in order to remain in office. However, the heavy anti-peasant bias of earlier regimes was retained. At least initially, the regime relied on extensive repression.

The Unfinished Experiment[49]

In the free elections that took place in 1962 the two principal candidates were Juan Bosch from the Partido Revolucionario Dominicano (PRD), and Viriato Fiallo from the conservative Union Cívica Nacional (UCN). Bosch won by a 2-to-1 margin.

Bosch was an intellectual who had criticized Trujillo and lived in exile for many years. He was in favour of economic reforms, but he was no revolutionary. He proposed for example a land reform and an extension of public services such as education, medical care, etc. However, once in office he did not attempt to carry out any far-reaching reforms. He did very little in the way of land reform and did not reduce the size of the armed force, probably fearing that such measures would lead to his overthrow. As Wiarda puts it: 'He demonstrated fiscal conservatism to the business community, avoided tampering with the sensitive armed forces, and tried to conciliate his opponents in the oligarchy and the church.'[50]

Nevertheless important sectors of the Dominican society were hostile towards Bosch. He provoked the resentment of parts of the military establishment since he had shown signs of wishing to curtail some of the unofficial privileges of the military. The military had long been able to make large profits from contraband and as commissioners in deals involving government purchases.[51] The landed elite mistrusted Bosch for his reform ambitions, as did the business community which, according to Bell, feared that he would favour the workers at the expense of employers.[52]

After only seven months in office Bosch was ousted by a military *coup*. The military was, according to various sources, supported by landowners, the church as well as the business community.[53] Bosch's 'mistaken' attempt to threaten powerful groups has been avoided by subsequent governments.

Interest Groups and Policies under Balaguer

According to North, a ruler will typically avoid offending powerful constituents. A ruler will agree to a property rights structure favourable to those groups, regardless of its effect on efficiency.[54] While Bosch indeed threatened the interests of powerful groups, at least in his pre-election rhetoric, Balaguer did not. Balaguer remained in power until 1978.

Balaguer maintained economic structures and policies which, while apparently being detrimental to development, suited the interests of important groups. Let us briefly review some of the economic conditions that prevailed in the Dominican Republic at the time, and describe the very important role that the state continued to have in economic affairs also after the death of Trujillo.

First, we have a very skewed distribution of land. This has at least two negative effects on overall development. It implies a low overall utilization of land since large landowners who control the bulk of cultivable land utilize this land poorly, and, due to the lack of land, landless peasants dedicate themselves to a slash and burn agriculture. The clearing of vegetation for small gardens, *conucos*, takes place in mountainous areas which leads to serious erosion.[55] Second, the industrial sector is small and poorly developed. It is protected from foreign competition and relies on government assistance, special concessions, etc. (this concerns 'larger' industry). Third, a factor of much importance was that the Dominican state took control over most of Trujillo's properties, much of the land belonging to the ex-dictator and many of his enterprises (including his sugar estates).

These factors were hardly compatible with the need to generate development. In Chapters 4 and 5 we discuss the negative effects of the unequal distribution of land. In Chapter 6 it is shown that industrialization policies, including distortions in credit markets, the provision of numerous privileges to classified firms, etc., have created an inefficient industrial sector. (We will mainly discuss policies after 1968 but these were largely a continuation of earlier policies and aggravated rather than initiated problems.) The negative performance of the state sugar producer, CEA, is discussed in Chapter 4.

The government was quite aware of the negative consequences for efficiency and distribution of the existing agrarian structure. We can for instance note what the comprehensive planning document *Plataforma para el desarrollo economico y social 1968–1985* from 1968 has to say about the agrarian structure prevailing in the Dominican Republic. Discussing the unequal distribution of land it is argued that:

> . . . there is not much chance that the agricultural sector will fulfil its important role in the economic and social development of the Dominican Republic without a previous, or concomitant, change of the existing agrarian structure.[56]

The government was also conscious of the fact that earlier industrialization policies had led to a high degree of industrial concentration since small and medium sized firms had been discriminated against.[57]

But the fact that Balaguer must have been aware of the adverse effects of existing structures and policies made him not adopt measures which would increase efficiency since such measures would be largely obstructed by strong interest groups. We will now briefly discuss some of the important interest groups in the Dominican Republic and then argue that their influence on policy accounts for much of the inefficiency generated. We will also point to the lack of influence of the Dominican peasantry.

The Military

Describing the constraint upon government, the political scientist Wiarda, writing in 1969, argues:

> Only at their own peril can Dominican governments disregard the interests of the armed forces; indeed before enacting any policy, the prudent Dominican president will first consider how the military, then how business, professional, and landowning elite, and then how other groups in descending order of importance will react.[58]

Atkins, in his *Arms and Politics in the Dominican Republic*, asserts: 'The Dominican armed force were the single most important political actor except for Balaguer himself.'[59]

As shown above, the importance of the military had increased under Trujillo. The military had been accustomed to be in a privileged position, receiving ample equipment, good salaries and the opportunity to earn money from public commissions. The situation had not changed after the death of Trujillo, and Balaguer was well aware of the strength of the military and did not curtail their privileges. Military spending continued to be high. In Table 2.1 we can compare military spending with what was spent on agriculture between 1966 and 1978.

Table 2.1: Government Spending on Armed Forces and Agriculture (million pesos, current prices)

	Armed forces	Agriculture		Armed forces	Agriculture
1966	33.5	19.2	1973	36.6	13.9
1967	30.8	15.8	1974	47.5	11.1
1968	32.6	10.1	1975	57.7	19.3
1969	30.2	12.2	1976	67.5	20.4
1970	31.5	13.6	1977	75.8	22.5
1971	32.0	13.7	1978	81.1	22.0
1972	34.5	13.5	TOTAL	591.2	206.7

Source: Figures from Oficina Nacional de Presupuestos in Centro de Estudios de la Realidad Social Dominicana (1978), p. 68.

Most of Balaguer's generals were able to become multi-millionaires through enterprises financed by government resources (the state sugar council, CEA, is one example), and by means of outright graft.[60] Many received vast tracts of land and now belong to the country's largest landowners. Frequently officers held military and civilian posts simultaneously. During Balaguer's presidency members of the armed forces held positions as foreign minister, director of customs and ports, minister of the interior . . .[61]

The army was used by Balaguer as an instrument of severe repression. He devoted substantial resources to create a well trained and armed counter-insurgency battalion. In particular between 1966 and 1970 many people belonging to the opposition parties, peasant leaders, etc., were killed.

Business and Landed Elite

Wiarda lumps businessmen and landowners into the same category: economic elites.[62] Businessmen and landowners have strong common interests since the latter have to a large extent moved into business while businessmen often own land. This economic elite is organized into various associations which have direct channels into government. This elite has so many connections that it is able to protect its interests no matter what direction the government in power actually takes. Several individuals from this group hold cabinet or other important government positions. Needless to say it can be assumed that the majority of this elite is opposed to major reforms, such as land reform.

The Peasantry

The Dominican peasantry is numerically the largest social sector. However its influence has been very small. Governments have traditionally been able to ignore the interests of the *campesinos*. Trujillo, who tried to control all sectors and social groups in the Dominican Republic, did not bother to organize or control the peasantry. The *campesinos* have continued to be isolated, unorganized, unable to impose their wants and desires on the government. Despite their being oppressed the Dominican peasants are not a revolutionary force and despite some illegal land occupations they have, on the whole, tacitly submitted to the 'rules of the game' which have been to their disadvantage.

The violence potential of the state combined with the free rider problem accounts, according to North, for the stability of states:

> The costs of the individual of opposing the coercive forces of the state have traditionally resulted in apathy and acceptance of the state's rules, no matter how oppressive.[63]

The failure of the Dominican peasants, who constitute the majority of the population, to organize themselves in order to exert pressure for better conditions can at least be partially explained in the following terms. First, the state has had a clear advantage in violence, which of course raises the cost for the individual of opposing the existing rules. Second, the free rider problem will give the individual little incentive to organize. Mancur Olson has shown that in order for large groups to be effective, members must receive exclusive individual benefits that are not available for non-members.[64] Large groups organized to create change that did not possess exclusive benefits for their members would be unstable and tend to disappear.[65]

The peasants constitute a *large* group compared to industrialists, urban workers, etc., in the Dominican society. In order for such a group to be effective, individuals who are actively working for changes in policies within an organization would have to receive exclusive benefits not available for those who do not take part. However, it is naturally difficult to provide such exclusive benefits. For instance, how could non-members be excluded from the benefit derived from an increase of government-regulated agricultural prices, a reduction of tariffs on industrial goods or a land reform? Without exclusive benefits, a peasant who can opt to take part in an organization fighting for land reform would not join if he knows that he would benefit from such a reform even if he did not take part in the organization. Hence the free rider problem may provide an important explanation of the lack of systematic opposition by peasants to the discrimination imposed upon them by different governments.

Policy Outcome

The above discussion indicates the unequal distribution of influence between different groups within the Dominican society. Now, it could perhaps be argued that elections and democracy should lead to policies accepted by the majority since, if the president wants to remain in power, he must be re-elected, and the poor after all constitute the majority of the population. Although the need for Balaguer to win votes was mitigated by the absence from the elections of the main opposition party, PRD, in 1970 and 1974, Balaguer also tried to win the support of the *campesinos* and the urban poor. Balaguer was thus in a far from enviable situation. He had to carry out programmes which would give him the support of the lower strata of the Dominican society and at the same time avoid threatening the important interest groups. In part, he tried to resolve this problem by the use of much rhetoric, such as the promise of land reform. This would give the support of the *campesinos*, which to large extent he in fact did obtain. Another way was to try to keep food prices low. This conflicts with the interests of the peasants but will satisfy the urban poor. We will discuss this price policy in later chapters.

This is one example of how different demands on government lead to policies which are inappropriate for the generation of development. This also characterizes the economic policy in general carried out by Balaguer and by subsequent administrations.

Many of the policies carried out by the Balaguer administration will be discussed in later chapters. Let us however portray some of the most salient features of these policies and point to some other aspects of policy, such as tax policy.

As will be shown in Chapter 6, industrialization policies carried out since the second half of the 1960s have mainly served the interests of 'large' business. This industrialization policy was to a considerable extent based on a classification system that sought mainly to protect classified firms from competition by providing them with different kinds of exemptions. It would appear that the credit system has favoured the 'large scale' business sector. These instruments have implied very high profits for some firms but have been inadequate to form the basis for a sound industrialization process.

One element of the industrial incentives law was to offer classified firms tax exemptions. Not only have these exemptions been prolonged, although it was originally intended that they would only be available for a finite period of time, they have also been extended to other activities. Under different 'incentives laws' tourism, banking, financial companies, etc., have been exempted from taxation.[66] Property taxes are insignificant, there is for instance no land tax and personal income taxes are small. The bulk of government income is made up by taxes on foreign trade and other indirect taxes. The reliance on taxes on foreign trade increases the vulnerability to changes in world market prices for Dominican exports.[67] The reliance on such taxes is in turn largely a consequence of the influence of wealthier groups on the tax system.

The anti-peasant bias of government policies is manifest. Credit policy, pricing policy, and government spending have discriminated against the peasant sector. For instance, Balaguer used large amounts of public money for the building of avenues and ostentatious government buildings in Santo Domingo. Resources were also spent on agriculture but these did not usually reach the poor peasants:

> When Balaguer did shift his attention from industrialization to agriculture, it was usually in the form of grandiose dam building and irrigation projects that benefited large landowners and left small farmers without sorely needed farm machinery, fertilizer, or more modern farming techniques.[68]

In the area of land reform little was accomplished despite considerable rhetoric by Balaguer and despite the urge for such a reform in official planning documents. The land reform was intended to redistribute both state and private land. Private land has in practice not been touched. The opposition to a redistribution of private lands is obvious. However redistribution of state land has also encountered serious obstacles. In fact much of state land is under the control of private landowners and members of the armed forces. As may be recalled from above, many members of the armed forces could convert themselves into *latifundistas* under both Trujillo and Balaguer.

Hans Illy has described the lack of determination and efficiency of the administration of land reform in the Dominican Republic.[69] Administrative bodies which were to execute the land reform have not been given adequate resources and civil servants are usually associated with landed interests through for instance family ties, or are themselves interested in the matter. As Illy argues, to possess a piece of land is a vital aspiration for all Dominicans. Balaguer's advisors on land reform were frequently accused of sabotaging the reform.[70] Consequently, Balaguer settled for a very modest programme offering unused state land, often of low quality, to peasants while in many cases not providing them with necessary additional services.

Concluding Remarks

The discussion in the present chapter reveals the nature of Dominican politics as a constant contest over the country's economic resources. The state has been used as an instrument to increase the wealth of those in power. Rulers have used the treasury for their personal benefit, indulging in theft, printing unsecured paper money . . . Evidently overall 'efficiency' has not been the aim of Dominican rulers.

Obviously the extent of the misuse of public office has varied with different governments and has probably diminished with the transition to democracy. Although persons related to recent governments have been able to make considerable economic gains from their position, ballot boxes and the spread of mass media inevitably set a constraint on the misuse of public resources which did not face previous rulers.

According to North there is usually a conflict between the property rights structure which maximizes the wealth of the ruler (and his group) and an efficient structure which encourages economic growth. Overall efficiency will not be promoted since the ruler will face a competitive and/or a transaction cost constraint. In the following chapters we will argue in somewhat more detail that these constraints on Dominican rulers have 1) contributed to the concentration of a large portion of the country's land resources (and other resources as well) in few hands; 2) stimulated the expansion of the dominant sector of the Dominican economy, namely the large sugar plantation sector; and 3) implied a constant discrimination of the peasant sector. In Chapter 3 we will discuss in general terms, the consequences of a predatory state for the pattern of international trade of a poor country. In Chapters 4 and 5 the argument will then be applied to the expansion of the plantation sector in the Dominican Republic.

Notes

1. Myrdal (1957), (1968) and (1977).

2. North (1981), p. 20.
3. Andreski (1966), p. 11.
4. Ibid.
5. Ibid., p. 211.
6. Lasswell and Kaplan (1950), p. 211.
7. Huntington (1968), p. 199.
8. North (1981), p. 21.
9. North uses the term 'efficient' and 'inefficient' to '. . . compare implications of two sets of constraints — in one, maximizing behavior on the part of the participants will produce increases in output; in the other, it will not produce increases in output.' North (1981), p. 7.
10. Ibid., p. 22.
11. Ibid.
12. Ibid., p. 28.
13. Tullock (1974), p. 19.
14. Lundahl (1985).
15. Spitzer (1972), p. 317.
16. Muto (1976), p. 15.
17. Moya Pons (1980), pp. 418–19.
18. Logan (1968), p. 45.
19. Ibid., pp. 42–7.
20. See Chapter 4.
21. See for instance Bell (1981), p. 59.
22. Ibid., p. 61.
23. Lundahl (1985).
24. Ibid., p. 34.
25. Bhagwati (1982), p. 989, defines as 'directly unproductive profit seeking activities' those activities that '. . . yield pecuniary returns but do not produce goods or services that enter a utility function directly or indirectly via increased production or availability of goods that enter a utility function.'
26. Different views on this issue are put forth by Knight (1928), Spitzer (1972) and Munro (1964).
27. Wiarda (1969), p. 34.
28. See Chapter 5.
29. North (1981), p. 27.
30. Discussing the role of the state in Haiti in the early nineteenth century Lundahl (1984a) and (1985) argues that Haitian rulers tried to reintroduce the plantation system in order to obtain foreign exchange. This would entail lower monitoring and transaction costs than a system based on smallholder production for exports.
31. See also more detailed discussion on this issue in Chapters 3 and 4.
32. Wiarda (1968), p. 83. Trujillo named Santo Domingo Ciudad Trujillo.
33. Ibid., p. 85.
34. Spitzer (1972), p. 379.
35. Ibid. and Bell (1981), p. 210.
36. Atkins (1981), p. 12.
37. Wiarda (1968), p. 44.
38. Ornes (1958), p. 132.
39. Wiarda (1968), p. 86. See also Ornes (1958), p. 236.
40. Wiarda (1969), p. 109 and Clausner (1973), p. 242.
41. Clausner (1973), p. 247.
42. Wiarda (1969), p. 44.
43. North (1981), p. 64.
44. Bell (1981), p. 227.
45. Wiarda (1968), p. 86. Wiarda (1975), p. 195 mentions the figure 1 billion.

46. International Monetary Fund (1983), pp. 196–7.
47. The most important political events and data during this period are:
1962–3 Council of State
1963 February to September Juan Bosch president
1963–5 The Triumvirate
1965 Civil fightings and US intervention
1965–6 Provisional Government
1966–78 Joaquín Balaguer from Partido Reformista president
1978–82 Antonio Guzmán from Partido Revolucionario Dominicano president
1982 Salvador Jorge Blanco from Partido Revolucionario Dominicano president.
48. Andreski (1966), p. 12.
49. The title of a book by Bosch. Bosch (1965).
50. Wiarda (1969), p. 60.
51. Spitzer (1972), p. 452.
52. Bell (1981), p. 81.
53. Wiarda (1969), p. 61, Spitzer (1971), p. 461.
54. North (1981), p. 28.
55. See Chapter 4.
56. Oficina Nacional de Planificación (1968), p. 124.
57. Ibid., 209.
58. Wiarda (1969), p. 189.
59. Atkins (1981), p. 33.
60. Ibid., p. 44.
61. Ibid., pp. 32–9.
62. Wiarda (1969), pp. 101–4. See also Wiarda and Kryzanek (1982), p. 65.
63. North (1981), p. 31.
64. Olson (1982).
65. Ibid. See also Olson (1983), p. 14.
66. See for instance Moya Pons (1983), pp. 156–7.
67. Between 1972 and 1980 on average 47 per cent of total tax receipts came from taxes on exports and imports. More than 70 per cent of taxes on foreign trade were import taxes. Moya Pons (1983), p. 131.
68. Wiarda and Kryzanek (1982), p. 109.
69. Illy (1978).
70. Ibid., p. 184.

3 THE PREDATORY STATE AND INTERNATIONAL TRADE

As was shown in Chapter 1, a salient feature of the Dominican economy is its extreme reliance on one export crop: sugar. Such large amounts of production resources are devoted to sugar production that the Dominican Republic has, by different observers, been termed both 'monoculture' and 'plantation economy'. In the present chapter we will outline a framework which will help to explain the concentration of considerable amounts of resources to a plantation export sector. Adopting the predatory state as our point of departure, we will argue that both a competitive and a transaction cost constraint may lead the ruler to favour the development of a plantation sector. In Chapters 4 and 5 we will then employ this framework explicitly in relation to the Dominican Republic. To analyse the cause of the present shape of the Dominican foreign trade structure is interesting *per se* since this could not, it will be argued, be fully explained by 'traditional' economic theory. However, the discussion on the expansion of the plantation economy will also shed light on several factors behind Dominican underdevelopment: extremely skewed distribution of land, neglect of the peasant sector, etc.

Before presenting this framework, we will briefly consider some 'mainstream' views on international trade and economic development as well as some other approaches which emphasize political/institutional factors in explaining both the structure of foreign trade and its impact on distribution.

Traditional Theory and Comparative Advantage

The core concept of mainstream trade theory is that of comparative advantage. With given resources, technology and tastes, perfect competition prevailing in factor and product markets, no externalities, etc., countries will specialize, in production, according to comparative advantage. The static gain from trade is usually illustrated by a movement along the transformation curve, from a point where autarchy prevails to a point where income at world market prices, and society's welfare, represented by social indifference curves, are maximized.[1]

Which factors do then determine a country's comparative advantage? While the classical theory emphasized differences in labour productivity between countries, modern theory singles out differences in factor endowments as an explanation of why trade takes place and why it is beneficial. The most renowned explanation of trade patterns in modern trade theory is the Heckscher-Ohlin theory. According to this theory, countries export commodities whose production requires the intensive use of the production factor that is relatively abundant in the country. The basic model is a 2×2×2 (two commodities, two factors of production and two countries) framework.[2]

The Heckscher-Ohlin theory has been presented explicitly as an attempt at explaining the structure of foreign trade rather than establishing welfare propositions and is the 'model most frequently used in positive trade theory'.[3] The empirical support for this theory is, however, not overwhelming.[4] In Chapter 4 it will be argued that the Heckscher-Ohlin theory cannot satisfactorily explain why the Dominican Republic is so heavily geared towards sugar exports.

Trade and Development

In addition to the comparative static welfare gain, illustrated by a movement along the transformation curve, trade is said to have important indirect, dynamic, effects. These indirect effects are often said to be more important than the static effect.[5] Yet, while the static advantages are subject to rigorous formal analysis and proofs, there has been a lack of rigor in the discussion of dynamic effects of trade. Compare Ronald Findlay's view on the way the relation between trade and development is treated in the literature:

> . . . the 'trade and development' area presents a rather chaotic appearance, rich in historical anecdotes and intuitive insights but lacking any unified framework.[6]

Positive indirect effects of trade are supposed to arise since for example, '. . . trade is means and vehicle for the dissemination of technological knowledge, the transformation of ideas, the importation of know how, managerial talents and entrepreneurship.'[7]

Trade also provides material means, in the form of capital goods, necessary for development. These rather standard neoclassical arguments[8] lead for instance Gottfried Haberler to assert that:

> . . . trade has made a tremendous contribution to the development of less developed countries in the 19th and 20th centuries and can be expected to make an equally big contribution in the future, if it is allowed to proceed freely.[9]

Trade and Domestic Impediments

While Haberler's view on trade and poor countries is shared by perhaps most neoclassical observers, it has also been acknowledged within this body of thought that in many cases the indirect effects of trade may turn out to be rather small. First, it has been recognized that there might be a potential conflict between trade and growth, and, second, domestic factors which prevent or limit the positive effects of trade on development have been discussed.

The indirect, dynamic effect can be described in analytical terms as an outward shift of the production possibility curve. According to the traditional view of trade, the choice of a point on the production possibility curve conforming with comparative advantage will both maximize welfare at a given point in time and cause an outward shift of the curve. An important question that arises is then the following: could another allocation lead to a faster outward movement of the transformation curve? This issue has been raised by, for instance, Gerald Meier and Hollis Chenery.[10] In his article from 1961, *Comparative Advantage and Development Policy*, Chenery argues that the market mechanism may discriminate against the manufacturing sector.[11] According to Chenery factors such as economies of scale, training effects, which are supposed to be most important in industrial activity, are insufficiently reflected in the price system. An allocation that conforms with comparative advantage may thus turn out not to be the best alternative for growth if it entails specialization on primary exports. A more 'balanced' pattern of production, with a larger industrial sector than would obtain under free trade and static allocative efficiency, could give a faster rate of technological change and faster overall growth.

Several development economists argue in terms of the nature of the export commodity or the 'export base' and of domestic factors, such as the presence of market imperfections, to account for the slow pace of development of many primary exporting countries.

Authors like Robert Baldwin[12] and Gerald Meier[13] argue that the nature of the export commodity can be decisive for the effects of export growth on economic development. The most important aspects considered in this context are: a) the presence of 'linkages'; b) the nature of the production function of the export commodity; c) the extent of dissemination of new technology; and 4) the structure of demand and saving propensities.

When production of the export commodity is growing, it provides a stimulus for expansion in industries supplying inputs for this production. This can be called backward linkage. In a similar way, the output of an export industry may be used as an input in other industries, thus providing forward linkages. In the presence of strong linkages, export growth has wide-spread effects in the economy. The importance of linkages was originally stressed by Albert Hirschman.[14]

The technological nature of the production function for the export activity is important not merely for the presence of linkages but also for the dissemination of new technology and the distribution of income. The growth of export production:

> . . . will provide only weak stimulus if its techniques of production are the same as those already in use in other sectors, and if its expansion can occur by a simple widening of production without any change in production functions.[15]

According to Meier this has been a feature of some peasant export sectors.[16]

More favourable effects on learning originate from exports requiring skilled labour than from those using unskilled labour. Baldwin argues that in this respect, mineral exports have been more favourable than plantation crops. Since mineral activities demand a fairly large number of positions requiring semi-skilled to highly skilled labour, training opportunities emerged. The knowledge acquired in the export sector could be disseminated to other sectors through movement of workers.[17] The labour-intensive plantation production has, on the other hand, not induced much learning stimulus.

The nature of the export commodity will also influence the distribution of income and hence the pattern of consumption and savings. The shares of wages, profits and rents, can be expected to vary according '. . . to whether the export sector product comes from mining, plantation agriculture, or peasant farming'.[18] Exports requiring large-scale employment of unskilled labour may provide a stimulus to the domestic market through the high propensity to consume domestic consumption goods of this group. Another product and production function may result in higher incomes for groups with higher saving propensities and thus favour capital accumulation.

Due to different degrees of market imperfection, the effectiveness of the price system will differ among countries. In an economy characterized by considerable market imperfection, or as Meier puts it, domestic impediments, the impulse to economic development from export growth may be quite limited. Less developed countries are usually characterized by factor immobility, price rigidity, restrictive tendencies in both factor and goods markets, limited knowledge of market conditions, etc. According to Meier, these domestic obstacles are decisive in explaining the poor development performance of many countries exhibiting large exports.

Some Alternative Views on Trade

The mainstream has given very little, if any, consideration to political/institutional factors, either in explaining the pattern of trade or in discussing the relation between trade and development. In this section we will briefly refer to some studies which include such factors in their discussion of international trade.

Enforced Bilateralism

Gunnar Myrdal, who rejects the comparative statics of traditional theory, includes such factors in his analysis. Myrdal emphasizes the colonial heritage to explain both the structure of poor countries' trade and why trade has not been beneficial for development. The structure of poor countries' trade is much a consequence of, Myrdal argues, 'enforced bilateralism'.[19] The colonial empires have had an obvious interest in monopolizing the dependent countries' trade as far as possible, both by providing market outlets for their own industrial products and as a source of cheap raw materials. The metropolitan countries fortified the protection of their monopolistic interests using the whole structure of legislation and administration, cementating the economic and political dependency which tends to remain also after liberation.

In an article by Ephraim Kleiman, *Trade and the Decline of Colonialism*, it is empirically shown that there is a visible relation between political status of poor countries and their *regional* trade patterns.[20] The commodity trade of poor countries tended to be heavily concentrated on the metropolitan, or formerly metropolitan, countries. This model is however not applicable to the Dominican Republic, which has been independent for a long period.

Group Behaviour and International Trade

Charles Kindleberger has argued that it is necessary to go beyond the pure market model in analyzing different countries' adjustment to external change. Kindleberger analyzed the very disparate response in different countries to the change in the wheat world market in the 1870s. The result of the British response (free trade) to the decline in the world market price of wheat was to 'complete the liquidation of agriculture as the most powerful economic group in Britain'.[21] Due to a different political situation, in countries like Germany and Italy, the farmer was protected by tariffs.

Inspired by Kindleberger's work Stephen Hymer and Stephen Resnick use a framework that includes political as well as economic factors in order to explain the structure of poor countries' trade and the historic origins of underdevelopment.[22] They argue that international trade theory only tells a portion of the story of the gains and losses from trade. A realistic model must include 'power' relations. Hymer and Resnick divide their analysis into three subperiods and in order to illustrate their way of reasoning, let us briefly review their argument about what they call Mercantilism II (approximately the period from 1870 to the Second World War).

The expansion of trade under Mercantilism II reflected in large parts the policies of colonial rule. The high elasticity of exports during this period reflected *government policy* as well as market response. A similar pattern emerged in different countries where the traditional economy is squeezed in order to create an elastic supply of labour for export production. The gains from trade were very unequally distributed. The gains went mainly to local and foreign elites and to government (in the form of taxes), while there was (at least initially) a decline in the standard of living for many of the individuals who were coerced into export production.

Political Factors and Plantation Exports

Studies on the presence of plantations in developing countries are of course of particular relevance for the present work.

Some studies discuss the impact of political change on plantation exports. In his study on Haiti, Lundahl shows that with the fall of colonial rule, the prerequisites for the existence of plantations no longer existed.[23] With independence, the forced labour system, which had prevailed under colonial rule, was abandoned and a land reform was initiated. There was a drastic reduction in the production of traditional export crops when peasants turned to production of subsistence crops.

Also in Indonesia, independence implied a decline in plantation production. In colonial times, the Dutch had exercised 'dictatorial and monolithic power' to back plantations.[24] Under different arrangements, the populations of Java and Sumatra had been forced into plantation production. The rulers of independent Indonesia could not, due to popular pressure, support the plantation sector, which implied that plantation production was drastically reduced.

A more comprehensive work on the role of plantations in developing countries is George Beckford's *Persistent Poverty*.[25] Beckford, who can be said to be a Caribbean representative for the 'dependency school' (see below), discusses the reasons for the domination of plantations in many poor countries' economies and the impact of plantations on development. Beckford argues that institutional factors play an important role in determining patterns of production and resource use in plantation economies. The state has throughout the 'plantation world' acted on behalf of plantations in several ways, creating a bias in resource use in favour of the plantation sector.

Although Beckford also points to the importance of domestic institutional factors, underdevelopment is said to be largely a consequence of the openness of plantation economies, and measures to bring about some degree of closure are needed. The openness leads to a 'dependency syndrome'. Beckford argues that the policies favouring the plantation sector are to a great extent a consequence of an alien ideology, that policy makers have based their decisions on models developed in industrial countries and they have not recognized that the plantations have had a low, not to say negative, development impact.[26]

Beckford points to an important aspect of plantation economies namely the state's backing of plantations, but fails to explain why the state has provided this support. It is misleading to argue that policy makers have based decisions on alien ideologies and that they have not realized that plantations have had negative effects. A framework which tries to explain the behaviour of the state, in this context, is presented below. It will be argued that a state which aims at earning income and obtaining access to foreign exchange will have incentives to promote a plantation system.

However, before presenting this framework, a few words are required on 'dependence'.

'Dependence'

Beckford's view, that the openness, as such, of developing countries, is the main cause of underdevelopment, characterizes much of the writings of the so-called 'dependency school'. Although authors within this body of thought stress to varying degrees the importance of domestic vs. external factors as causes of underdevelopment, the emphasis on external factors is a common denominator.[27] Trade is one of the vehicles through which the rich metropolitan countries dominate the poor, 'dependent', countries, and through which surplus is transferred from the latter to the former. Development and underdevelopment are simultaneous processes, the development of the rich countries conditioning the underdevelopment of the dependent countries.

This approach does not appear to have been particularly successful in the study of development problems, and has been abandoned by most of its original advocates. We will, however, not spend any further time on a discussion of the 'dependency school'. What is of interest in the context of the present book is that this body of literature may have created an attitude among many politicians, scholars, etc., according to which many of the domestic difficulties are blamed on external factors. This is certainly the case in the Dominican Republic, where the word 'dependence' is constantly used by politicians, scholars, journalists, etc. We will in subsequent chapters criticize some of these views put forth by Dominican economists.

The 'Predatory' State and International Trade

In the traditional model, we have a decentralized world where the range of activities of the economic actors is limited to the quantities to be produced and consumed. As shown above, Kindleberger argued that it is necessary to account for the behaviour of groups in international trade theory. In Chapter 2, we referred to the work by Mancur Olson and Douglass North which has given considerable attention to the behaviour of groups and the state and their impact on economic performance.[28] Below we will use the ideas on the behaviour of groups and the state developed by these two authors, in a framework of international trade for an underdeveloped country. It will be shown that the outcome for trade structure and the ensuing distribution of income may be quite different from what would be predicted in the traditional economic model when individuals or groups exert a decisive influence on the economic system.

The behaviour of the state is of fundamental importance to North's analysis and according to the 'predatory' view of the state, the state serves as an instrument of the ruling group or class to redistribute income in favour of that group or class.[29] This 'predatory' view of the state is based on the assumption of the state's inherent superiority in the use of force. Given this strong state and, assuming that its main interest is the maximization of wealth of those in power, what will be the impact on overall economic efficiency?

The state has a strong impact on the structure of ownership, and, according to North, there is a tension between the ownership structure which maximizes the rent of the ruler (and his group) and an efficient system which encourages economic growth. In fact, the argument presented in Chapter 2 is that a predatory state will specify a set of property rights that maximizes the revenue of the group in power regardless of its impact on the income of society as a whole.[30]

Let Figure 3.1 depict the production possibility curve of a country. Both X and Z are agricultural commodities, of which X is a plantation crop (exportable). The straight line represents relative prices on the world market. In the decentralized world of traditional theory the country will settle at point A, where national income at world market price is maximized. At A the marginal return to an input factor is equal in X and Z.

Figure 3.1: Equilibrium in Economy Characterized by Competitive Conditions (A) and Economy Ruled by Predatory Government (B)

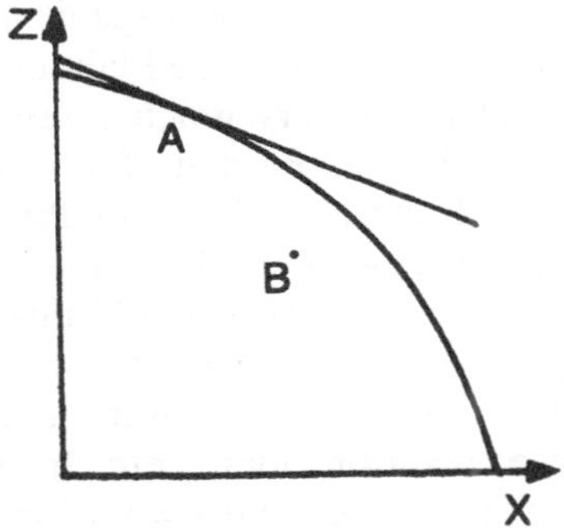

Let us now assume that the country is ruled by a 'predatory' state. The question can now be asked whether a ruler that aims to maximize the wealth of the group in power would opt for point A and then use taxation to extract income for the state? The outcome for production and trade structure would then be identical to what would obtain in the decentralized world.

If the ruler had no competitor and there were no transaction costs this would reasonably be the case. If the ruler could introduce a, say, proportional tax (t) which does not entail transaction costs, a policy that maximizes national income (Y) will also maximize the revenue of the ruler (tY). This could only be done if he had no competitors. If there were competitors to his rule he would be forced to make concessions to important groups and this could take the form of grants or monopolies, etc., which would reduce national income.

But rulers will normally face one or both of these constraints. Let us start by assuming that the ruler has no competitors and that consequently he only faces a transaction cost constraint. There are monitoring, metering and collecting costs associated with taxation. Let us, in terms of Figure 3.1, assume that Z is produced by peasants. Let us also assume that these are widely scattered and since we are discussing an underdeveloped country we can reasonably assume that communications are poor and that there is no efficient administrative apparatus. Thus to collect taxes from peasants would entail very high, perhaps prohibitive, costs. There is thus no, or a very weak, relationship between peasant output and the income of the ruler.

Instead, let us assume that the income of the state is related to production of commodity X, a plantation crop. The plantation system entails a special way of organizing production. The plantation relies on strictly supervised labour under conditions of slavery, or conditions that very much resemble slavery. Special arrangements in the labour market, for instance promotion of immigrant labour, will increase the profitability of plantations.

Under the above conditions, a ruler will not opt for point A, but for a point to the right of A. How could this be done? The state could carry out plantation production itself or it could promote a group of plantation owners on whom it could then rely for financial assistance, taxation, loans, etc. In both cases, the state would devise a structure of land ownership that would not be consistent with the maximization of national output. The state would enforce property rights which would ensure the state or plantation owners a large share of the country's resources.

This could, in analytical terms, be treated as a 'distortion' in the land market. The state or private plantations would obtain control of land at (implicit) prices below social opportunity cost. This distortion would mean that national output would not be maximized, since the marginal productivity of land in production of Z would exceed that in sector X, which has obtained land at lower cost. This can be illustrated by point B, which represents lower output than that which would be possible given the resource base and technology. In a world with transaction costs, point B could represent the combination of output which would maximize the ruler's wealth.[31] This example shows that in order to maximize his own income, the ruler may induce overall inefficiency.

A similar way of reasoning is applicable to the situation where the ruler has a strong desire for foreign exchange. The ruler's demand for exchange may derive from 1) the need to import military equipment (which may be necessary to keep him in power), 2) his and his group's desire to consume imported goods, and 3) the wish to place money in foreign banks (in the case of a *coup* or a revolution forceing him to leave the country it would of course be convenient to have money placed in foreign banks).

Theoretically, the ruler could opt for a situation where smallholder production for exports is stimulated. Again, this would entail high transaction costs. The peasant tends to produce subsistence goods. In order to change the product mix in favour of exports, the ruler would have to devise an incentive system stimulating (or forcing) the peasant to produce export crops.[32] This would entail extremely high costs. Once again, the ruler will choose the plantation system, whose output can more easily be measured (and taxed) and where workers are tied to estates and supervised tightly. Point B may again be the outcome.

The outcome may be similar in the case when the ruler has competitors and thus, in North's terminology, faces a competitive constraint. He will then be forced to make concessions to important groups. This could take the form of granting monopolies, giving away state land or selling it at below-market prices, offering these groups a large share of the treasury, etc. The granting of monopolies and vast tracts of valuable land would be tantamount to the introduction of imperfections or distortions and would thus reduce overall efficiency. Such important groups may be large landowners or (particularly relevant in our case) plantation owners. These groups are small in comparison with the peasants and will, in accordance with Olson's line of thought, have a greater incentive to try to obtain a (for the group) collective good than has the peasant community. Consequently they could easily turn their support to a rival of the present ruler.

Can then this assumed behaviour of the state conform with 'real life'? Lundahl discussing Haiti in the early nineteenth century argues along these lines.[33] The restoration of the plantation system, which had broken down during the wars of independence, was motivated by the need of the rulers of independent Haiti for income and particularly for foreign exchange, in order to secure both military strength and income for powerful groups. The choice of the plantation system, instead of a smallholder system, to achieve these aims, was motivated, Lundahl argues, precisely by the fact that transaction costs connected with the smallholder system were so high as to be almost prohibitive.

In Chapter 2 it was argued that in the Dominican Republic rulers have been primarily concerned with maximizing their own income and security. The need to gain control over foreign exchange was for example an important aim of Trujillo. Rulers have implemented policies which have served these objectives. A satisfactory method by which the state may earn income or secure political support has been to grant privileges to different groups, i.e. to sugar estates. As will be shown in Chapter 4, the Dominican state had promoted the concentration of land to the plantation sector. Land policy, immigration policy, government spending, etc., have also served this aim.

Concluding Remarks

In this chapter we have merely touched on the vast 'trade and development' area. Emphasis has been placed throughout on the fact that political/institutional factors have usually been excluded in the 'mainstream' view on the subject.

Prominent authors such as Baldwin and Meier argue that the nature of the production function for the export commodity has important consequences for the growth impact of exports and for income distribution. Domestic 'impediments' or distortions have limited the development impact of primary exports. In this context, they do not consider the role of the state in inducing these 'impediments' or the importance that the very unequal distribution of land has for income distribution in for instance plantation export economies.

In contrast we have presented an approach which emphasizes the role of the state in causing distortions and an unequal distribution of income. Rulers who have personal welfare as their primary government objective may find it rewarding to favour the concentration of resources, particularly land, in a plantation export sector. Although this policy will provide the ruler with foreign exchange and the political support of important plantation owners, it will also generate a very skewed distribution of income.

In the next chapter, we will argue that the Dominican Republic conforms with this latter approach. 'Distortions' favouring the plantation sector have been induced by Dominican rulers intent on the maximization of their own utility. The behaviour of the Dominican state is thus an important factor in trying to explain the expansion of the plantation sector and the predominant role played by this sector in Dominican society today.

Notes

1. See for instance Chacholiadis (1978), p. 144, Grubel (1977), p. 38 and Meier (1968), p. 14.
2. See for instance Chacholiadis (1978), pp. 258–65.
3. Jones and Neary (1984), p. 4.
4. See for instance Stern (1973), and Jones and Neary (1984), p. 4, and Deardorff (1984).
5. Compare for instance Haberler (1959) arguing 'If we were to estimate the contribution of international trade to economic development, especially of the underdeveloped countries, solely by the static gains from trade . . . we would indeed grossly underestimate the importance of trade.'
6. Findlay (1984), p. 212.
7. Haberler (1959).
8. Efforts to mould these rather 'loose' arguments, about the growth inducing effects of trade, into more formal frameworks, have been made e.g. by Johnson (1953), Ball (1962), Hultman (1967), Massell (1964), Stern (1973), Voivodas (1973) and (1974). Emery (1967), Maizels (1968) and Michaely (1977) in different ways employ econometrics to investigate the relation between trade and growth.
9. Haberler (1959), p. 5.
10. Meier (1968), pp. 216–7, Chenery (1961). Compare also Schumpeter's general argument on statics vs. dynamics: 'A system — any system economic or not — that at every point of time fully utilizes its possibilities to the best advantage may yet in the long run be inferior to a system that does so at no given point in time, because the latter's failure to do so may be a condition for the level or speed of long-run performance.' Schumpeter (1976), p. 83.
11. Chenery (1961).
12. Baldwin (1963).
13. Meier (1968) and Meier (1976), pp. 719–23.
14. Hirschman (1958).
15. Meier (1968), p. 243.
16. Ibid., pp. 243–4.
17. Baldwin (1963), p. 86.
18. Meier (1968), p. 241.
19. Myrdal (1957).
20. Kleiman (1976).
21. Kindleberger (1951), p. 33.
22. Hymer and Resnick (1971).
23. Lundahl (1979), Chapter 6. Early rulers of independent Haiti, however, tried to reintroduce the plantation system, but suceeded in doing so only for a short period, Lundahl (1984a) and (1985), see also below, section The Predatory State.
24. Gordon (1983), see also Geertz (1970).
25. Beckford (1972).
26. Ibid., pp. 217, 219 and 231.
27. Blomström and Hettne (1981).
28. Olson (1965), (1982) and (1983).
29. Ibid., p. 22; see also this book, Chapter 2, for a longer discussion on the predatory state, particularly on the predatory nature of the Dominican state.
30. Ibid.
31. It would be more correct to represent the consequence of the distortion as an inward shift of the production possibility curve. We, however, use Figure 3.1 for the sake of illustration.
32. Lundahl (1984a).
33. See Lundahl (1984a) and (1985).

4 THE DEVELOPMENT OF THE EXPORT ECONOMY: SUGAR

About 50 per cent of the Dominican population live in rural areas. The majority of this rural population have incomes below or near what is considered the rural poverty line.[1] Data indicate that agricultural production *per capita* has been more or less stagnant since the 1940s[2], and rural tension in the form of, for instance, illegal land occupations, has been an important aspect of rural life during the last decade.[3]

An argument throughout the present work is that these rural problems are to a considerable extent a consequence of a discrimination of the peasant sector. This discrimination is in turn largely a consequence of the low political influence of peasants. The peasant sector has suffered from a double discrimination. First, the *latifundios* in general, and the sugar plantation sector in particular, have often been favoured at the expense of the peasant sector. Second, the rural sector has been discriminated by policies favouring industry and the urban sector. The discrimination imposed on the rural sector by industrialization policies will be discussed in Chapter 6.

In this chapter, we will show how political-institutional factors have favoured the expansion of sugar exports at the expense of peasants. The purpose of the chapter is thus twofold: 1) to discuss some of the institutional factors which have made sugar production and exports such a dominant activity in the economic life of the Dominican Republic; and 2) to show how the peasant sector has been discriminated against in this process. The relation between sugar exports and resource use and living conditions in the agricultural sector will then be more explicitly discussed in Chapter 5.

It will also be shown that the distribution of land outside the plantation sector is extremely skewed, and, it will be argued, the concentration of land in a few hands has been consistent with the preference of Dominican rulers.

The Creation of the Export Economy

As was shown in Chapter 1, sugar plays a dominant role in the economic life of the Dominican Republic. Traditionally about 50 to 60 per cent of exports have consisted of sugar and a substantial share of the country's land resources are devoted to sugar cane production. In this section, the opening up of sugar exports and the early development of the sector, up to 1930, will be discussed.

Traditional economic theory views the opening up of trade as a movement along a production possibility curve. Fixed amounts of production factors are assumed and institutions are assumed (implicitly) not to change. According to the Heckscher-Ohlin theorem, different fixed amounts of production factors yield divergent relative prices of goods (before trade) and thus gains from international trade.

We will however show that the opening up of sugar exports in the Dominican Republic was not a result of a movement along a transformation curve based on fixed supplies of production factors. In fact, important production factors for large-scale production and exports of sugar were lacking in the Dominican Republic. In addition, institutions were changed in order to facilitate production and exports of sugar.

The story of the modern Dominican sugar industry began in the 1870s. Up until then cattle ranching and subsistence agriculture had been the dominant economic activities in the country. The opening up of sugar exports was not a response to an increase in sugar prices which could have motivated Dominican factors of production to move into this sector.[4] Sugar prices were in fact declining at the time.[5] The rise of large-scale sugar exports was instead the indirect outcome of the Cuban war and the consequent movement of production factors to the Dominican Republic. In the 1870s, seeking refuge from the war of independence, Cuban immigrants invested their capital in the purchase of land for sugar plantations. With the arrival of the Cubans the modern *ingenio* replaced the older *trapiche*. The *trapiche*[6] was a small and rudimentary mill operated by human labour. It was typically located in rural areas and produced for the local market. The *ingenio* is a large mill, originally powered by horses or oxen, after 1875 by steam and today by fuel.[7]

Cubans did however not dominate the sugar industry for very long. US interests soon found their way into the Dominican sugar fields and by the end of the century the industry was dominated by North American companies.

In addition to capital, management and skilled labour also came from abroad. Much of the unskilled labour had also to be provided from abroad. The production factor which was initially relatively abundant was land. But the structure of land ownership was changed in order to facilitate the expansion of sugar plantations. Let us take a somewhat closer look at some of these factors.

Investment

Investment requirements of large-scale sugar production are substantial. It is improbable that the capital needed for investments in sugar could have been provided within the Dominican economy. At the time of the arrival of the Cuban immigrants and the consequent rise of the sugar industry, the Dominican banking system was just incipient and not in a position to finance the large investments needed. The Cuban immigrants put between 30 and 35 *ingenios* into operation between 1875 and 1882, the total of capital invested amounting to US$ 6,000,000.[8] This was a large sum at the time.

The sugar companies were later tied to foreign (mainly American) shipping companies and banks. The Cuban-Dominican Sugar Company (American owned) had strong links to the National City Bank and the United States South Porto Rico Company was tied to the American dominated Royal Bank of Canada. The National City Bank created the International Banking Corporation whose only task was that of financing sugar operations. In 1920, during the sugar boom, the Cuban Dominican Sugar Development Syndicate was organized in order to furnish capital to sugar companies.[9] On the relations between foreign banks and sugar companies, Melvin Knight comments: 'Americans prefer to loan money to American planters, or better still to big sugar corporations whose directorates interlock with that of the lending bank.'[10] In Table 4.1 we can clearly see the foreign influence in the sugar sector.

Table 4.1: Nationality of Sugar Estates in 1925

Number	Nationality	Area in acreage	%	Value in mill. US$
12	American	355,000	81.4	33.5
2	American-Dominican	10,000	2.2	0.7
5	Italian	50,000	11.5	5.0
1	Italian-Dominican	12,000	2.9	n.a.
2	Dominican	9,000	2.0	1.3

Source: Knight (1928), p.139.

Labour

Skilled labour was imported: '. . . the wellpaid directive and technical personnel was largely foreign',[11] and so was also much of *unskilled labour*. At the wage level offered by the sugar industry, Dominican labour was not sufficiently plentiful. Knight argues: 'Peasants were not tempted by the low rates of pay to leave their small plots. Hence a type of black labour not wanted by the Dominicans as a permanent settler was imported from Haiti and the West Indies.'[12]

As early as 1884, it was calculated that 35 *ingenios* used 5,500 domestic and 500 foreign labourers.[13] Especially the immigration of Haitians has played a major role in the Dominican sugar industry, from its start up to the present. In 1920, more than 28,000 Haitians were legally resident in the country. This is probably an underestimate of the true number since clandestine immigration, which can be assumed to have been substantial, is not included.[14]

During the American occupation (1916–24) legal provisions were taken in order to secure the supply of workers for the sugar industry.[15] The import of Haitian labour was perhaps not in accordance with the preference of the majority of the Dominican population. Knight states: '. . . the Dominicans would be glad to dispense with their 100,000 or so of annual Haitian visitors.'[16]

Land

Land was relatively abundant in the Republic at the time of the rise of the sugar industry. The low density of population had made cattle ranching the dominant economic activity during the eighteenth century. Difficulties in dividing the extensive ranches, *hatos*, usually led to the establishment of the system of communal lands, *terrenos comuneros*.[17] Heirs received shares, *acciones* or *pesos*, of the inherited land. These shares would not necessarily remain in the hands of the heirs since they could be traded. The original *hato* could with the passing of time be considered a cooperative association.[18] The *accion* or *peso* did not give a property right to any specific parcel of land, but a right to use land for cattle or cultivation.

This system often made land titles and property rights unclear. When the value of land rose with the extension of the sugar industry, falsification of land titles was frequent, and, according to Harmannus Hoetink, foreign investors benefited especially from these frauds.[19]

But as time went on the sugar companies considered the collective titles too insecure. Measures were taken in order to clarify land possession and ownership. In 1920 during the American occupation a Land Registration Law was issued in order to give owners of communal shares an undisputed title. Ten years possession would give the right to such a title. According to Knight: 'The Military Government's Land Registration Law of 1920 was just what the sugar companies had wanted for years.'[20] One example of such 'clarification' of land titles is given by Knight. The American Central Romana Company obtained a title to land that up to then had been two villages, Caimoni and Higueral. 'Both villages had been burned, and a hundred and fifty families were under the sky.'[21] A case similar to this took place when the American owned Consuelo estate expanded its land holdings for sugar cultivation.[22]

The historian Bruce Calder argues that the eviction of peasants by the use of force was not something exceptional. For instance he quotes a US Marine colonel who reported a battle between some peasants and the workers of one Johan Leevy, who was rapidly increasing his sugar holdings, as merely a '. . . normal fight between Leevy's men and the natives they are attempting to oust'.[23] 'It would appear', Calder argues, '. . . that the colonel had seen such affairs before and that they were not unusual'.[24]

According to an investigation from the early 1920s, it is alleged that sugar companies commonly took and held land '. . . more by force than by legal process'.[25] Juan Bosch comments: 'The sugar companies needed land, and the means to take it away from the peasants was supplied by the US Marines.'[26] In his autobiography, the US Marine Officer Smedley Butler actually acknowledges that he and his troops paved the way for American sugar interests in the Dominican Republic.[27]

In fact, the 'clarification' of land titles carried out by the US military government caused a peasant rebellion against both the American sugar holdings and some national *latifundistas* who had benefited. US forces put the rebellion down.[28]

Now, it has been argued that the confusion of land titles and the increasing number of frauds, had made an agrarian reform necessary.[29] However, the reform as such seems to have been motivated primarily by the desires of US sugar estates. The latter would in fact appear to have profited most from the reform. Both the new land law and its factual implementation reflects the distribution of power at the time. The court that was to administer the law was of course dominated by American judges.[30] According to Calder through the laws and administrative procedures concerning the adjudication of land titles the military government '. . . completely capitulated to foreign interests, ignoring those of the Dominican people'.[31] The land area controlled by sugar companies increased from 350,000 *tareas* in 1915 to 1 million in 1923.[32]

Dominican Rulers and Sugar Interests

Not only the US military government favoured the sugar sector. During the decades preceding the occupation, several measures, which had favoured the sugar sector, had been undertaken. This policy was also a consequence of the connections between sugar interests, both foreign and domestic, and political control. For instance, in the late nineteenth century, the sugar magnate Juan Batista Vicini had strong links with the dictator Ulises Heureaux by providing, *inter alia*, him with large credits. In fact Heureaux is supposed to have said that he considered Vicini the 'real' president of the country.[33] Vicini received special government favours, obtaining exemption from import duties, special concessions of land for the construction of sugar mills, irrigation facilities, etc. Later, in 1922, Vicini was elected provisional president. The land law which had been promulgated in 1911 had, according to Hamlet Herman, been designed to satisfy the desires of the sugar companies. This law and the one subsequently promulgated by the military government '. . . made it possible for the *ingenios* to obtain control of vast areas paying ridiculously low prices and, at times, without the need to pay anything at all'.[34]

Other legislation was also geared towards the desires of the sugar sector. Machinery imports to the sugar industry was exempted from duties. Profits from sugar were exempted from taxation.[35] On this legislation the United States Receivership reported: '. . . [it] is understood to reflect . . . the desires and wishes of those investors who have come into the Dominican sugar fields.'[36]

The building of infrastructure was geared towards the needs of the sugar sector. Around 1920 sugar estate lines made up 80 per cent of Dominican railway truck.[37] Special provisions were taken under the Agricultural Concessions Law of 1911:

> One privilege was really extraordinary: Where roads, railways, port improvements or other connecting works were found

> necessary, the state exercised its right of eminent domain in the interest of the foreigner expropriating the required land.[38]

Sugar output expanded rapidly at the turn of the century. Output in 1886 was 8,000,000 pounds. By 1896 it reached 35,000,000, a figure which was tripled by 1905.[39] In Figure 4.1 we can see the development of sugar exports from 1905 until the first years of Trujillo's dictatorship.

The long-run trend is one of substantially increased exports. During the post-First World War period, area under cane and sugar production rose considerably in the whole Caribbean, during what has been called the Dance of the Millions.[40] From what we can see from Figure 4.1, Dominican output increased rapidly even afterwards, when prices fell markedly.

The rapid increase of sugar exports was made possible by an inflow of foreign factors of production. The pre-existing supply of factors could not explain the export structure.[41] Political-institutional factors facilitated the expansion of sugar exports. Political decisions increased the profitability of private investment in sugar. These political decisions have, *ceteris paribus*, contributed to increase the size and importance of the sugar sector in the Dominican economy. Sugar interests and political decisions were interlacing, both during Dominican rule and during the US military occupation. The peasants, on the other hand, were politically inarticulate and weak. Government policies, such as the encouragement of labour imports and the land reform discussed above, certainly did not aim at improving conditions for the peasants. The resistance to the expansion of sugar estates, that they tried to establish, had to be armed. However, peasant rebellions were easily crushed by the US Marines.

Chapter 3 provided an explanatory framework for the heavy concentration of resources in the plantation sector. This hinged on two assumptions: 1) the ruler is primarily interested in obtaining security and income; and 2) the presence of transaction costs. It was argued that in the face of a competitive constraint the ruler would agree to a property rights structure favourable to important groups and that the presence of transaction costs induces the ruler to favour the expansion of activities, whose taxation entails low transaction costs. The argument was that plantation production constitutes such an activity.

The period under discussion was, up to the US occupation in

Figure 4.1: Raw Sugar Exports 1905–30: Price and Quantity

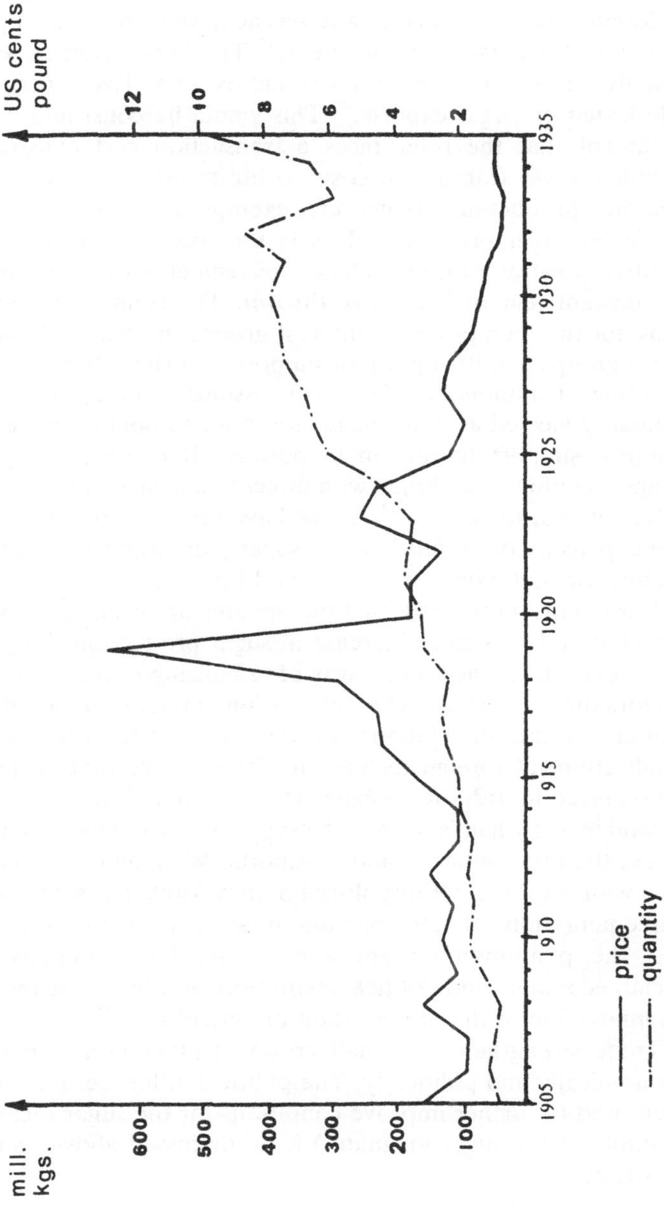

Source: Muto (1976), p. 62.

1916, characterized by a constant struggle for power between different *caudillos*. Once power was achieved, the state apparatus was used for personal enrichment.[42] The Dominican state relied heavily on taxes on both imports and exports. Taxes were generally levied on sugar exports.[43] This would be consistent with the argument that the ruler faces a transaction cost constraint. It entailed lower transaction costs to tax foreign trade than to tax peasant production. However, exemptions were occasionally made for sugar producers. This in turn conforms with the competitive constraint on the rulers. Governments were unstable and in constant fear of being overthrown. The ruling *caudillo* could thus not threaten powerful interest groups, by taxing them, since these groups had the option of supporting a rival. In this case, the granting of monopolies, large concessions of land, etc., may be primarily viewed as a means for the ruler to obtain the necessary political support to remain in power. Of course, this political support could be combined with direct financial advantages for the ruler: bribes, loans, etc.[44] As we have seen Heureaux promoted the expansion of *latifundios* and sugar plantations in return, as it seems, for *both* political support and financial assistance.

It is important to stress that the opening up of sugar exports was not confined to a mere increase in sugar production. Large-scale sugar exports implied a new way of organizing production and the surrounding society. The plantation system required large amounts of unskilled labour at low wages, strictly supervised by a small group of foreign technicians. The surrounding society was reorganized in order to mobilize cheap labour. The concentration of land in a few hands pushed the supply curve of labour outwards, as did the promotion of labour imports. We may draw a comparison with what the anthropologist Sidney Mintz has said about the implementation of the plantation system in the Caribbean: '. . . the plantation system was an absolutely unprecedented social, economic and political institution, and by no means simply an innovation in the organization of agriculture'.[45]

Trade strengthened a small group of plantation owners both economically and politically. The political influence obtained was then used to further improve conditions for the sugar sector. The example of the sugar magnate Vicini, discussed above, is a good illustration of this.

Trujillo and Sugar

Rafael Trujillo became President in 1930. As was argued in Chapter 2, Trujillo's power came to extend to almost every aspect of Dominican life. He used it to transform the whole of Dominican society according to his own wishes.[46] Trujillo became highly involved in economic affairs and came to dominate large sections of the Dominican economy. Particularly his involvement in the sugar sector was to have a vast impact on the subsequent agricultural development of the country.

During the first decade of Trujillo's rule, sugar prices were very low and the sugar industry appears to have made losses. Roberto Cassá asserts that Trujillo guaranteed the survival of the sugar industry by providing subsidies, but fails to tell us why Trujillo undertook such a measure.[47] Trujillo's personal engagement in sugar production started in 1948. From this time on, he expanded his activities in sugar until he controlled two-thirds of total sugar production by his death. The acreage dedicated to sugar cane increased substantially during this process.

Two aspects of Trujillo's engagement in the sugar industry are of particular relevance for our analysis: 1) the motivation for his involvement in sugar on such a large scale does not seem to have been solely for profit; and 2) the fact that he could expand the sugar sector without incurring substantial personal costs or risks. These factors contributed to make the sugar sector inefficient and much larger than it would have been under competitive conditions. After the death of Trujillo the Dominican state inherited both Trujillo's *ingenios* and his vast land holdings, and since subsequent governments have not carried out any significant structural changes, the inefficiencies generated by Trujillo still persist.

Let us start with Trujillo's *motivation* and turn to the cost aspect later. Had Trujillo's only motivation for engagement in sugar production been the desire for profits, the outcome, regarding the size of the sugar sector, would have been identical with what would have obtained in the competitive case (disregarding the cost aspect). But Trujillo's engagement in sugar production and exports would *also* seem to have been motivated by the power aspect of controlling the country's most important economic activity, and by his desire to gain access to foreign exchange.

Several observers argue that Trujillo's sugar activities were not mainly motivated by his interest in profits but by its power aspect and by political reasons. Robert Crassweller argues: 'The fact is that Trujillo was not essentially a good business man, and he was not interested in business as such. It was the power aspect of business that appealed to him.'[48] Cassá asserts: 'Trujillo decided to take possession of the sugar industry primarily for political motives, in order to eliminate a power parallel to his own.'[49] In fact, by the end of the 1940s Trujillo's control over Dominican society was almost total. He controlled the army, the church, the schools, the university, etc. The large sugar industry was probably the only important independent centre of power in the country.

Bosch tries to explain Trujillo's desire for economic power in more profound psychological and sociological terms in his *Trujillo. Causas de una dictadura sin ejemplo*.[50] In brief, Bosch attributes great importance to the fact that Trujillo was of very humble origin and to his ambition of being accepted by the upper class. The only people that did count in Dominican society were those belonging to the landed gentry, whom Bosch calls *los de primera* (the first, the best). Trujillo was ostracized by this group when he was head of the armed forces in the late 1920s. He was politically a very important person, indeed one of the country's most influential persons, but was rejected on the ground of his humble origin and his lack of economic power. Bosch goes on to argue that Trujillo's deep involvement in economic affairs was much a consequence of the humiliation inflicted upon him by the people of *primera*. As dictator he had to show, beyond all doubt, that in economic affairs he was also the most important person in the country.[51] One way of doing so was to engage in the country's most important industry: sugar.

It is of course difficult to asses the plausibility of this reasoning. However the agreement among different observers gives *some* weight to the argument that Trujillo engaged in large-scale sugar production partly for 'political' reasons.

But more important is perhaps the 'foreign exchange motive' for engaging in sugar. The running of the sugar industry gave Trujillo direct control over the most important source of foreign exchange. The importance of direct access to foreign exchange is a factor stressed by Gustavo Volmar. Trujillo's activities in sugar, Volmar argues:

> . . . were the result of a desire to dominate the sources of foreign exchange no matter what export prices were at the time . . . due to the special relationship between the government as such and

> the Trujillo family, the latter could operate the sugar industry at a profit almost under any conceivable condition while controlling at the same time the most important economic activity as far as foreign exchange earnings were concerned.[52]

Trujillo did certainly have use for foreign exchange. He and his family deposited substantial sums in foreign banks. Trujillo, for instance, kept the receipts from sales from the *ingenio* Río Haina abroad.[53] He also needed foreign exchange to buy military equipment (necessary if he wanted to remain in power), for consumption of imported goods, and to run his numerous import firms.[54]

From this we may infer that the utility that Trujillo derived from sugar production and exports was not solely a matter of the profits that the industry yielded him. The control of sugar production also gave him ready access to foreign exchange and, assumedly, 'power'. Trujillo thus faced a trade-off between profits, on the one hand, and foreign exchange receipts and 'power' on the other. If we take the volume of output (x) as a proxy for both foreign exchange and 'power'[55] there is thus a trade-off between profits, π, and volume (x), giving the π−x locus illustrated in Figure 4.2. The technological assumption behind this curve is that after a certain level of output, profits decrease within the expansion of x. Both π and x provide utility to Trujillo, represented by a convex indifference curve, UU. Utility maximization must then occur at a point on the negative slope of the π −x locus. Sugar is produced at a point beyond that which maximize profits.[56]

Figure 4.2: Utility Maximization Problem Faced by the Dictator Trujillo

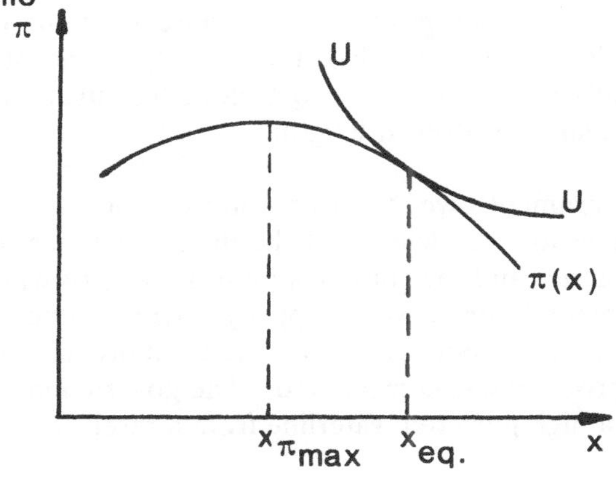

It is of course difficult to test empirically whether Trujillo tried to maximize profits or not. Some factors, however, indicate that the sugar industry may not have been too profitable. Sugar prices were in fact declining during the period in which Trujillo took an interest in expanding sugar production (1948–60)[57] and, as a reflection of this, he spent much money on lobbying for obtaining a larger quota on the US market.[58] We do not have figures on the performance of Trujillo's sugar industry but several observers argue that it was not very lucrative.[59]

Independent of the 'true' motives for Trujillo's engagement in sugar, the impact of Trujillo's expansion of the sugar sector, on the Dominican economy, was both considerable and devastating due to the *instruments* that he employed to satisfy this aim.

The land that he required could be obtained by use of force and intimidation. According to Ian Bell his methods of aquisition ranged '. . . from purchase at knockdown price by intimidation or blackmail to outright confiscation'.[60] Peasants were evicted from their land to give space for Trujillo's production of sugar cane. For instance, the land surrounding the large *ingenio* Río Haina, and occupied by Trujillo, had formerly belonged to peasants.[61] It is assumed that up to between 50 and 60 per cent of the arable land, often of best quality, ended up belonging to Trujillo or his family.[62] Much of the labour needed for the operation of the plantations continued to be provided from Haiti. Despite a massacre of 15,000 to 25,000 Haitians in 1937, and much anti-Haitian rhetoric, Trujillo signed various recruitment treaties with Haiti.[63]

Trujillo used government resources in various ways. He used the reserves of the *Banco Central* to finance the construction of his *ingenios*. He used government resources for the construction of the infrastructure needed for his sugar industry. Regarding Trujillo's use of the state to benefit his sugar interests we can quote Daniel Spitzer at length:

> Government owned construction equipment was used free of charge for the clearing of the dictator's lands, the building of refineries and the construction of roads (for which special governmental funds were tapped). Army equipment and manpower for labor were employed extensively on Trujillo enterprises as was convict labor. The government provided funds for a high powered waterline from a reservoir to Trujillo's first

> sugar property at Catarey. The huge Río Haina complex was built largely with forced labor under the auspices of the army. Tractors and bulldozers for the mill came from the Department of Public Works.[64]

Trujillo could use his power in other ways. Trujillo's sugar holdings were declared 'new industry' thus affording them tax exemptions. A Labour Code was enforced, but only on those holdings that did not belong to Trujillo.[65]

Trujillo could thus expand the sugar industry without giving any particular consideration to the costs. Considering the distortions thus introduced (Trujillo could obtain resources, land, etc., at (implicit) prices far below the social opportunity cost) resources were inoptimally allocated between different producers. The sugar sector turned out to be too large from a social point of view. In fact the consequence of Trujillo's activities appears to be a reduction of overall economic performance. We will consider this further in Chapter 5.

But why should Trujillo promote overall inefficiency? Would it not be better to implement policies that maximize national income and then use the state power to extract income by taxation?

If Trujillo, in accordance with the discussion above on Trujillo's motives, engaged in sugar production partly because of the 'power' aspect of controlling the industry, he could sacrifice some income in order to control sugar production. But this explanation does not suffice to explain why Trujillo implemented policies which may have lowered overall performance.

Even if we assume that Trujillo did try to maximize his personal income, Trujillo had nevertheless reasons for promoting overall inefficiency since he faced a transaction cost constraint. As argued in Chapters 2 and 3, a policy which leads to better overall performance may well reduce the income of the ruler, since the collection of taxes entails transaction costs. Theoretically, Trujillo could have opted for a smallholder system, where the structure of land ownership (more equal distribution) could promote better utilization of land and thus higher overall output. However, the collection of taxes on small-scale producers may entail very high transaction costs. Peasants are widely scattered, communication is poor,[66] the administrative capacity is low.

In addition, the peasant tends to produce subsistence goods, and Trujillo was interested in obtaining foreign exchange. Trujillo could of course have stimulated or forced peasants to produce for exports. Again, this would entail high transaction costs. The plantation alternative implied lower transaction costs. Trujillo could, by the use of force, concentrate land ownership to himself and his family. He promoted the import of labour for plantation work. This labour could then, in a military fashion, be strictly supervised.

Due to Trujillo's activities, the acreage dedicated to sugar cane in the Dominican Republic doubled between 1948 and 1960, as did sugar exports.[67] This occurred despite falling sugar prices and deteriorating terms of trade during the same period. An investigation carried out by the US Department of Agriculture in 1963 observed with some amazement: 'In the early 1950s . . . despite growing world supplies of sugar, the Dominican Republic began to increase production of sugar and to expand total investment in the industry.'[68]

This rapid expansion of sugar production and exports could not be fully explained by traditional trade theory. The fact that the Dominican Republic was under dictatorial rule, the dictator's motivations and the instruments at his disposal such as the eviction of peasants from their lands by the use of force, were crucial factors for the expansion of sugar exports.

Sugar in the Post-Trujillo Period

Political-institutional factors are also important in explaining why production and trade structures have not significantly changed during the period following Trujillo's death. Numerous official publications have stressed the need to decrease the influence of sugar in the economy and to diversify production and trade structure. However, policies have not been in accordance with these proclamations.

Trujillo's property was taken over by the state after the dictator's death. His sugar properties were initially administered by the Corporación Azucarera Dominicana (CAD) but were reorganized in 1966 under the Consejo Estatal de Azucar (CEA). In addition to this state producer there are two private producers, one national, Vicini, and one American, La Romana, owned by Gulf and Western. The CEA is the largest of these companies, producing about two-thirds of total sugar production and controlling by far the largest sugar land areas (see below).

A conspicuous feature of sugar policies in the post-Trujillo period has been the continued reliance on labour imports. An official investigation estimated that 75 per cent of the labour force in the sugar industry in 1980 was Haitian.[69] The policy of promoting labour imports, pursued during the American occupation and by Trujillo, has thus not come to a halt. At the same time as imports of Haitian labour are promoted, politicians blame the high levels of unemployment on the presence of Haitians in the country.

The institutional character of the Haitian immigration can be seen for example from the fact that various contracts on Haitian labour have been signed by the Haitian and Dominican governments. In 1966, when Balaguer came to power, a contract was signed giving the Duvalier government 60 Dominican pesos for each worker provided. For the 1980–1 *zafra* (harvest), the price of a Haitian worker had risen to 182 US dollars.[70] Table 4.2 shows the extent of Haitian immigration supervised by the CEA.

Table 4.2: Legal Immigration of Haitian Sugar Workers, 1966/67–1979/80

Year of *zafra*	Number of Legal immigrants
1966–67	14,000
1967–68	10,000
1968–69	n.a.
1969–70	12,000
1970–71	n.a.
1971–72	12,000
1972–73	12,000
1973–74	12,000
1974–75	n.a.
1975–76	12,000
1976–77	12,000
1977–78	0
1978–79	15,000
1979–80	16,000

Source: Veras (1981), p. 63.

The living conditions of these Haitians is not enviable. Their conditions have been compared with those of slavery.[71] Haitians may not belong to a labour union.[72] These labour imports imply that the sugar sector (both CEA and the two private producers) has been able to maintain low wages.[73]

The favourable position of the sugar industry also concerns access to land. Above we have described how the sugar industry has been able to benefit from the promulgation of laws that suit the sugar industry and not least, the use of military force. The (implicit) price of land paid by the sugar industry has thus been considerably lower than its social opportunity cost.

The sugar industry does not use land obtained at such low price very efficiently. This applies particularly to the large state producer, CEA. The CEA does for instance not impute any cost of using its vast sugar lands in its calculations. The social opportunity cost of using land for cane production is however considerable. We have tried to make a rough estimate of the (social) opportunity cost of land used by CEA. To carry out an accurate estimate of opportunity cost we would need accurate figures on the amount and quality of land owned by CEA and on land prices. Neither is available. Perhaps not even CEA itself knows exactly how much land it controls. Eduardo Latorre, a senior official at CEA, affirms that CEA owns about 4.8 million *tareas*.[74] Information on land prices, share-cropping arrangments, etc., is scanty. According to IICA no systematic survey on rents, share-cropping arrangements, etc., has been carried out.[75] Piecemeal information can however be found. Fernando Ferrán affirms that under tenancy arrangements, the tenant may have to pay 20 pesos per year and *tarea*.[76] This figure refers to 1976. Multiplying this figure by the extension of land controlled by CEA gives a figure of 96 million pesos. In order to give an idea of the size of this sum we can mention that CEA's total entries in 1976 were 270 million.[77] In 1979, when sugar prices were lower, CEA's total receipts were 168 million,[78] while, if we extrapolate the land 'cost' of 1976 with the rate of inflation, this amounted to 123 million.

We do not pretend that these figures are exact estimates of the social opportunity costs involved in using land for sugar production by CEA. Our point is that the social opportunity cost involved is considerable but the CEA does not consider land a scarce resource.

What we have described is a serious distortion. While the CEA can use a substantial part of the country's land resources at no cost the peasant may have to pay up to more than 35 pesos per *tarea* under tenancy arrangements or more than 100 pesos under share-cropping arrangements.[79] This is reflected in an inefficient utilization of land by the sugar industry while the peasant cultivates the small plot he has access to very intensively. We will have more to say about this in Chapter 5.

Hence we have several factors of an institutional character that favour sugar production: government promotion of labour imports, use of state land free of charge (concerns the CEA) and an infrastructure, transport system, irrigation, etc., heavily geared towards the needs of the sugar sector. Despite these benefits, state sugar production runs at a large deficit. When the sugar industry inherited from Trujillo was reorganized in 1966, the state wrote off losses that it had been accumulating during the first half of the 1960s. These amounted to more than 30 million pesos.[80] During the 1970s, the CEA made losses every year except in 1975 when prices reached their peak.[81] However, it must be acknowledged that the overvaluation of the peso influenced the result (reducing the amount of domestic currency received per unit of exports).[82] But even accounting for the overvaluation of the exchange rate, the CEA would be making losses most years, and the results would be far from covering even a very moderate estimate of the opportunity cost of land dedicated to sugar.

There are several peculiarities in the policies concerning the huge state producer. One such peculiarity is that even when it has been making losses, the CEA has had to pay export taxes. In order to finance its operating costs, the CEA has then had to be subsidized by government and has had to take up foreign loans. How can one try to explain such an oddity and the fact that despite very low world market prices and continuing losses, no efforts to diversify production have taken place? To try to get at least a partial explanation of this state of affairs, we must identify different interest groups and discuss their motivation.

Let us start with the *government*. The behaviour of the government is conditioned for instance by the short election periods and the need for the president and ministers to reward supporters. The election period in the Dominican Republic is four years. This does not motivate the government to carry out changes that will only have a visible result in the long run. To carry out a programme to diversify agricultural production is a difficult task and the possible positive results would probably not be manifest within the election period. While losses by the sugar industry would be carried by the Dominican society at large (in the form of taxes, or inflationary financing) and could be blamed on external factors, a rise in sugar prices would, on the other hand, provide the government with ample resources to squander on prestige buildings, to divert into its own pockets, etc. Thus if things go bad (low export prices),

Dominican society will lose, while if things go well, government and its bureaucracy will win. Traditionally, political power in the Dominican Republic has been used to enrich not only those in power, but also political supporters, relatives, friends, etc. One way of rewarding such allies has been to provide them with prestige employment in the public sector and thus possibly also with the largest industry in the country, the Consejo Estatal de Azucar. In the mid-1960s, John Bartlow Martin wrote: '. . . the Consejo could not withstand political pressure to put on the Haina payroll thousands of people that did not work at all'.[83] Things have probably not changed much since that date.

The *CEA bureaucracy* does not appear to have any incentives to decrease sugar production despite losses. We may well assume that CEA managers aim at maximizing the size of the bureaucracy and the level of output (this would give them more prestige and power) since they will not be responsible for economic losses.[84] It is also important to stress that many CEA officials have been able to make large personal economic gains from their position in the company. Agricultural diversification does therefore not appear to be an interesting alternative for CEA managers.

We may note that the CEA argues that the land not dedicated to sugar cane is not suitable for other production. According to independent observers this is false.[85] Much of the land which the CEA controls is of very good quality and perfectly suitable for other cultivation. One can frequently observe sugar cane and, for instance rice, cultivated side by side. If anything, much of the land owned by CEA is not suitable for cane.[86] This kind of argument from the CEA is instead a reflection of the CEA bureaucracy's personal interest in maintaining production at present levels rather than the true state of land conditions.

Another important interest group is the set of independent sugar producers, *colonos*, who sell cane to CEA *ingenios*. This class of producers expanded under Balaguer, who in order to secure political support from important persons gave them state land on which they were supposed to produce cane. Many of those who received land in this way were high ranked members of the armed forces. These *colonos* operate under extremely favourable conditions, receiving subsidized loans from the CEA, who actually often carry out most of the work on these holdings. The price to these *colonos* for the cane they deliver is two to three times higher than the cost for CEA of raising its own cane, and can be considered a 'political price'.[87] These *colonos* can thus be assumed to be interested in maintaining the existing production structure.

We would not deny that diversification is a difficult task and that there are many issues to be settled before even a moderate programme of diversification could be implemented. What we have tried to show is that important individuals have no incentives to undertake changes.

We have so far limited our discussion to the state sugar producer, who is, as we have mentioned above, the most important one, as far as sugar output and control of land is concerned. The CEA controls about 80 per cent of all sugar land. The remaining production is carried out by two private producers, Gulf and Western and Vicini. The former amalgamated with the ancient South Porto Rico Sugar Company in 1967.

Gulf and Western is a conglomerate particularly engaged in food production, but is also involved in tourism and in industrial free zones. The company seems to have taken less and less interest in sugar production after the mid-1970s.[88] The company has moved away from its dependence on sugar. It has started production of a series of agricultural products, citrus fruits, tomatoes, etc. A large share of Gulf and Western's land holdings is used for the raising of cattle. It uses the sugar by-product, *melaza*, for the feeding of this cattle stock. It also carries out production of *furfural*, a sugar by-product used in plastic, chemical and pharmaceutical industries.[89]

In June 1984, Gulf and Western announced that it intended to sell its sugar interests in the Dominican Republic.[90] This, if anything, shows the decreasing interest in sugar shown by this multinational.

Information on costs and profits is not made public by these two private companies. 'Informed guessers' assume that the production cost of raw sugar for these producers are about 10 per cent lower than that of the CEA.[91] This means that at the world market prices that have prevailed during the last years, they would have been making losses.[92] However, both producers have reduced the amount of sugar sold at world market prices. Vicini today produces exactly what it can place on the preferential US market.[93] This also appears to be the strategy of Gulf and Western, which in addition, as we have seen, has ventured into agricultural diversification. We may also note that Gulf and Western has a larger share of the Dominican quota, i.e. the quota which the United States offers the Dominican Republic, than its actual share in Dominican production and exports would entitle it to.[94] This perhaps reflects the political influence of the company in the Dominican Republic.

To a large extent both producers use imported Haitian labour. Most of the land controlled by the companies has been in their domain for a very long time. The expansion of American sugar companies during the American occupation, and the connection between the Vicini family and political decision makers, has been discussed above. The example given by Knight on the burning of two villages for the expansion of the sugar industry actually concerned the Central Romana which today is run by Gulf and Western. There have been recent controversies concerning the status of some of the land the companies control. Gulf and Western has, for instance, been accused of illegally occupying state land,[95] and as late as 1983, 200 persons invaded 19,000 *tareas* cultivated by Vicini, claiming that this land belonged to them.[96]

In the same way as the CEA, both these producers argue that the land dedicated to cane is not suitable for other agricultural production.[97] The argument does not appear to be more valid than CEA's. For instance, Gulf and Western controls most of that land in the eastern region which is considered to be of high value for production of other crops. This is supported by the fact that the company has ventured into other agricultural production. Peasant pressure for land, and confrontations with the sugar industry, has taken place in the eastern region which is dominated by Gulf and Western.

These large private producers are considered to have a strong political influence in the country.

Resource Use in a Plantation Economy

In traditional economic theory resources are allocated via 'impersonal' market forces, through the smooth working of the price system. In competitive models, prices are given to the individual producer and consumer, both being too small to decide on anything but quantities to produce or consume. From the exposition above we can, however, discern individual persons or groups whose activities have been decisive for the allocation of resources and whose decisions have not been confined to mere quantity adjustment to given prices.

These persons or groups have been able to influence political decisions that have an important bearing on allocation. American sugar interests and domestic *latifundistas* could clearly benefit from the land legislation enforced by the US military government. This legislation was in turn a reflection of the influence of the sugar industry. Trujillo could use the entire state apparatus for his personal benefit and that implied a substantial expansion of the sugar sector. Different interest groups have since the death of Trujillo been able to present obstacles to changes in the production structure. It is also important to stress that considerable *force* has been used in the process of expanding the sugar sector. The military was used to evict peasants from their land and to suppress peasant resistance. Trujillo used force to get control over about half of the country's land resources. The sugar sector has thus obtained land at (implicit) prices far below social opportunity cost. This distortion implies much more land under sugar cane than would have obtained under competitive conditions.

The bulk of cultivable land is in farms. Land in farms actually decreased during the 1970s.[98] Erosion may decrease the amount of cultivable land in the future. Large devastations of Dominican forests starting during the American occupation and continuing under the regime of Trujillo have contributed to the erosion process.[99] Inadequate management has resulted in rich land becoming less productive. Already in 1952 the country had lost about 15 per cent of its total amount of arable land due to erosion.[100] Trujillo did little to enforce conservation laws and subsequent governments have done little to reverse this process.[101]

Shortage of cultivable land has forced the farm population to expand into mountainous areas. The cutting of forests in order to make *conucos*, small gardens, has reinforced the erosion process. Today, food is clearly produced on land which is unsuitable for this activity.[102] The scarcity of land will force the Dominican society to use its land resources in the best possible way if it is to have any chance of feeding its rapidly growing population. This is not done today and the fact that sugar producers control a considerable part of the country's land resources, and utilize the land they control poorly, contributes to a socially inefficient use of resources.

According to an official Dominican publication, *Plandes*, the pattern of land use was as follows in 1971.

Table 4.3: Land Use in 1971

	thousands of hectares
Seasonal crops	292
Permanent crops	533
Fallow	142
Pasture	1,432
Forest	250
Other	37

Source: Oficina Nacional de Planificación (1974), p. 108.

According to an OAS survey on land capability, only 600,000 hectares were found to be of good quality for cultivation.[103] In addition there were 360,000 hectares whose production capacity was limited or marginal. How much of this land is then occupied by the three sugar producers?

No accurate data on the extension of sugar land is available. According to Hans Illy, the sugar holdings are outside official statistics for mainly political reasons.[104] Above we assumed that the state producer CEA controls about 300,000 hectares. Gulf and Western controls about 110,000 hectares, of which 60,000 are used for cultivation of cane, while Vicini controls about 15,000 hectares.[105] In total that would make 375,000 hectares used for cane production. These figures clearly indicate the importance of sugar in the use of a scarce production resource in the Dominican Republic. The fact that this estimate of cane land may for political reasons be an underestimate strengthens this inference.

Considerable attention has been given to the role that legislation and the use of force has played in securing a large supply of land for the sugar sector. This has created very disparate conditions between the sugar sector and peasant production. However, the concentration of land in a few hands, other than sugar producers, the creation of *latifundios* in general, can be analyzed in similar terms. The dictator Heureaux secured political support for himself by creating a class of *latifundistas*.[106] He '. . . based the stability of his regime on friends whom he gave free hands to establish themselves as *latifundistas*, and in every region in the country there were two or three friends of Heureaux who took hold of the best land.'[107] Domestic *latifundistas* and American lumber companies could benefit from the land laws promulgated by the US military government.[108] Friends and political supporters of Trujillo were granted land by the dictator. Political allies to Balaguer were also able to gain possession of considerable land.[109] These are factors which have contributed to make the distribution of land extremely unequal in the Dominican Republic. Table 4.4 shows the distribution of land in the country in 1971. The table indicates that 1.2 per cent of farms occupy almost 45 per cent of the land. This is one of the most unequal patterns of land distribution in the world.[110]

Table 4.4: Land Distribution in 1971

Range in ha.	No. of farms	%	% of area
0.5–5	182,222	71.9	12.7
5–101	69,995	26.9	42.9
101–803	2,658	1.0	19.1
803–	425	0.2	25.3

Source: Oficina Internacional del Trabajo (1975), p.145.

According to Carlos Dore y Cabral there are also about 50,000 *microfincas* of less than 0.5 hectares. [111] These are outside the official statistics. There are also about 190,000 rural families with no land at all, according to the same source. These two last groups comprise about 36 per cent of the rural population.[112]

There is a connection between the size of a land holding and the intensity with which it is cultivated. The larger the size of the holding the less intensively it is generally cultivated.[113] There is also a connection between the size of the land holding and the composition of crops cultivated on it. Farms of up to 80 *tareas* produce food for domestic consumption. Two-thirds of rice production come from 25,000 farms of size less than 80 *tareas*.[114] Farms of between 80 and 800 *tareas* devote about half of their area to production of food for domestic consumption, and the rest to production of export crops, mainly coffee, cocoa and tobacco. Larger holdings are almost completely dedicated to export production, mostly sugar and cattle.[115]

The pattern of land distribution does accordingly seem to have a significant impact on both the structure of production and the structure of the country's foreign trade.

Concluding Remarks

In this chapter we have argued that in order to explain why the Dominican economy is so heavily geared towards sugar exports considerable attention must be paid to institutional factors. We have tried to show that the opening up and expansion of trade was not the result of a movement along the country's production possibility curve, with institutions remaining unchanged as assumed by traditional trade theory. In fact, production factors have been supplied from abroad and institutions have been changed in order to facilitate sugar expansion. The available supply of production factors in the Dominican Republic could not have yielded a comparative advantage in large-scale sugar production. Management and capital was lacking. The required amounts of plantation labour have not been forthcoming within the Dominican economy at the wage levels offered.

American sugar companies, the US military occupants, Trujillo and Dominican sugar barons such as Vicini represent groups or persons who have been able to influence the institutional setting.

The structure of land ownership changed during the process of expansion of sugar production. Legislation seems to have been designed in the interest of sugar business and *latifundistas*. Organization based on *terrenos comuneros*, communal lands, was abandoned. The *latifundios*, which are a relatively recent development in the Dominican Republic, thus gained importance with the expansion of the sugar industry in the economy. This process was reinforced during the Trujillo dictatorship. Trujillo became the country's largest single landowner by means of force. Trujillo's activities, in Bell's words, '. . . created latifundia on a scale unprecedented in the Dominican Republic'.[116]

The dictator not only got hold of the best land by fraud and the use of force. Public resources were also used to expand his sugar industry. The road system was geared towards the needs of Trujillo's sugar industry. Trujillo could thus expand the sugar industry without due consideration to costs.

The use of force has been an integral part of the process of concentrating land in a few hands. The US Marines were used to protect the interests of the sugar industry. The backbone of the Trujillo regime was the armed forces. They were in fact the prerequisite for the expansion of Trujillo's sugar interests. Force has also been used to prevent a land reform.[117]

The interests of the sugar industry have given rise to the massive importation of Haitian labour. The state has acted on behalf of sugar interests signing contracts with Haitian governments for the supply of Haitian labour. This policy has certainly not been in the interest of *minifundistas* or landless rural workers.

The state has neglected the interest of the peasant sector in a number of other ways. A very small fraction of formal credit has been directed to the peasant sector. The peasants have thus had to rely on informal sources of credit at very high rates of interest. Government constructed infrastructure has neglected peasant areas. Irrigation has been neglected (most of the land which has received irrigation is sugar land).[118] While the transport system has satisfied the needs of the sugar sector, it has disregarded the needs of the peasants. Transportation costs for the *campesino* can be exorbitant. The policy of the price regulation institute INESPRE operates against the interests of most of the peasants who produce for the market.[119]

These are all important factors in explaining why we can observe a secular stagnation in *per capita* agricultural production (other than sugar) at the same time as sugar production has been increasing. These factors also influence the trade structure: large sugar exports and substantial food imports. The trade structure cannot be independent of institutional factors and power relations.

In Chapter 3 we briefly discussed George Beckford's book on the plantation economies of the Third World. Beckford's analysis considers explicitly the importance of institutional factors in the allocation and growth of resources. An important element in Beckford's work is his emphasis on distortions present in the plantation economies. The plantation system has created a situation which gives the peasants very limited access to land and capital. According to Beckford these distortions have mainly been induced by governments: 'Everywhere in the plantation world at present and in the past the state has acted on behalf of plantations in several ways.'[120] From our analysis in this chapter, it may be inferred that the Dominican Republic clearly falls into this pattern. But while Beckford attributes the behaviour of government to 'alien ideologies', we have argued that it has been to the personal benefit of the Dominican ruler to promote the plantation system, and although we have stressed the importance of institutional factors, thus agreeing with Beckford, we would not put the blame for the present state of affairs on 'dependence' or argue for a 'closure of the economy' as does Beckford.[121] Many Dominican economists 'explain' the Dominican trade structure purely in terms of dependence. Lucas Vicens argues: 'Imports of food, and agricultural products in general is evidence . . . of the dependence on the world market and the law of unequal exchange which characterize semicolonial countries.'[122] Roberto Cassá argues along similar lines.[123] But none of them actually explains how 'dependence' has determined the trade structure. 'Dependence' resembles some kind of Pandora's box from which everything considered bad originates. It seems as if the world market as such is something to be seriously distrusted.

We cannot, however, disregard the fact that foreign interests have had an influence on domestic political decisions. American sugar interests have, as we have argued above, exerted such an influence. But then the trade structure has to be discusssed in terms of the mutual interests of Dominican policy makers and foreign business, and should not, in abstract terms, be blamed on the 'world market' or 'unequal exchange'.

It should also be noted that sugar exports grew particularly during the 1950s. This was the decade during which Trujillo engaged in sugar production, evicting peasants and disrupting the agricultural organization of the country. These activities were not conditioned by foreign interests but by Trujillo's. Similarly, it is domestic rather than foreign interests that account for the conditions which plague the peasants today; unequal distribution of land, discriminatory price policy, lack of rural infrastructure, etc., with their consequences for production and international trade.

Notes

1. See Chapter 1.
2. See Chapter 5.
3. See for instance Moya-Pons (1982c), p. 14, and Illy (1978), p. 181.
4. A sequence which would correspond to the textbook version of the opening up of trade.
5. The price had fallen during the 1850s, and did not increase during the 1860s. Between 1870–2 and 1884 the price fell by more than 50 per cent and remained at this low level, except during a brief period, until the exceptional years towards the end of the First World War and immediately afterwards. See Thomas (1971), p. 272.
6. Muto (1976), p. 333.
7. Bell (1981), p. 317.
8. Moya Pons (1980), p. 409.
9. Knight (1928), p. 133.
10. Ibid., p. xv.
11. Ibid., p. 141.
12. Ibid., with 'black' labour Knight intended coloured immigrants.
13. Lundahl and Vargas (1983), p. 118.
14. Ibid., p. 119.

15. Ibid., p. 121.
16. Knight (1928), p. 125.
17. Hoetink (1965), p. 5.
18. Ibid.
19. Ibid., p. 13. See also Calder (1984), p. 104.
20. Knight (1928), p. 140.
21. Ibid., p. 118.
22. Calder (1981), p. 44. Spitzer (1972), p. 351 argues: 'By 1920, a considerable amount of land had been confiscated from the peasantry as a result of "clarification" of land titles by the military government.'
23. Calder (1981), p. 44.
24. Ibid.
25. Ibid.
26. Bosch (1959), p. 104.
27. See Schori (1981).
28. Moya Pons (1980), pp. 476–7. See also Calder (1984), pp. 115–83, and Spitzer (1972), p. 351.
29. This is argued by Clausner (1973), pp. 194–5.
30. Ibid., p. 201.
31. Calder (1984), p. 31.
32. Muto (1976), p. 36. 1 *tarea* = 0.063 hectares.
33. Herman (1981), p. 163.
34. Ibid., p. 167, translation from Spanish by the present author.
35. Spitzer (1972), p. 331.
36. Quoted in Muto (1976), p. 96.
37. Muto (1976), p. 181.
38. Knight (1928), p. 48.
39. Ibid., p. 24.
40. As a consequence of the war, with the European sugar fields in ruin, the price of sugar soared, reaching a peak in 1919. With the recovery of the beet industry, prices returned to 'normal' levels.
41. This is consistent with, for instance, Johathan Levin's analysis of the trade structure in Peru. Levin (1960).
42. See Chapter 2.
43. Herman (1981), p. 169. See also Muto (1976), p. 41.
44. Herman (1981), p. 169, argues that sugar estate owners generally supported government financially by loans, grants, etc. According to Knight, President Morales *sold* exemption from tax to sugar planters. Knight (1928), pp. 35–6. See also Knight (ibid.), p. 36 on the efforts of governments to tax sugar and the resistance to such a tax by sugar estates.
45. Mintz' foreword in Guerra y Sanchez (1964), p. xiv.
46. See biographies on Trujillo by Crassweller (1966), Wiarda (1968), Ornes (1958) and Galindez (1962).
47. Cassá (1980), p. 263.
48. Crassweller (1966), p. 263.
49. Cassá (1980), p. 264. See also Wiarda (1968) arguing that 'power' as such was the predominant motive for most of Trujillo's activities.
50. Bosch (1959).
51. Ibid., pp. 37–9.
52. Volmar (1971), p. 79.
53. Academia de las Ciencias en la República Dominicana (1977), p. 250.
54. See Chapter 2.
55. We thus assume that the larger the volume of sugar production the larger both foreign exchange receipts and 'power'.

56. Compare the model of the behaviour of a bureaucracy having 'non-profit' motives, Mueller (1979), p. 165.
57. The average price in 1947–8 was 4.7 US cents per pound compared with 3.1 in 1959–60, see Cassá (1982), Table III 11.
58. See for instance Martin (1966), p. 161.
59. 'In short, Trujillo made almost every technical mistake in operation of this industry that it was possible to make, and on cash flow basis the entire operation lost money.' Crassweller (1966), p. 259. Bell (1981), p. 243, puts forth similar arguments.
60. Bell (1981), p. 306. See also Cassá (1982), p. 243.
61. Cassá (1982), pp. 127–8. See also Franco (1967), p. 48.
62. Wiarda (1968), p. 83.
63. Lundahl and Vargas (1983), p. 125.
64. Spitzer (1972), p. 395.
65. Ibid.
66. An illustration of the poor communications prevailing at the time is given by the fact that even in the 1960s, according to Muto, the only producers who could supply urban markets were those living along the main highway constructed in the 1920s. Muto (1976), p. 104.
67. Cassá (1982), p. 222 and 264.
68. US Department of Agriculture (1963), p. 18.
69. See Lundahl and Vargas (1983), p. 138.
70. Ibid., p. 127.
71. Anti-Slavery Society (1979), p. 1.
72. Bell (1981), p. 316.
73. On wages in the sugar industry, see Oficina Nacional de Planificación (1981). On the effects of labour imports on the labour market see Lundahl and Vargas (1983) pp. 140–1.
74. Latorre (1973), p. 10. Latorre was at the time Assistant to the Under-Executive Director.
75. Information given to the author by IICA, Institute for Co-operation on Agriculture, Santo Domingo.
76. Ferrán (1976), p. 100.
77. Figure from Oficina Nacional de Presupuestos in Moya Pons (1982d), p. 27.
78. Ibid.
79. Figures obtained by extrapolation of 1976 figures using the consumer price index to the end of 1983. The figure for share-cropping presented by Ferrán, for 1976, shows that a share-cropper may have to pay up to 60 pesos.
80. Instituto de Capacitación Tributaria (1982).
81. Figure from Oficina Nacional de Presupuestos in Moya Pons (1982d), p. 27.
82. On the exchange rate see Chapter 6.
83. Martin (1966), p. 162.
84. See the discussion on the behaviour of the bureaucracy in Mueller (1979).
85. Information received at IICA and from officials at the Ministery of Planning, section Azucar y Diversificacion.
86. See, for instance, Vicens (1982), p. 309, and Bookers (1975).
87. Information received from officials at CEA.
88. Dore y Cabral (1981), p. 44.
89. See Del Castillo *et al.* (1974), p. 217.
90. Listín Diario (1984).
91. See Moya Pons (1982d), pp. 45–6.
92. For example, the world market price of raw sugar averaged about 7 US cents per pound in 1983 and in 1984, about 5 cents. Production costs of CEA were estimated to be about 20 centavos per pound in the beginning of 1983. Official exchange rate one to one. On the exchange rate see Chapters 6 and 7.

93. According to the Ministry of Planning.
94. See Del Castillo *et al.* (1974).
95. Ibid., p. 139.
96. *Hoy* (1983), 22 April.
97. See, for instance, speech by Felipe Vicini in Instituto Azucarero Dominicano (1982).
98. Oficina Nacional de Planificación (1974), p. xii.
99. Spitzer (1972), p. 512.
100. Ibid., p. 513.
101. Ibid. See also Palmer (1976) discussing land use along the Haitian-Dominican border, argues that soil productivity has decreased on both sides.
102. Moya Pons (1982c), p. 42.
103. World Bank (1978a), p. 387.
104. Illy (1978), p. 70.
105. Ibid., pp. 70–1.
106. Bosch (1959), p. 39.
107. Ibid., see also p. 88.
108. Knight (1928), Chapters 12 and 13.
109. See Chapter 2.
110. The Dominican Republic ranks 12th in terms of its Gini index in a sample of 54 countries in Taylor and Hudson (1975), p. 267.
111. Dore y Cabral (1979), p. 28.
112. See Moya Pons (1982c), p. 103.
113. See Chapter 5.
114. Senauer (1982).
115. See Vicens (1982), pp. 162–3.
116. Bell (1981), p. 281.
117. See Chapter 2.
118. Dore y Cabral (1981), p. 23.
119. See Chapters 6 and 7.
120. Beckford (1972), p. 181.
121. Ibid., p. 221.
122. Vicens (1982), p. 161, translation from Spanish by the present author.
123. Cassá (1982), p. 202.

5 PLANTATION EXPORTS AND ECONOMIC DEVELOPMENT

In the preceding chapter we discussed the development of the important sugar sector. We will now discuss some of the economic consequences of the secular expansion of sugar exports. The most conspicuous effect of the expansion of the sugar sector has been the negative impact on resource allocation within the agricultural sector, and the concomitant discrimination of the peasant community. Stagnation in the rural sector is also evident, both with regards to agricultural technology and growth of non-sugar output. We will start with a brief discussion of the opening up of trade and the period of foreign dominance of the sugar industry. The way trade was opened up and the consequences for the economy deserve, we think, some attention *per se* and may differ from what can be predicted from traditional trade theory. The consequences of Trujillo's engagement in sugar exports will be analyzed, and finally we will examine the post-Trujillo period. It must be emphasized, however, that the concentration of much of Dominican land in the hands of sugar producers is just one aspect of a generally extremely skewed distribution of land which has had a negative effect on rural development. This is an aspect which will also be considered in the present chapter.

Opening Up of Trade and Foreign Dominance

Reference has already been made to the limited availability of data. It goes without saying that this problem is particularly pronounced when we are discussing the end of the nineteenth century and the beginning of the twentieth. Our discussion will accordingly have to be narrative in character, since few quantitative data can be provided.

According to the textbook exposition, the opening up of trade will involve a reallocation of factors of production and the remuneration of factors used intensively in export production will increase. As was described in Chapter 4, the opening up of large-scale sugar exports was however not a result of a mere movement along the Dominican transformation curve. Production factors for sugar production were supplied from abroad and institutions were changed in order to facilitate sugar production and exports. In 1884 it was calculated that via capital imports, the capital stock had increased by more than 21 million US dollars since 1870, and that about 500 foreign technicians and engineers were employed in sugar production. Moreover capital imports continued after that date.[1] As a result of the inflow of foreign capital and management we would, *ceteris paribus*, expect the marginal products of land and labour to increase and accordingly that it would lead to higher land rents and wages. Although land prices did rise, wages, after tending to increase prior to 1890, appear to have decreased after the 1890s.[2] The increase in population is one factor that can contribute to explain this development. But in addition, *political* measures were taken to increase the profitability of the sugar industry. The most important measures were the concentration of land in a few hands and the promotion of labour imports for plantation work. These measures are likely to have reduced wages by pushing the supply curve of labour outwards.

Along with the increasing price of land, the structure of land ownership radically changed. In Chapter 4 we discussed how arbitrary assignments and fraudulent titles to communal lands made possible the expansion of sugar plantations on land previously belonging to independent peasants. The legislation promulgated by the US military government favoured the sugar industry. Much force was used in order to evict peasants from their lands. Accordingly, with the opening up of international trade on a large scale, not only the structure of production changed but also the structure of land ownership. Some contemporary observers deplored the change that was taking place. Pedro Francisco Bono, observing the demolition of small scale agriculture, in 1884 states: '. . . [earlier] even if poor and rude, they were proprietors, and now poorer and more rude, they have ended up as proletarians. What kind of progress is this?'[3] As we will see below the conditions which generated a change in the structure of land ownership also had negative repercussions on allocative efficiency within the agricultural sector.

Plantation owners were not satisfied with the supplies of labour available in the Dominican Republic and the trends towards rising wages. Providing imports of cheap labour from the British West Indies and Haiti, they could not only prevent wages from rising, but even, as it seems, lower them. Evidently Dominican labour had no reason to be particularly happy about these imports of cheap labour. Others, however, defending the sugar industry saw the black immigration as a 'gift from heaven': 'Thanks to it the sugar industry has escaped ruin . . . In this manner, the sugar mills have been able to survive the drop in sugar prices.'[4]

The scant data available support our argument. According to Baez Everszt, in 1893, labour in the sugar industry received about 2 pesos a day. In 1925 wages were only 80 centavos.[5] According to Knight, the basic wage at the time (1926) was 60 centavos.[6] Jesus de Galindez affirms that the daily wage in the sugar industry in the period 1935–40 was 50 centavos.[7] Cassá presents figures that show slightly lower wages during the same period.[8] In addition to the factors we have mentioned above, the change in *demand* for plantation labour may help to explain the lowering of wages in the 1930s. The world depression affected the sugar market and prices were considerably reduced. But as will be shown below, real wages for plantation work do not appear to have increased after the 1930s when the world market recovered.

The experience of the Dominican Republic is in no way unique. In his book on the sugar economy of Cuba, Ramiro Guerra y Sanchez asserts that throughout the Caribbean the opening up and expansion of large-scale sugar production has 'always produced an identical cycle of events'.[9] The most conspicuous changes brought about by the sugar plantations are 1) the substitution of one population for another and 2) a transfer of property ownership. The expansion of sugar exports on Barbados implied a lowering of wages for the working class, in fact a large part of the white population emigrated due to the massive imports of plantation labour. In Cuba perhaps more than half the arable land came under foreign dominated sugar plantations. This change created, according to Guerra y Sanchez, fortunes for a few through the subjugation of the farmer community, while impoverishing large segments of the rural population.

Remittance of Earnings

With the participation of foreign factors of production the question arises as to the extent to which export earnings are retained locally. Jonathan Levin argues that an important characteristic of the export economies is the substantial remittance of earnings abroad.[10] An indication of the magnitude of remitted earnings can be obtained from an examination of the balance of trade.

In fact during the period 1905 to 1930, the Dominican trade balance exhibited a substantial export surplus. An exception was 1921 when prices fell markedly.[11] Table 5.1 shows the trade balance for this period.

Table 5.1: Trade Balance 1905–30 (million US Dollars)

Average	1905–09	1910–14	1915–19	1920–24	1925–30
Exports	7.7	11.1	24.2	30.2	25.6
Imports	4.2	7.5	15.8	24.2	23.6
Trade balance	3.5	3.6	8.4	6.0	2.0

Source: Muto (1976), p. 85.

The export surplus made possible an outflow of export earnings. Knight argues:

> The favourable balance . . . was so large, in fact, to be ruinous. Practically half of the entire value of exports was sugar, which was almost purely a foreign industry. What interests was paid on investments went chiefly to Americans and Italians. Even the wages paid to laborers were collected almost entirely by foreigners — British West Indians and Haitians — and the salaried personnel was also mainly foreign.[12]

A strong argument in favour of international trade is that export earnings can be used to finance the import of capital goods, that are necessary for economic development. The above figures, however, show that a large fraction of export earnings were remitted. In addition, out of the foreign exchange available for imports, only a small part was used for capital goods imports. For instance, in 1918 only 11 per cent of imports constituted machinery and equipment, half of which was destined for the sugar industry itself.[13] The contribution of sugar exports to capital formation thus appears to have been rather limited.

Other Effects

Along with increased exports, increasing amounts of food were imported. It appears as if the expansion of sugar plantations and the decline of small-scale farming provoked a shortage of vegetables and fruits. Eugenio Maria de Hostos had observed rising prices for such products at the end of the nineteenth century.[14] Muto argues: 'The growing cities depended upon local *campesinos* for much of their food supplies, but the repeated expansions of the sugar estates reduced land around many cities which might have been used for local food production.'[15] In 1918 about 25 per cent of imports was food.[16] The share of food had increased to 35 per cent in 1935.[17]

Although increased exports stimulated activities in the main ports, such as Santo Domingo, the Republic's domestic economy appears to have developed at a much slower pace than did its international trade.[18] Repatriation of profits and wages of immigrant labour and the lowering of wage levels for native workers limited the stimuli to commercial and industrial activities. Shopkeepers complained about the habit of immigrant labour of saving as much as possible and bringing these savings back to the home country. Furthermore when the sugar enterprises grew larger, they started to perform many commercial activities themselves. One way was to set up their own stores:

> With Dominican and immigrant laborers living in plantation settlements, the companies enjoyed a natural monopoly. Distance, intimidation, and payment in company script forced workers to buy all their necessities from the sugar mills' field and central stores. By 1915, the Dominican Republic's sixteen sugar mills operated some seventy-four commercial establishments; only one mill did not run its own stores.[19]

This implied very few stimuli to the society surrounding the sugar plantations. An American visitor seeing a large sugar mill in 1919 observed: '. . . it looks like a bit of the United States set down in the tropics'.[20]

Trade and Distortions under Trujillo

Efficient allocation of resources, in the sense that it would not be possible to increase output of any good without decreasing the amount of any other good, within the agricultural sector, will be achieved, *inter alia*, if different producers pay the same price for production factors.[21] Production factors will then be allocated in such a way that the value of their marginal products will be equalized among different uses. To simplify our subsequent discussion we will divide the agricultural sector into two distinct parts: 1) the plantation sector producing mainly for exports and 2) a peasant (import competing) sector producing food for the domestic market. Ideally, these two sectors would then meet the same set of factor prices. But a distinctive feature of Dominican development is that this has not been the case.

In Chapter 4 we argued that a set of distortions has had a decisive impact on the shaping of the production and trade structure. We can express this as a violation of the marginal conditions whose fulfilment is necessary for the achievement of allocative efficiency. The conditions facing these two sectors have been quite different. Before turning to the disparate conditions facing the two sectors we must first discuss an additional factor which may have contributed to generate overall inefficiency in the agricultural sector. This factor is Trujillo's motivation for engagement in large-scale sugar production.

We know that the optimality of perfect competition requires profit maximization by the producer. Given another production criteria, say maximization of output, the outcome for allocative efficiency may be negative. In the previous chapter, it was also argued that motives other than profits may have driven Trujillo into sugar production. The power aspect of large-scale sugar business and the pursuit of control over foreign exchange seem to have been important motivations for his activities in sugar. Given such incentives economic efficiency will not even be achieved *within the plantation sector*. We argued that there were reasons to assume that Trujillo was operating in the range where $\delta \pi / \delta x < 0$, i. e. where the volume of sugar output was larger than that which would have maximized profits.

Trujillo's exceptional power enabled him to use any means whatsoever in order to increase sugar production. In particular his actions regarding land had important repercussions. We discussed how Trujillo used intimidation to obtain access to the best land at arbitrary prices or simply confiscated the land he needed. Eviction of peasants from their lands does not appear to have been unusual. Analytically, although it might appear a euphemism, we could express this as a factor price distortion in the land market. The cost of acquiring land was quite different for Trujillo and his relatives and friends on the one hand and the peasant on the other. Limiting the analysis to a plantation sector (controlled by Trujillo) and a peasant sector, we can express this distortion as follows:

$$r_T < r_P \tag{5.1}$$

where r_T is the (implicit) price of land paid by Trujillo and r_P the price paid by the peasant.

This inequality in no way pertains only to Trujillo's activities. The American and other national sugar estates had also gained control of land in ways similar to those used by Trujillo. These holdings, for instance, could by the use of force obtain land at prices far below social opportunity cost, so 5.1 can be generalized to include the whole plantation sector. We can express this as:

$$r_{pl} < r_p \tag{5.2}$$

where r_{pl} is the (implicit) price of land paid by the plantation sector.

This distortion in the land market implies that from a social point of view, too much land ended up in the plantation sector and too little in the peasant sector. It also means that the value of the marginal product of land in the subsistence sector will exceed that in the plantation sector and that overall output will be lower than would have been possible, given the amount of land. Production could be increased by transferring some land from the plantation sector to peasant production (see also below).

The distortion in the land market may also have been the main reason for the highly skewed distribution of credits to different agricultural activities. In 1953, for instance, 83 per cent of the loans from the Banco Agricola, a bank operating with government resources, were allocated to the sugar industry.[22] This in fact seems to indicate that there were distortions in the capital market. This is likely to occur since, as shown for instance by Keith Griffin,[23] highly unequal access to land normally generates distortions in the capital market, in the sense that the difference in interest rates paid by different producers exceeds what could be motivated by difference in risks, collateral, etc. The distortion in the capital market means that peasants will have to pay a higher rate of interest (above the competitive level) than will the plantation owner (who is likely to pay an interest rate below the competitive level). Capital will not be allocated in a way that would maximize output. 'Too much' will end up in the plantation sector and 'too little' in the peasant sector.

A highly skewed distribution of land is likely to lead to monopsony power in the labour market.[24] If land is highly concentrated within a locality where few alternative occupations are available, the land owner will be a 'price maker' rather than a 'price taker'. Such a situation would imply both reduced employment and lower wages since at the monopsonist's point of profit maximization, the number of employed and the level of wages will be lower than would have been the case in a competitive situation. However, the return to the *minifundista* on his small plot and the wage for work on the plantation should, at the margin, be equal. Otherwise the *minifundista* would have no incentive to accept employment on the plantation.

We can summarize the characteristics of the factor markets as follows:

$$r_{pl} < r_p \quad (5.3)$$
$$i_{pl} < i_p \quad (5.4)$$
$$w_{pl} = w_p \quad (5.5)$$

where i is interest and w is wage.

A consequence of these factor markets characteristics is that the two sets of producers will combine production factors in different ways. The peasant will thus employ more labour per unit of land than will the plantation owner. The latter will combine more capital with labour than the peasant, while the capital to land ratio will depend on whether $(i/r)_{pl} \lesseqgtr (i/r)_p$. If we assume that the capital market is less imperfect than the land market, i.e. $(i/r)_{pl} > (i/r)_p$, the capital-land ratio will be higher on the peasant plot.[25] Given these factor combinations then, the peasant will cultivate his land more intensively and, if both producers have access to the same technology, achieve a higher output per unit of land than will the plantation owner.[26] Now, the plantation owner may have better knowledge about production techniques, on how to make better use of fertilizers, etc. Given such knowledge, he could in theory produce more per unit of land in spite of the fact that he employs less labour and capital.

We do not have figures that enable us to compare factor proportions, or output per unit of land, in the respective sectors. However, there are indications of very low utilization of sugar land. According to a study by the US Department of Agriculture, yields per hectare in 1960 were very low considering the favourable climate and fertile soils.[27] Using more intensive cultivation practices yields per hectare could be greatly increased. This appears consistent with our argument that the price the plantation sector has had to pay for land has been quite low. Besides, evidence of more recent date, which is presented below, shows that output per hectare is higher on smaller farms. There is no apparent reason why the outcome should have been different in the 1950s, considering that distortions were of the same type.

Trujillo's Use of Public Resources

In the preceding chapter we discussed how Trujillo used public resources for the construction of his sugar mills, and for the carrying out of the work on the estates. The use of public resources and the eviction of peasants from their lands implied that Trujillo's personal costs for sugar production must have been substantially lower than the social cost. Since Trujillo's personal costs were lower than social costs, production is expanded beyond the level which would have obtained under competitive conditions. The other side of the coin is of course too low a level of peasant production.

We have pointed to two factors which have contributed to raise sugar production above the level on which it would otherwise have been under competitive conditions: Trujillo's non-economic motives, and his use of force, public resources, etc. But we would also wish to stress the fact that Trujillo's use of public resources implied that he did not take any significant risk in being involved in sugar production.

For a market to be perfectly competitive, economic agents have to be able to predict prices correctly. In practice, however, where prices are difficult to predict, they will have to maximize profit or utility, given a probability distribution of future prices. Sugar prices are subject to rather substantial price changes, making correct predictions extremely difficult. Our argument is that Trujillo's use of public resources to compensate for losses made him unsusceptible to the risk of economic loss through low export prices, biasing his production choice in favour of large-scale sugar production. If prices turned out to be high, Trujillo would profit. On the other hand, he was protected against losses when prices were low. The Dominicans had an expression for Trujillo's business engagement: 'If it loses money, it's government owned, but if it makes money it's Trujillo's.'[28]

Trujillo's hope of influencing export prices may also have biased his activities in favour of sugar production. In fact, Trujillo spent much government money on lobbying to obtain a larger sugar quota on the US market. In an official publication from the 1950s, *La industria azucarera en marcha*, Trujillo's lobbying is described as:

> . . . one of the most brilliant campaigns ever developed by our government in the field of international relations . . . it has also obtained the valuable support of highly reputable official and private circles in the United States. The Dominican sugar industry relies on the government to keep up this far-reaching activity, under the judicious direction of its great leader, the Generalísimo Trujillo.[29]

It is also argued that the aspiration of this policy is only to obtain 'justice' on the world market. This kind of argument has repeatedly been put forward in the Dominican Republic up until the present.[30]

However, Trujillo's lobbying does not appear to have been particularly successful. The Dominican quota did not increase, and sugar prices fell during the 1950s, and were lower than they had been at the end of the 1940s.[31] Furthermore, the country's terms of trade fell, from an index of 120 in 1948 to 86 in 1960.[32]

Outcome for Agricultural Production

We have given much attention to Trujillo's activities since up to 50 or 60 per cent of the arable land may have ended up belonging to him and his family. The decisions Trujillo took did accordingly have a considerable impact on agricultural organization in the Dominican Republic. His decisions affected the structure of production and trade, and the distribution of the gains and losses from trade.

The inefficiencies generated by Trujillo were particularly serious considering the fact that land is a very scarce resource in the Dominican Republic. The figure for land under cultivation per inhabitant, during the 1950s, 0.9 hectare, was one of the lowest in Latin America. Only El Salvador had a lower ratio among the 18 countries recorded.[33] The acreage dedicated to sugar cane appears to have doubled during the period Trujillo engaged in sugar production.[34] At the same time the proliferation of *minifundios* continued. For example, there were 132,000 more farms of less than 1 hectare in size in 1960, than in 1950.[35]

The distribution of land was already very skewed when Trujillo came to power. But it seems reasonable to assume, considering the evidence put forth in Chapter 3 and above, that the *degree* of distortions in the land market increased due to Trujillo's activities. What were then the consequences for agricultural output?

While sugar output doubled during the period, production of several food products stagnated or fell. On the development of the agricultural sector a US study argues:

> Agricultural development and diversification in the Dominican Republic suffered a setback during the decade 1950 to 60. The rapid expansion of the sugar industry during this period, through greatly increasing exports, disrupted the organization of agricultural resources.[36]

Production of such important products as beans, sweet potatoes, yuca and *guandules*,[37] fell between the end of the 1940s and 1960.[38] Agricultural production *per capita* declined from an index of 111 in 1936–40 to 104 in 1954.[39] Total agricultural output *per capita*, measured in Dominican pesos of 1960, decreased from 24.3 in 1950 to 20.7 in 1960.[40] The level of rural wages were, according to Cordero, substantially lower at the end of the 1950s than they had been in the mid-1930s.[41] These trends are corroborated by figures on wages in the sugar sector, which fell by about 20 per cent between 1942 and 1960.[42]

The average daily food intake in the Dominican Republic in the beginning of the 1960s was one of the lowest in Latin America. Only Costa Rica had a lower average among the 13 countries recorded.[43] The Dominican food price index was 15 per cent higher than the average for Latin America.[44]

While individual data must be treated with utmost care the *pattern* which emerges from these figures indicates that Trujillo's policies had negative repercussions on Dominican agriculture. A US study, discussing the 1950s, noticed: 'Notable increases in a few export crops have not resulted in any economic betterment of the rural people.'[45]

Distortions in the Post-Trujillo Period

Much of the inefficiency generated by Trujillo during the 1950s has remained during the decades after the dictator's death. The institutional set-up after Trujillo has maintained several of those characteristics which are important in determining the distribution of resources and the degree of efficiency with which resources are used.

In Chapter 4 we presented data which illustrated the importance of cane production in the use of Dominican land resources. Figure 5.1, which also shows how arable land is used, gives perhaps a more tangible illustration of the importance of sugar in the use of this resource.

The conditions facing the sugar sector and the rest of the agricultural sector are still quite different. Thus the inequality

Figure 5.1: Land Use in the Dominican Republic in the Second Half of the 1970s

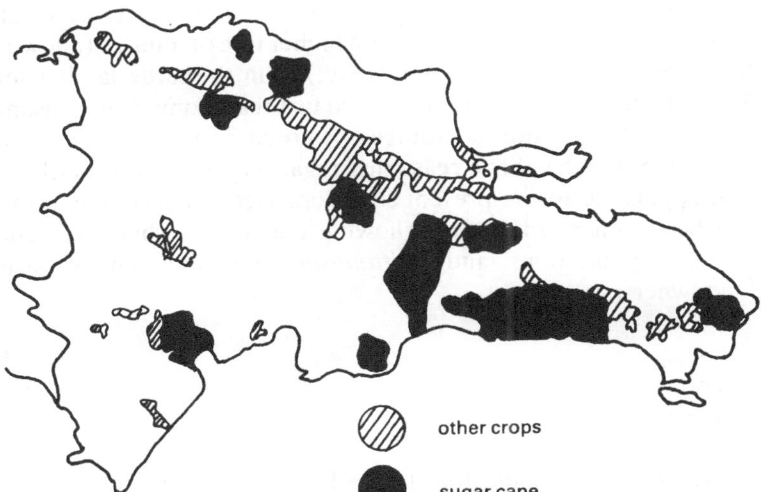

Source: World Bank (1978a).

expressed in equation 5.2 is still valid. In Chapter 4, for instance, we argued that while the State Sugar Council, CEA, does not impute any cost for the use of land, the peasant may, under share cropping arrangements, have to pay up to more than 100 pesos per *tarea*. Thus the sugar sector, which does not pay a price that corresponds to the social opportunity cost of land, does not perceive the 'true' scarcity of this resource. Accordingly, it does not use the land which it controls very efficiently.

As shown in Chapter 4 (Table 4.4), the concentration of land resources in the plantations is just one facet of a generally very skewed distribution of land. In addition to the plantation owners, *latifundistas* control a large share of the land. The bulk of Dominican land resources is thus in the hands of a relatively small number of large landowners. This situation in the land market is of course not unique for the Dominican Republic, but is notorious throughout Latin America.[46] As argued by Keith Griffin, this situation creates a distortion in the land market in the sense that the price of land will be higher for the peasant than for the large landowner.[47]

As argued above, the distortion in the land market is also likely to generate a distortion in the capital market. Accordingly we would expect Dominican peasants to pay a higher rate of interest (allowing for difference in risk, collateral, etc.) than the large landowner. This argument is corroborated by the fact that Dominican peasants have to rely on informal sources of credit at very high rates of interest. Since the above reasoning regarding the labour market is also applicable to the present situation, factor market conditions can be summarized in the following equations, where we lump together plantations and *latifundistas* into one set of large landowners:

$$r_l < r_p \qquad (5.6)$$

$$i_l < i_p \qquad (5.7)$$

$$w_l = w_p \qquad (5.8)$$

where l thus stands for large landowner (plantations and *latifundistas*).

As a consequence of these factor price distortions, we would expect large landowners to adopt techniques characterized by high land to labour ratios, while the peasant will use a large amount of labour per unit of land.[48] This argument is supported by empirical evidence. Data presented by Eric Graber show that labour is on average much more intensively used on small than on large farms. Employment per hectare of utilized land on small farms amounted, in 1975, to 82.3 man-days, medium sized farms employed 39.0 man-days while large farms employed 17.8 man-days.[49] These figures do not include employment in sugar cane production. An estimate based on figures for CEA employment and land ownership yields a figure of 32 man-days per hectare.[50] Another kind of information which indicates highly labour intensive cultivation on small plots is the repeated observation that serious erosion is taking place in peasant areas as a consequence of excessively intensive cultivation practices.[51]

As a consequence of this difference in the way of combining production factors, output per unit of land appears to be higher on the small farm than on the large. In 1975, gross output per hectare in small farms amounted to 452 Dominican pesos. For large farms the corresponding figure was 345.[52] It must be remembered, however, that 1975 was a year when export prices, particularly sugar, were exceptionally high. Since these crops are produced on large farms, the difference, between small and large farms, in a year with 'normal' prices, would be substantially larger. Another factor which points to low utilization of sugar land is that according to the World Bank the yield per hectare is far below agricultural potential.[53] Sugar cane output per hectare has even decreased.[54]

A factor which contributes to a low allocative efficiency in the agricultural sector, is the low utilization of land by *latifundistas* due to their lack of interest in agricultural production. The majority, 64 per cent, of owners of farms of size larger than 5,000 *tareas* did, according to a study carried out in 1969, not consider agriculture their main occupation,[55] and as much as 86.5 per cent of land controlled by these *latifundistas* was very poorly utilized. The corresponding figure for farms of size less than 50 *tareas* was 16.8.[56] This very unequal access to land for different groups thus implies a low overall utilization of Dominican land resources. These figures are also consistent with the presence of a factor price distortion in the land market.

These distortions would seem to imply a lack of 'dynamics' in the agricultural sector, although we cannot argue that the *degree* of distortions has increased after the death of Trujillo. Thus we cannot, in a comparative static sense, simply affirm that these distortions have reduced agricultural *growth* although they have implied allocative inefficiency. But there is of course a connection between allocative inefficiency and the low level of growth in the agricultural sector. Fewer distortions that discriminate against the peasant sector would not only mean improved allocative efficiency, but also higher incomes for the peasant. This would in turn increase the opportunities for savings and investment, factors which positively affect the rate of agricultural growth. More formally, John Hicks has shown, in a two sector model, that imperfect transferability of production factors may reduce growth considerably.[57] Thus distortions in the Dominican agricultural sector and the locking up of resources (see also below) is likely to have reduced growth. What has then happened with agricultural output after the death of Trujillo?

Agricultural production has continued to lag behind during the last two decades. Food production *per capita* decreased, according to UNCTAD, between 1961 and 1974.[58] According to the FAO, food production *per capita* has been practically constant during the 1970s. The FAO index of food production which was 101 in 1970, reached 102 in 1981.[59] Production of several food crops fell in absolute terms between 1973 and 1981.[60]

Other factors than those mentioned above have contributed to lagging agricultural production. Industrialization policies have neglected the needs of the agricultural sector both through its protection and subsidization of industry and through a price policy which has aimed at keeping food prices low. This has implied a deterioration of internal terms of trade between agriculture and industry. We will return to this issue in Chapter 6.

As we argued in Chapter 4, massive imports of Haitian labour have continued under the auspices of the Dominican government. In 1980 more than 75 per cent of the labour force in the sugar industry consisted of Haitians.[61] At the same time taking into account the seasonality of work, the equivalent of about 300,000 Dominicans out of a working force of 800,000 in the rural sector are unemployed.[62] Labour imports do depress wage levels in the rural sector. Thus the welfare of Dominican rural labour is reduced as a result of the government's interest in supplying the country's most important industry with as cheap labour as possible. This policy is made possible, it seems, by the fact that the peasant sector has minimal political influence.

Plantation Exports and Capital Accumulation

In the early debate on development, the importance of savings and capital accumulation for economic growth was emphasized.[63] Empirical studies have, however, shown that capital accumulation can only explain a minor part of growth. Much of actual growth has to be explained by other factors, such as improved technology, improved quality of labour due to better nutrition, education, etc.[64] Even though savings do not seem to have the overwhelming importance attributed to them by earlier growth theories, it is however difficult to conceive of development without capital accumulation, and in this section we will briefly discuss the connection between sugar exports and capital accumulation in the Dominican Republic, starting with the Trujillo period. In the next section, the impact of plantation Exports on technological change will be discussed.

Table 5.1 indicated that repatriation of profits up to the 1930s must have been substantial. But also after Trujillo came to power, capital exports continued to be of considerable importance. Export surpluses also continued after 1930 (a total export surplus of 265 million pesos for the period 1930 to 1949 can be compared with total imports for the same period amounting to 384 million)[65] and rose to particularly high levels during the 1950s as did capital exports. In the 1950s, Trujillo's export of foreign exchange must be added to the repatriation of profits by foreign sugar estates. In Chapter 4 we argued that one motive for Trujillo's engagement in sugar production was his desire to control the most important source of foreign exchange. Nobody knows exactly how much money Trujillo sent out of the country. One estimate reaches the figure 800 million dollars.[66] These figures can be compared with the value of total Dominican sugar exports between 1950 and 1961, which amounted to 710 million in current prices. Table 5.2 shows Dominican exports and imports and trade balance for the period 1950 to 1961.

The trade surplus illustrated in Table 5.2 is counterbalanced by an outflow of foreign capital in the form of income on investment and, particularly, by the entry 'error and omissions'. Between 1957 and 1961 the latter averaged a minus of 29 million. This figure probably hides substantial capital outflows. The low reserves of gold and foreign exchange in the Banco Central in 1961, equivalent to 9.0 million dollars, is another indication of a heavy outflow

Table 5.2: Exports, Imports and Trade Balance 1950–61 (million Dominican pesos, current prices)

	Exports	Imports	Trade balance
1950	86.8	43.6	43.2
1951	108.5	58.6	49.9
1952	115.4	96.9	18.5
1953	105.3	86.5	18.8
1954	119.7	82.8	36.9
1955	114.9	98.0	16.9
1956	121.5	108.3	13.2
1957	147.4	116.4	31.0
1958	128.2	129.5	−1.3
1959	130.1	117.5	12.6
1960	174.4	87.0	87.4
1961	143.1	69.5	73.6

Source: Cassá (1982), p. 391.

of capital.[67] This figure is particularly low when viewed against the substantial export surplus generated during a long period. On average imports of capital goods accounted for 22 per cent of total imports.[68] This means that only a minor part of exchange earned through sugar exports was used for capital accumulation. Nevertheless, considering the small resources of the country, this contribution may not have been altogether negligible.

Exports and Savings in the Post-Trujillo Period

Following the death of Trujillo the bulk of sugar exports has been carried out by a state producer. Consequently expatriation does not appear to be a conspicuous aspect of sugar production during recent decades. But to what extent have sugar exports contributed to savings and investment during this period?

A recurrent argument in the development literature has been that the savings propensity in the rural sector is very low. Hence a squeeze of the rural sector in favour of the urban sector and industrialization will promote more rapid capital accumulation and development, it has often been argued.[69] By analogy, distortions favouring the 'modern' sugar sector *could* lead to a higher saving level in the economy if this has a larger saving propensity than the peasant sector.[70]

However, the argument that savings in the rural sector are generally very low has seriously been questioned by, for instance, Michael Lipton. Lipton argues that careful estimates on rural savings reveal much higher agricultural saving propensities than those calculated from national income statistics.[71] Also, national income statistics seriously underestimate non-monetized activities which can be considered as farm saving embodied directly in investment, for instance '. . . time spent by a small farm family in desilting its own field irrigation channel'.[72]

Information on savings in the Dominican rural sector is very scant. However, one investigation on incomes and spending in the sector shows that 95 per cent of the families were not able to save. The remaining 5 per cent could on average save 3 per cent of their income.[73] It is difficult to judge the accuracy of the estimates given by this investigation and, needless to say, these figures should be interpreted with utmost care. Nevertheless, they seem to indicate that the savings capacity, at least the capacity to save in 'monetary' terms, is limited in the rural sector. Considering the discrimination against this sector this should not come as a surprise. What about saving out of income generated by sugar exports?

Savings on labour income in sugar production have probably been small. First, all incomes have been, and still are, very low for the large fraction of the labour force within the industry. Second, a large part of the labour force have consisted of foreigners, and what little they have been able to save, assumedly very little, they have brought back to their country of origin, mainly Haiti. The contribution from sugar taxes may however have been positive, since after Trujillo's death a tax was imposed on sugar exports. (Trujillo had exempted sugar from taxation.) The contribution of export taxes to government revenue during the 1960s was however small. Up to 1971 *total* export duties varied around 4 per cent of total government revenue. Thereafter they have been more important. With increased tax rates they have varied around 13 to 14 per cent (up until 1976) with a peak of 23.4 per cent of revenues in 1975, when sugar prices soared.[74] Trade *may* thus, especially during periods of high export prices, as in 1974–5, have contributed to savings and investment. The tax was, however, abolished in 1982 in the face of low export prices.

A method of estimating the effects of exports on savings has been proposed by Alfred Maizels. Maizels analyses whether savings are more closely related to the value of exports than they are to gross domestic product as a whole, or to the product of the non-export sector.[75] This is done by estimating the following equations:

$$S(t) = a + b\,Y(t) \tag{5.9}$$
$$S(t) = c + d\,(Y(t) - X(t)) + e\,X(t) \tag{5.10}$$

If the savings propensity out of exports is larger than that out of non-exports, equation 5.10 should produce a larger R^2 than equation 5.9 and the regression coefficient of exports would be larger than that of non-export income. Maizels estimates these equations on a sample of eleven countries and finding a higher R^2 for the second equation contends: ' . . . the regression results can reasonably be taken as supporting the view . . . that there is likely to be a positive association in many primary-exporting countries between exports and savings.'[76] Jong-Koon Lee using Maizels' approach reaches analogous conclusions.[77] We have estimated equations 5.9 and 5.10 on the basis of Dominican data for the period 1963–78, but using sugar exports instead of total exports. This gave the following results:[78]

1) $R^2 = 0.83$ $b = 0.15$ $SE = 0.02$
2) $R^2 = 0.96$ $d = 0.09*$ $SE = 0.01$ $e = 0.88*$ $SE = 0.11$
* significant at 1 per cent level

These results that conform with Maizels', could indicate that the propensity to save out of sugar income is higher than the one out of non-sugar income. We must however be very careful when interpreting these figures. First, as suggested by Lipton national income statistics may seriously underestimate savings, both monetized and non-monetized, in the rural sector. Second, as we argued in Chapter 4, CEA has made losses almost every year. The government has anyway taxed CEA forcing the company to take up foreign loans. What we then observe as government receipts from taxation of sugar is thus *de facto*, to a large extent *foreign* and not domestic savings. It is therefore risky to draw any clear-cut conclusions from such regressions in the present case.

Now, even *if* the propensity to save in rural areas is lower than elsewhere, this would not necessarily constitute an argument in favour of a pro-plantation (or pro-industry for that matter[79]) bias. Three main reasons can be considered.

First, consumption by the peasant is in many cases likely to increase his productivity.[80] Thus peasant consumption may increase output potential more than the saving 'forgone' might have done. Second, as argued by Lipton, 'cash spent is not spent for ever'.[81] If peasants spend most of their income, those who produce the goods the peasants buy may save much of their receipts. Lipton shows, in a simple economy with only two sectors, agriculture and industry, that even if peasants save nothing out of an extra income and industry everything, the ultimate effect on the volume of savings is independent of whether an extra $1,000 accrues to agriculture or to industry.[82] Third, even *if* distortions favouring the export sector would increase total savings, the outcome for development will depend on how savings are used. For instance, savings generated by sugar exports could be expatriated or could be invested in projects with low return. Above we argued that savings which have been generated by sugar exports up to 1961 appear to have mainly been expatriated. Concerning the subsequent period it is probable that profits made by the two private producers, particularly the US owned Gulf and Western, have been expatriated. But this is difficult to substantiate. It is also difficult to trace the use that has been made of government tax receipts from sugar exports. However, much of government spending, particularly in the first half of the 1970s when export prices and export taxes were high, was used for ostentatious public buildings in Santo Domingo. The return, in terms of potential for future output, might have been substantially higher if savings, even if lower, might have been controlled and used by peasants for irrigation, sewerage, pesticides, fertilizers, etc. Again, it is difficult to draw any general and clear-cut conclusions. However, on the basis of the above arguments we may infer that there is no apparent reason why a pro-plantation bias would generate a more rapid increase in output potential due to higher levels of savings and/or that savings generated by sugar exports would be invested in projects with a higher return.

Plantation Exports and Technological Change

Empirical studies have shown that a large fraction of growth has to be explained by improved methods of production. What is the impact of plantation exports on improved techniques, improved skills, etc? Many authors discussing the extent to which exports contribute to increased skills and spread of new techniques to other sectors emphasize the 'technological nature of the production function for the export industry'. Baldwin argues that the limited effect of plantation exports on technology in many developing countries is a consequence of the particular composition of the labour force in plantation production: on the one hand, a small staff of technicians with a high skill component and, on the other, a large amount of unskilled labour performing simple tasks.[83] As this skilled labour is supplied from abroad, the possibility for local people to advance within the industry has been very limited. The simplicity of tasks performed by the majority of labour employed in plantation production and the limited vertical mobility within the industry explain the fact that local people '. . . did not acquire much in the way of new skills by working in the sugar industry'.[84]

While the production function, or the nature of the export sector, is important it must not obscure the importance of institutional factors for the improvement in production methods and dissemination of knowledge. The fact that government policy has systematically favoured plantation production is perhaps as important as the pure 'technical' aspect of the production function.

First we have the organized imports of Haitian labour. As we discussed above this has enabled the sugar industry to secure necessary labour inputs without the need to raise wages. Salter has observed that factor prices and the introduction of techniques are closely interrelated.[85] A wage increase creating a gap between wage and short-run labour productivity will induce the producer to adopt policies economizing labour and raising its productivity. Myint argues that the 'cheap' labour policies (through for instance promotion of migrant labour) in plantation economies has 'fossilized' wages at their low initial levels, through a vicious circle of low wages and productivity.[86] With depressed wages as a consequence of massive imports of Haitian labour (but also as a consequence of the concentration of land in a few hands), there has been a very limited need to introduce labour-saving technologies within the sugar industry in the Dominican Republic. The data available (which however must be considered with care) indicate that real wages in the plantation sector have decreased during a long time. It was shown above that wages for plantation labour showed a downward trend between the 1890s and the 1930s, and it does not appear as if wages have increased since that period. Galindez affirms that in the second half of the 1930s, the wage rate was about 50 centavos per day. In 1962 a *family* could earn about 1.1 pesos a day, according to Wiarda.[87] Consumer prices increased during the same period from an index of 100 in 1936 to 264 in 1962.[88] This indicates that a considerable decrease in real wages took place. In 1982 the daily wage for plantation work was about 2 pesos, compared then with slightly more than 1 peso in the early 1960s.[89] Consumer prices increased from an index of around 35 in the first half of the 1960s to 115 in 1982.[90] The negative consequences of the Dominican 'cheap' labour policies may be far from negligible since the introduction of labour saving techniques is an important contributor to economic growth.

It is not just the availability of abundant and cheap labour that has prevented technological change in Dominican plantation production. Another important aspect is the sugar sector's acquisition of land at low prices (below the competitive market price) or by means of fraud. This has led to limited efforts to economize with land resources. We have observed above that sugar yields per unit of land have been far below what have been considered possible considering the quality of land. We also pointed to the fact that sugar yields per hectare have decreased. Eric Graber, estimating a production function for the sugar sector, agricultural plus industrial phase, has shown that no technical progress has taken place during the period 1950–73.[91] In the pure industrial phase, in the transformation of cane to raw sugar, productivity seems to have been stagnant since the end of the 1930s.[92] The factors discussed contribute to a low rate of technological change *within* the plantation sector. Has plantation production had any positive effect on the spread of skills outside the plantation sector?

The technique employed in the agricultural phase of sugar production is generally very rudimentary. Most of the work is carried out with the mere use of a *machete*. This work is very hard and monotonous and most of it is carried out by Haitians who live under conditions which are comparable with slavery.[93] Under such conditions it is difficult to perceive of any dissemination of knowledge coming from this activity to the surrounding agricultural community. The industrial phase of sugar production has given more scope for improved skills. Traditionally skilled labour has been foreign, although domestic participation has increased during recent time. The skills acquired in the industrial phase may thus have spread to surrounding society.

The state of agricultural technology is on the whole still at a very rudimentary level in the Dominican Republic. A very small proportion of farms use chemical fertilizers, irrigation or some kind of mechanical force. As much as 83 per cent of farms do not use chemical fertilizers. The farms on which such inputs are used are usually large (over 800 *tareas*).[94] On the smaller farms, the implements that are most widely used are the *machete* and the hoe, while oxen may provide traction power.[95]

We may point to two factors[96] which have contributed to this low level of technology. First, peasants have had extremely limited access to credit. We have observed that Dominican peasants have had little access to official credit. The Banco Agricola was created in the 1940s to provide credit to agricultural enterprises. However, these loans were generally restricted to large commercial firms, and particularly to the sugar estates. Thus peasants have had to rely on mainly informal sources of credit at very high rates of interest.[97] Griffin has shown that distortions in capital markets may impede the introduction of new technologies in the peasant sector. If the price of capital is too high, certain types of technological changes will be economically irrelevant for the peasant.[98] Distortions in the Dominican capital market have undoubtedly had a negative impact on the rate of technological change in the Dominican peasant sector.

Second, Dominican governments have neglected education in general, and education in the rural areas in particular. For instance, the percentage of the national budget spent on education was under Trujillo the second lowest in Latin America.[99] The discrimination against education in rural areas in more recent times has been discussed by José Luis Alemán.[100] The majority of rural teachers have inadequate preparation. A tangible illustration of the standard of rural education is provided by the fact that 60 per cent of rural schools lack a chair for the teacher.[101] The difference in standard between rural and urban education is striking. The lack of interest in the agricultural sector shown by Dominican governments can also be illustrated by the fact that up until 1968 there was no programme for agricultural education at university level within the country.[102] Although we do not know the exact relation between education and technological change, the '. . . presumption appears to be that the connection is strong'.[103] More educated farmers tend to be more willing to innovate.

The origin of both of these factors, unequal access to credit and neglect of rural education, lies in the distortion in the land market which discriminates against the peasant sector. The discrimination of the peasant sector is in turn, as argued above, largely a consequence of the expansion of the sugar sector.

Distortions and Transformation

According to economic theory a change in relative prices will induce the economy to alter the composition of output. For instance, a decrease in the price of the export good will cause a shift of resources to the import competing sector. However, developing countries allegedly often lack the capacity to reallocate resources. The voluminous debate[104] on the terms of trade is mainly pertinent to countries whose economy lacks the capacity to respond to price changes. If an economy had the capacity to reallocate resources instantaneously, there would, for example, be no strong need to forecast the future price of an export good. Future price changes would simply induce a reallocation of production.

Different views are put forth as to the causes of the limited transformation capacity of developing countries, but they usually emphasize the nature of the export good and the production function. Griffin argues: 'Bolivia cannot transform tin mines into potatoes.'[105] 'Ecuador and Colombia cannot easily and quickly expand their banana and coffee plantation sectors or convert them to other crops without undertaking large investments which, in some cases, have long gestation periods.'[106] And '. . . once a particular structure of production has been selected, for whatever reason, labour and capital tend to become immobile because they become incorporated into the productive process in the form of durable and specific skills and equipment.'[107] While these factors are also of importance in the Dominican case, the institutional set up has, in our view, a major influence over decisions regarding reallocation of resources.

Firstly we reiterate the fact that plantation production has been highly concentrated in the hands of Trujillo and, subsequently, the Dominican government. Hence the incentives for these decision makers are of crucial importance when production changes in the face of, say, a deterioration in the terms of trade. If incentives other than profit maximization exist, the outcome may well be different from what would have been the case under competitive conditions. As discussed above, there are reasons to assume that

Trujillo's activities in sugar production were *also* motivated by the power aspect of this large-scale business and by the desire to control foreign exchange. As argued in Chapter 4, there is reason to believe that subsequent governments have also had other motives than profits for their sugar policies. For example, decision makers such as the CEA bureaucracy will not reduce production in response to lower export prices since losses incurred by the sugar industry are paid for out of taxes or foreign loans.

Neither Trujillo nor the present CEA management (or the government for that matter) would incur personal losses if sugar prices turned out to be low. On the other hand if prices turned out to be high, they would profit. Trujillo would profit directly, through his owning of the sugar industry, the CEA management through increased opportunities to spend on larger desks, larger offices, etc. As we argued above, many CEA officials have also been able to make personal profits from the running of the sugar industry.[108]

The reaction to low sugar prices has generally been confined to a general complaint on 'unfair' world market conditions. The need to make international efforts to improve terms of trade is constantly stressed. This has been a traditional Dominican way of looking at the problem.

These factors render production less responsive to price changes and contribute to the 'transformation problem'. This transformation problem has aggravated the economic problems of the country. Confronted by extremely low export prices during recent years,[109] and poor prospects for the future, very limited efforts have been made to reallocate resources.

Concluding Remarks

In Chapter 3 we quoted Haberler regarding the standard neoclassical arguments for the positive effects of trade. Haberler asserted that '. . . trade has made a tremendous contribution to the development of less developed countries in the 19th and 20th centuries . . .'[110] The analysis in this chapter has, we think, cast considerable doubt on the validity of such an assertion for the Dominican Republic. The argument here is not that there is something intrinsically wrong with international trade, but rather that those institutions and policies that have favoured exports have had negative repercussions on other sectors. These policies have implied:

(1) allocative inefficiency
(2) a negative effect on distribution
(3) limited 'dynamic' effects from exports

The most important factor in this process has been the concentration of land in a few hands. The sugar sector has got control of land by the use of methods that range from fraud to the use of military force to evict peasants from their land. This 'distortion' in the land market has thus also affected distribution negatively. The concentration of land in a few hands has increased the man/land ratio outside the plantation sector. This means lower output per man in the peasant sector. The 'dynamic' effects of exports have been limited due to the large expatriation of foreign exchange and the lack of technological change induced by sugar production.

It should be reiterated that the control by sugar producers of a large share of the country's land resources is just one facet of a generally extremely unequal distribution of land which has had negative consequences for rural development. Thus although we have emphasized several negative aspects of the involvement in sugar exports, it could not however be argued that in the absence of sugar exports things would have been better. What can be said is that despite a secular involvement in large-scale sugar exports, living conditions in rural areas are still deplorable and working conditions for plantation labour are comparable to slavery.

In Chapters 4 and 5 our discussion has been confined to the agricultural sector. We have pointed to some of the institutional factors which have concentrated land in a few hands and pushed the supply curve of labour outwards. The outcome has been low living standards in the rural sector and considerable migration to urban areas. As we will show in the next chapter, the industrial sector has not been able to absorb this inflow of labour. Recent policies favouring industrialization, have by discriminating against the rural sector, reinforced the problems that have been discussed in this chapter. In the next chapter we will thus discuss industrialization policies and some of their consequences.

Notes

1. Hoetink (1965), p. 15.
2. See below.
3. Quotation in Hoetink (1965), p. 15. See also Calder (1981), p. 94.
4. Quotation in Muto (1976), p. 165.
5. Evertsz (1978), p. 45. Hoetink (1965), p. 18, presents figures from 1893 corresponding to Evertsz'.
6. Knight (1928), p. 141.
7. De Galindez (1962), p. 161. See also Franco (1967), p. 36.
8. Cassá (1982), p. 603.
9. Guerra y Sanchez (1964), p. 5.
10. Levin (1960), p. 174.
11. See Figure 3.1.
12. Knight (1928), p. 33. Part of the outflow of capital reflects repayment of the debt of the Dominican state. See Chapter 2 on how this debt has been accumulated by fraudulent rulers during the second half of the nineteenth century.
13. Dominican Custom Receivership (1919), pp. 55 and 47.
14. See Evertsz (1978), p. 23.
15. Muto (1976), p. 77. See also Hoetink (1965), p. 18.
16. Dominican Custom Receivership (1919), p. 55.
17. Dominican Custom Receivership (1923), p. 70.
18. Muto (1976), pp. 83–8.
19. Ibid., p. 106.
20. Quoted in Muto (1976), p. 71.
21. See for instance Scitovsky (1971), Chapter 8.
22. Duval Perez (1977).
23. Griffin (1974), pp. 26–30.
24. Griffin (1969), pp. 70–4, and Griffin (1974), pp. 30–4.
25. This is not an unrealistic assumption considering the extreme concentration of land ownership and the fact that plantation owners, particularly Trujillo, could in many cases incorporate land at virtually no cost.
26. If on the other hand the plantation owner employs more capital per hectare than the peasant, the former *might* produce a higher output per hectare. The outcome will depend on the difference in capital to land ratios between plantations and peasants and on the shape of production functions.
27. US Department of Agriculture (1963), p. 19. See also Cassá (1982), p. 226.
28. Spitzer (1972), p. 394.
29. *La industria azucarera en marcha* (1955), p. 71.
30. See Chapter 1.
31. Cassá (1982), Table III 11.
32. Ibid., Table V 7.
33. Clausner (1973), p. 240. Countries recorded: Argentina 8.8, Bolivia 10.8, Brazil 3.7, Chile 4.1, Columbia 1.9, Costa Rica 2.0, Cuba 1.4, El Salvador 0.6, Guatemala 1.3, Honduras 1.7, Mexico 5.6, Nicaragua 2.2, Panama 1.7, Peru 2.1, Uruguay 6.4 and Venezuela 4.3.
34. Cassá (1982), Table III 8.
35. Moya Pons (1982c) pp. 124–5.
36. US Department of Agriculture (1963), p. 18.
37. Pidgeon peas.
38. Cassá (1982), pp. 120–1.
39. Cordero (1959), p. 52.
40. Oficina Nacional de Planificación (1968), p. 142.
41. Cordero (1959), p. 52.

42. Figures from Oficina Nacional de Estadística presented in Espinal (forthcoming).
43. Clausner (1973), p. 242.
44. Ibid., p. 241, Table V.10.
45. US Department of Agriculture (1963), p. 2.
46. See for instance Griffin (1969), pp. 75–80, Griffin (1974), pp. 18–22, and Barraclough and Domike (1966).
47. Griffin (1974), pp. 22–6. For a rigorous formulation see Lundahl (1984b).
48. See for instance Griffin (1974), pp. 34–8.
49. Graber (1978), p. 123, small farms: < 5.0 hectares, medium farms 5.0–49.9, large farms > 50 hectares.
50. Of a total CEA labour force of 60,000, about 80 per cent are employed in the agricultural phase of sugar production. (Bell (1981), p. 316.) During a good sugar year the *zafra* lasts for about 200 days. (Lundahl and Vargas (1983), p. 138.) This gives 9.6 million man-days on 300,000 hectares of sugar land controlled by CEA.
51. See Chapter 4.
52. Graber (1978), p. 118.
53. World Bank (1978a), p. 27.
54. Ibid.
55. Alemán (1982), p. 29.
56. Ibid.
57. Hicks (1983).
58. UNCTAD figures in Lundahl (1979), p. 99.
59. FAO (1982), p. 79.
60. Moya Pons (1982c), p. 95.
61. See Chapter 4.
62. Moya Pons (1982c), p. 201.
63. See Nurkse (1953), Lewis (1955), particularly pp. 225–6, Rostow (1971).
64. See Kuznets (1966), p. 81.
65. Cassá (1982), Table V 1.
66. See Chapter 2.
67. See Banco Central (1961), p. 56.
68. Average 1950–61. Figures from Oficina Nacional de Planificación (1965), Table 11.
69. See Lipton (1976), Chapter 10.
70. The difference in saving propensities must be large enough to compensate for the reduction of overall income which results from distortions favouring the sugar sector, if total savings are to be higher.
71. Lipton (1976), pp. 246–7.
72. Ibid., p. 246.
73. Oficina Nacional de Planificación (1975), pp. 88–9.
74. World Bank (1978a), p. 321, Moya Pons (1983), p. 131.
75. Maizels (1968), pp. 93–6.
76. Ibid., p. 96.
77. Lee (1971).
78. Data from UN Yearbook of National Accounts and IMF International Financial Statistics, various issues.
79. For a more explicit discussion on the arguments in favour of pro-industry bias see Chapter 7.
80. Lipton (1976), pp. 243–5.
81. Ibid., p. 253.
82. Ibid., pp. 252–7. The only difference is that savings will be *delayed* if the income accrues to the agricultural sector.
83. Baldwin (1963), p. 87.
84. Ibid.

85. Salter (1969), pp. 66–73.
86. Myint (1964), p. 57.
87. Wiarda (1969), p. 92.
88. Cassá (1982), Table VI 21 for 1936–8 to 1960. Consumer price index from IMF (1983) for extrapolation of index, presented by Cassá, to 1962.
89. Oficina Nacional de Planificación (1981).
90. IMF (1983).
91. Graber (1978), pp. 106–8.
92. Cassá (1982), p. 226.
93. See Chapter 4.
94. Secretaria de Estado de Agricultura (1982/3).
95. Vicens (1982), p. 164.
96. For additional factors which may retard technological change in a peasant economy see Lundahl (1979), Chapter 12.
97. See for instance World Bank (1978a), pp. 23–4.
98. Griffin (1974), pp. 48–51.
99. Clausner (1973), p. 242.
100. Alemán (1982), pp. 372–5.
101. Ibid. See also Graber (1978), p. 148.
102. Bell (1981), p. 291.
103. See Lundahl (1979), p. 607.
104. See for instance UN Economic Affairs Department (1949) and Prebisch (1950).
105. Griffin (1969), p. 95.
106. Ibid.
107. Ibid.
108. See Chapter 1.
109. Ibid.
110. Haberler (1959).

6 THE POLITICAL ECONOMY OF IMPORT SUBSTITUTION

In the two preceding chapters, we have discussed the expansion of the large sugar sector and its impact on Dominican society. In Chapter 4 we showed that, in addition to market forces, institutional factors have played a very important role in making the Dominican Republic an economy heavily biased towards sugar production and exports. In Chapter 5 we then argued that the heavy reliance on sugar exports for more than a century has not generated development. In the present chapter, we will turn our attention towards industrialization. The industrialization policies which have been pursued since the second half of the 1960s will be discussed. We will identify the most salient elements of this policy and discuss some of its important consequences.

The Rationale for Industrialization Policies

Trade and industrialization strategies in developing countries have been the subject of much economic analysis during the last decades. Two comparative studies, those carried out under the auspices of the OECD and the National Bureau of Economic Research, respectively, on industrialization strategies belong to the most comprehensive and discussed analyses on economic development.[1] The OECD study examines the experience of Argentina, Brazil, India, Mexico, Pakistan, The Philippines and Taiwan, while the NBER project covered Colombia, Brazil, Chile, Ghana, Egypt, India, The Philippines, Israel, South Korea and Turkey. Both studies converge on a critical appraisal of import substitution strategies. Countries pursuing import substitution policies have experienced similar problems: inefficient high cost production, underutilization of both labour and capital, lagging agricultural production and stagnating exports. As we will show below the import substitution policy pursued in the Dominican Republic has generated similar problems.

Let us first briefly discuss why this kind of policy has been pursued. The rationale for the implementation of import substitution policies is briefly discussed in the OECD volume, *Industry and Trade in Some Developing Countries*, by Ian Little, Tibor Scitovsky and Maurice Scott.[2]

Little, Scitovsky and Scott emphasize the role of the great depression and the Second World War for the fostering of industrialization. The former implied that the developing countries' ability to import was reduced by the fall in the value of their exports of primary commodities, while, during the war, the industrialized countries could not supply manufactured goods.

'These experiences', Little, Scitovsky and Scott argue, 'induced a strong desire for self-sufficiency and economic independence, and hence for industrialization.'[3] General arguments in favour of industrialization have also contributed to the implementation of industrialization policies. It is argued that there are substantial benefits to be derived from technical progress and innovation associated with industrialization. Historically, it is observed that industrialization accompanies rises in the standard of living.[4]

While the factors discussed by Little, Scitovsky and Scott are undoubtedly important in explaining why inward looking strategies have been chosen, the explanation is not exhaustive. The authors do not discuss the motivation of government and the connection between political decisions and different interest groups. It is reasonable to assume that inward looking strategies were chosen because important interest groups thought that they would profit from them. This kind of discussion is absent in the book by Little, Scitovsky and Scott.

The Rationale for Dominican Industrialization Policies

We have in the preceding chapters argued that there is a clear connection between the interests of important groups and government policies in the Dominican Republic. This applies also to the choice of industrialization policies. The industrialization policies promulgated under Trujillo were a direct consequence of the dictator's personal interest in industrial production. Most industries at the time were controlled by Trujillo, his family, and a small group of Trujillo supporters.

In 1950 an industrial promotion law was promulgated giving tariff protection and generous tax exemptions to industrial activities.[5] Aided by tariffs and government subsidies, the incipient industry was able to make substantial profits.[6] The policies used protected the small industrial group controlled by Trujillo and relatives/friends, from both foreign and internal competition. Tax exemptions and government support were highly selective, which prevented competition. As we will see below, more recent industrialization policies have maintained this kind of arbitrariness and selectivity. During the 1950s the combination of an authoritarian regime, firmly controlling salaries, and a high concentration of industrial (and agrarian) property generated, as it seems, a very unequal distribution of income.[7]

After Joaquín Balaguer had become president in 1966, the work on a new law of industrial promotion was initiated. The rationale for the new law was given in a planning document from 1968, *Plataforma para el desarrollo economico y social de la República Dominicana 1968–1985*.[8] In this document the authorities emphasize the non-viability of the 'traditional model for growth'.[9] The 'traditional model' was excessively dependent on the 'occasional dynamism' of the external sector and has failed to generate welfare to the large segments of the Dominican society. To try to promote savings through a high concentration of income is considered to be incompatible with a truly democratic regime. The rapid growth of the population makes industrialization necessary in order to alleviate the pressure on agricultural land.

The development strategy was to be based on the creation of incentives for industrial activities — incentives to produce for the domestic market. This inward looking industrialization was to be supported by a substantial involvement of the state in economic activities which would provide additional stimulus to domestic industry. Finally, the work on an agrarian reform should be intensified. Such a reform should be carried out because an important aim of the new strategy was to generate welfare, not only for a privileged minority, as in the past, but for the masses.[10] Such a reform would also, it is argued in the *Plataforma*, facilitate the industrialization process since the domestic market would be enlarged if the incomes of the lower strata of the Dominican society increased.

This is the official explanation for the implementation of the import substitution policy. However, in order to understand why a certain policy has been chosen we must go beyond these official phrases and discuss the interests of strategic groups in the Dominican society at the time.

In the beginning of the 1960s a class of industrialists had emerged. Much of the landed oligarchy had gone into business.

Political scientists argue that the political influence of this class of industrialists was considerable. Business groups were, according to Howard Wiarda and Michael Kryzanek, influential in overthrowing Bosch's democratic government in 1963 and under Balaguer business 'had direct pipelines into government'.[11] There is thus reason to assume that the policies more reflected the interests of this group than Balaguer's concern about the welfare of the Dominican masses. Rather, Balaguer's policies in general showed a lack of interest for the Dominican masses but a very strong concern for remaining in power. It is reasonable to assume that Dominican import competing producers demanded restrictionist policies, since protection from foreign competition increases the producer's surplus. As will be shown below, 'large scale' business has been able to make ample profit thanks to the policies pursued. It is important to stress that the industrialization policies carried out are very much a reflection of the interests of an influential group. In part this explains why these policies have generated considerable inefficiency. In a sense Balaguer's 'new model' was just a continuation of the 'traditional model', with the number of privileged extended from Trujillo and a small group surrounding him to a larger group of industrialists.

Instruments of Dominican Industrialization Policy

The instruments of the Dominican industrialization strategy to be considered below are: tariff protection, tariff exemptions on capital goods, fiscal incentives, the exchange rate policy and the provision of cheap finance for industrial activities.

The basis for the present *tariff policy* is a tariff structure in force since 1950 where all imports are subject to an *ad-valorem* tariff plus various additional import charges. Exemptions from tariffs on imports of capital and intermediate goods are available for selected activities. The Industrial Incentives Law (IIL) promulgated in 1968 established a classification scheme according to which *tariff exemption* for such imports would be granted. The IIL also provides ample *fiscal incentives*. The objective of the IIL was: '. . . to promote the most rapid and effective industrial promotion of the country's economy with the purpose of obtaining permanent sources of employment and income for our population and a diversification of our national economic basis . . .'[12]

The IIL established three categories of industrial firms to be given incentives: A for firms exporting their production, B for import substituting firms producing goods for which there was no domestic production and C for firms producing goods which where already produced domestically, but for which installed capacity was not sufficient to fulfil domestic demand. In addition, firms applying for classification in category B have to be of 'high development priority for the development of the country'.[13] This means that producers have to specify to what extent they will satisfy a set of criteria put up by the authorities.[14] Exports are allowed only after the authorities consider domestic demand to be fulfilled. Firms applying for category C do not need to be of 'high development priority' but they have to provide employment and save foreign exchange. For firms classified in categories B and C, a tariff rate of 5 per cent on imports of capital goods was applied (increased to 10 per cent in 1972 and 20 per cent in 1977) while exemptions of up to 95 per cent on imports of intermediate goods and raw materials has been conceded. In practice there does not seem to be any clear criteria regarding the level of exemption for the individual firm, although the authorities claim that the level of exemption is linked to the firm's profitability. Firms with lower profits should receive higher exemptions.[15]

Firms included in category A, i. e. producing only for exports, have to be located in export processing zones. There are several such zones in the Dominican Republic and virtually all firms that have settled in these zones are foreign, mainly American. These firms are totally exempted from tariffs on imported machinery and equipment.

The combination of high nominal tariffs on final goods plus the system of exemption on different inputs has implied very high rates of effective protection. According to a study from 1971, the dispersion of effective rates of protection among sectors has been pronounced, from −48 per cent on distilleries to 874 for electrical apparatus and 1,067 for wine industries, with an arithmetical average of 165 per cent.[16]

Fiscal incentives have been an important element of government policy. Firms included in category A are totally exempted from taxes on wages and capital income. B and C firms will also be exempted from taxes on capital income, for an amount of up to 50 per cent of investment costs if profits are reinvested.

All these benefits, tariff and tax exemptions were to be granted for a period of eight years in Santo Domingo, while firms established in other parts of the country would benefit for up to 20 years.

The choice of *exchange rate arrangement* has of course important repercussions on the working of the economy. Since 1967 a dual exchange market has legally been in operation in the Dominican Republic. In that year, in response to balance of payments difficulties, the monetary authorities prohibited the import of a number of goods using exchange from the Central Bank. These goods could, however, be imported by using foreign exchange from the parallel market.[17] Foreign exchange for imports of capital and intermediate goods and some consumer goods were thus available at the official rate, while the remaining consumer goods could only be imported by means of foreign exchange provided from the parallel market.

During the 1970s and early 1980s, an increasing amount of goods have been transferred to the parallel market.[18] The supply of foreign exchange to the parallel market has come mainly from: tourism, remittances from Dominicans resident abroad, under-invoicing of exports and over-invoicing of imports. Table 6.1 shows the supply and use of foreign exchange on the parallel market.

Table 6.1: Supply and Use of Foreign Exchange on the Parallel Market in 1979

Supply		Use	
1) tourism	115.9	1) tourism	112.2
2) remittances	137.3	2) private short term deposits in US banks	171.5
3) over-invoicing of imp.[a]	158.2	3) imports	227.6
4) under-invoicing of exp.[a]	86.8		
5) other	13.1		
	511.3		511.3

Note: a. Estimated residuals.

Source: Banco Central (1980).

The premium, above the official rate, at which foreign exchange can be obtained on this market was 10 per cent around 1970. As will be shown below, this premium has tended to rise continuously.

Credit Policy has also been an instrument of the industrialization strategy. The goverment has provided cheap finance for the promotion of industrial activities. The *Fondo de Inversión para el Desarrollo* (FIDE) was created in 1966 to provide finance for machinery and equipment. FIDE charges an interest rate of 9 per cent, below the legal ceiling on commercial lending, both rates often below the domestic rate of inflation.[19] This cheap credit has not been available for all applicants and has therefore been rationed.

Summarizing then, the industrialization strategy has largely been based on high levels of protection, a tariff and tax exemption scheme, a dual exchange rate system and loans at low rates of interest for selected activities. In terms of ratios of import tax yields to cif. import values, the level of protection in the Dominican Republic in 1970 was the second highest in Latin America.[20] This ratio was 32.1 per cent compared with an average in Latin America of 13.5 per cent. Only Ecuador with 34.5 had a higher ratio. According to a study carried out by Walter Robichek and Carlos Sanson, the Dominican trade regime became more restrictionist after 1966. In fact, according to the same study, the Dominican Republic and Peru were the only Latin American countries that had appreciably more restrictive exchange and trade regimes in 1970 than in 1966.[21]

Industrialization Policy and Static Efficiency

Let us now turn to a discussion of the effects on the Dominican economy of the industrialization policies portrayed in this section. Analysing the effects of restrictionist strategies Jagdish Bhagwati, in *Anatomy and Consequences of Exchange Control Regimes*, distinguishes between the effects on static or allocative efficiency and the effects on dynamic efficiency. Static effects are the effects on investment among alternative activities, choice of technique, capacity utilization, holding of inventories, etc., while dynamic effects are the effects on savings and capital formation, export performance entrepreneurship and innovation.[22] Let us start with a discussion of the static effects.

Summarizing the experience of the NBER Project countries, Bhagwati asserts that the effects of more restrictionist regimes on static efficiency is adverse[23] in the sense that 'excess' holdings of inventories have been piled up, methods of production have been biased in favour of imported capital goods, overall productivity has been lowered, etc. Little, Scitovsky and Scott reached analogous conclusions.[24] Data on industrial activity in the Dominican Republic are very scant, but the data which are available and which are presented below indicate that industrialization policies in the Dominican Republic have had similar effects on allocative efficiency.

Capital Output Ratio

One rough indicator of overall efficiency is the capital output ratio.[25] For instance, an increase in the marginal capital output ratio means that less output is produced per unit of capital. Data indicate that the policies implemented in the late 1960s led to an increase in the incremental capital output ratio in Dominican manufacturing. This ratio increased from between 2.0 to 2.4 in 1970 to 1973 to between 4.5 and 4.7 during 1974 to 1977.[26]

This conforms with the experience of other countries pursuing similar policies. Bhagwati argues that there is a relation between the overall capital output ratio and the type of foreign trade regime in Project countries. Countries with more liberalized regimes tend to exhibit lower capital output ratios. For example, when Brazil switched policies, lowering restrictions, the marginal capital output ratio fell from 3.8 for 1960 to 1966 to 2.1 in 1966 to 1973.[27]

Different factors may account for the increase of the capital output ratio in Dominican manufacturing. First, restrictionist measures lead to an allocation of investment that does not conform with comparative advantage. Investment in activities in which the country has a comparative disadvantage may imply lower return to capital. Second, as will be argued below, different measures have distorted factor prices in the sense that capital has been 'cheap' which means that the choice of technique has been biased in favour of capital. Third, the lowering of the price of capital may also have led to the building up of 'excessive' inventories. Finally, administrative procedures that delay routine decisions also usually increase the marginal capital output ratio.[28]

Choice of Technique

An important aspect of restrictionist trade and exchange regimes in general is that imported capital and intermediate goods are cheaper than they would have been if the exchange rate had been allowed to adjust to changes in demand and supply. Much of the capital and intermediate goods imports to the Dominican Republic have been carried out using foreign exchange from the Central Bank at the official one to one parity.[29] Import duties on such goods have been very low and have not offset the cheapening caused by the overvaluation of the exchange rate. In addition, loans to 'large scale' industry have been given at negative real rates of interest.

With this 'cheapening' of capital the producer's choice of technique will be distorted if capital can be substituted for labour. This is normally the case. The outcome will then be very high capital labour ratios. In the Dominican case, the data really indicate that the policies pursued have led to high capital labour ratios. The capital output ratio increased, after the promulgation of the IIL, by 35 per cent between 1968 and 1971.[30] The capital labour ratio for new firms established in category C up until 1973 amounted, on average, to 10, 144 US dollars per employed.[31] The capital labour ratio was much higher in the Dominican Republic than in other Latin American countries such as Venezuela where wages are substantially higher.[32] In fact, this is a ratio not much below that of the United States.[33] The wide dispersion of capital labour ratios between different categories also indicates that different sectors face very different conditions. Average capital invested per employee in category A between 1973 and 1977 amounted to 4,029 pesos whereas in the import substituting categories B and C, it totalled 15,748.[34] This difference cannot be explained by the fact that different goods with different factor intensities are produced in each respective category. Even within the same subsector, e.g. food processing, there is a very large difference in terms of investment per employed between firms in category A, on one hand, and firms in category B and C, on the other.

The high capital labour ratios in the Dominican Republic conform with the experience of countries pursuing similar policies. According to Little, Scitovsky and Scott, industry in countries pursuing import substitution policies have generally exhibited extremely high capital intensity.[35] Capital labour ratios have been much higher than would be expected considering available factor supplies: abundant labour and scarce capital.

The overvaluation of the exchange rate may affect the choice of technique in other ways. First, since imports are artificially cheapened, raw materials as well as capital goods can be imported at 'low' prices. This could imply that production was biased towards the intensive use of raw materials. We do not have figures to show that this has in fact happened in the Dominican Republic. But this is a likely outcome since there is plenty of general evidence which suggests that raw materials can substitute for capital and labour.[36] Second, the producers' choice of technique will also be distorted if imported capital and intermediate goods can be substituted for domestic. The figures presented in Table 6.2 conform with this presumption, although we cannot with certainty affirm that the substitution of imported for domestic inputs is a consequence of this price effect. In fact, a change in the sectoral composition of production, in favour of goods using substantial imported inputs, could explain the change portrayed in the table.

Table 6.2: Inputs in Dominican Industry

	Domestic inputs as share of total inputs (percent)
1966	70
1967	66
1968	62
1969	64
1970	64
1971	63
1972	61
1973	56

Source: Oficina Nacional de Planificación (1976), p. 232.

We would expect these effects, the substitution of imported raw materials for capital and labour and of imported inputs for domestic, to occur as a consequence of Dominican industrialization policies, not only for the reasons given above but also because the evidence from the NBER project is that the cheapening of imported inputs has distorted the choice of technique in that direction.[37]

Another indicator of inefficiency is the piling up of excessive holdings of inventories. Data on inventories in the Dominican Republic are, to my knowledge, not available. However, excess capacity may very well be stored up due to the way exempted imports are made available. The authorities will specify the importable quantity for each and every year of the period for which benefits are granted. If during a particular year a firm uses less than the quota for that year, the difference will not be allocated to subsequent years. The firm then has to choose between the loss of exempted imports, which it might need later, or incurring higher costs for stock piling. The administrative delays in connection with exemption of imported inputs and allocation of official exchange are also likely to have led to excessive holdings of inventories.

Utilization of Capacity

Another indicator of static inefficiency is underutilization of capacity. Data from the Dominican Republic reveal exceptionally high levels of underutilization of capacity in import substitution industries. In a study from 1979, 54 per cent of firms were shown to use less than 25 per cent of capacity.[38] Table 6.3 shows the extent of capacity underutilization.

Table 6.3: Underutilization of Capacity in 1979

Capacity not used (%)	Percent of firms
75–	54.1
50–74.9	29.0
25–49.9	9.8
–24.9	7.1

Source: Centro de Promoción de Exportaciones (1979), p. 38.

Different arguments are put forth to explain why capacity is substantially underutilized in many developing countries.[39] First, it is usually alleged that there is a great reluctance to work more than one shift, which in turn is explained by '. . . the shortage of managerial and supervisory staff to work at night in countries where their social prestige and standing in the income scale are very high'.[40] Second, the insufficiency of imported raw materials, components, etc., may force firms to leave capacity idle. Third, entrepreneurial efforts to minimize costs tend to become weakened in the face of excessively high profits.

All the enumerated factors may help to explain the underutilization of capacity in the Dominican manufacturing industry. The first factor, the reluctance of managerial staff to work more than one shift, is however difficult to substantiate. The second factor is also likely to have caused slack in Dominican manufacturing since many firms have complained about not getting regular deliveries of inputs (see below). The third factor is definitely important in the Dominican case.

The restrictionist policies pursued in the country imply reduced competition. Firstly, protection from imports of final goods is given. Secondly, the system of industrial classification discussed above allows firms a privileged position (see below on barriers to entry). The lack of competition for classified firms is likely to have made them less aware of the need to reduce costs, which may have resulted in slack capacity. Profits in Dominican industry in fact appear to have been very high. Food, beverage and tobacco, which made up the bulk of industrial expansion during the 1970s,[41] had an average return on invested capital of 62.5 per cent in 1977, the only year to my knowledge, for which information on profits is available.[42]

Additional factors may have been important in the Dominican case. First, firms classified according to the Industrial Incentives Law have had an incentive to build up capacity due to the way classification has been granted. If classified firms have been able to prove that they already had the capacity to satisfy domestic demand, non-classified firms applying for classification could be denied classification.[43] Building up capacity in this way could accordingly be a way of preventing competition. Second, the small size of the Dominican market places a limit on the utilization of equipment which has been largely imported from abroad and most likely designed for large production series.

Barriers to Entry

As we hinted above, the classification system may act as a barrier to entry. We will consider this more explicitly in this section and point at another factor that may work as a barrier to entry: the difficulties for small and non-classified firms to obtain credit.

A policy of limiting foreign competition through high tariffs will raise profitability of domestic production but is of course no barrier to entry for potential domestic competitors to existing firms. The Dominican industrialization policy has however not been limited to increasing the profitability of import substitution activities in general, through limiting foreign competition, but has also contributed to raising the profitability of a number of privileged firms. This is an important aspect of the policies pursued and an issue to which we will also return in the next chapter.

The classification system implies that classified firms, to varying degrees, are exempted from duties on imported capital and intermediate goods. This means that classified firms will have a considerable cost advantage over non-classified firms. This cost advantage may well prevent non-classified firms from entering the market. In addition, since different classified firms will receive different levels of exemptions, competitive conditions will be distorted between classified firms.

Who is then responsible for the decisions on which firms should be classified? This task has been assigned to the Directorio de Desarrollo Industrial (DDI). This consists of eight persons, four of whom are representatives of the business sector.[44] This means, in other words, that representatives from established and classified firms take part in decisions on whether new firms should be classified or not. One would expect that these would try to impede classification of firms which could affect their own interest. This in fact appears to have happened. The DDI has protected the interests of classified firms. This is the public opinion in the Dominican Republic and is also the view of officials at the Ministry of Industry.[45] The DDI has given in to pressure from established producers who have often argued that applicant firms should not be granted classification because existing firms already have the capacity to produce more than can be absorbed by the market.

The other factor which may work as a barrier to entry is the different access that different firms have to credit. As stated above FIDE has supplied credit for industrial activities at low rates of interest, usually below the rate of inflation. There has been no shortage of official credit for firms which have qualified for classification. However access to credit — both official and private — has been a problem for small non-classified firms. In an inquiry carried out by the Centro de Promoción de Exportaciones small firms have serious difficulties in obtaining credit of any kind.[46]

The exemption system and the unequal access to credit can give classified firms an 'absolute cost advantage'. According to Joe Bain in his classic book on barriers to new competition, a source of absolute cost advantage is that: 'There may be imperfections in the markets for productive factors purchased by all firms which permit established firms to secure such factors at lower prices than potential entrants can.'[47]

Since classified firms obtain capital and intermediate goods at lower prices and credits at lower rates of interest, they ought to have a considerable cost advantage over non-classified firms and potential entrants. These factors may be important in explaining the high level of concentration in Dominican industry, 3.2 per cent of firms accounting for 50 per cent of the capital stock, and the high profits of established firms.[48]

The negative consequences of unequal access to credits for the performance of the manufacturing sector in developing countries is stressed by many observers. For instance, Hla Myint identifies the distortion in the credit market as a major explanation of the dualism usually observed in the manufacturing sector in developing countries.[49] Large firms with access to 'cheap' credit adopt modern and 'excessively' capital intensive technologies, technologies that are too specialized to be transmitted to the traditional or small scale sector. By denying small firms credits, those myriads of simple improvements which do not require large amounts of investment, and which appear to be so important for the development of the manufacturing sector, will not take place.

Other Effects

Classified firms, which have benefited from the IIL, will have an incentive to perpetuate the system. They may have put more emphasis into trying to convince the authorities of the necessity of extending or prolonging grants than into increasing competitiveness. This may be rational behaviour from the point of view of the individual firm but not for the economy as a whole. The tendency towards perpetuation of the system can be illustrated by the following example. Exemptions were originally to be granted for a period of eight years in Santo Domingo. When this time period expired the concession period was extended. The argument from business was that since firms outside Santo Domingo would be receiving the benefits for an additional period of time, competition would be distorted. This argument was evidently accepted by the authorities.[50]

It is also evident that the system creates administrative costs. Applying for classification requires considerable paper work which gives rise to complaints from the firms. A lot of detailed information has to be given to the authorities. Once classification has been established, the normal running of business also requires much administrative work, since every exemption of import duties or taxes requires the involvement of different authorities. Delays are customary and a majority of firms complain about not getting regular provision of essential inputs due to administrative difficulties.[51]

Industrialization Policy and Growth

Discussing the 'dynamic' effects of foreign trade regimes, Bhagwati summarizes the evidence on the relationship between different phases, on the one hand, and domestic savings and capital formation, export performance, entrepreneurship and innovation, on the other. Except in the case of exports, where the more liberalized regimes clearly exhibit larger exports, the conclusions are not very clear-cut. Bhagwati for instance states: 'The evidence on the possible links between foreign trade regimes and domestic saving is thus not as clear-cut as the proponents or opponents of restrictionist exchange control regimes could wish.'[52]

In any case, according to Bhagwati, the results fail to support the notion that more restrictionist regimes, while creating static inefficiencies, are more 'dynamically' efficient.

However, the Bhagwati study encounters substantial difficulties in establishing empirical links between, for example, the exchange regime and savings and capital formation. Firstly, there is the problem of establishing a link between the trade regime and, say, functional (or regional, or sectoral) distribution of income. Secondly, it proved difficult to find a correlation between functional (or regional, etc.) distribution and savings/capital formation. We will not carry out a similar analysis for the Dominican Republic since data are deficient and returns, with the difficulties of the Bhagwati study in mind, in the sense of clear results, can be expected to be low. We will instead in a less formal way discuss the development of the Dominican economy since the implementation of the new strategy, trying to relate such variables as overall growth rates and growth of exports to the policies pursued. However, when comparing, say GDP growth, before and after a new policy has been implemented the reasoning can of course be subject to the criticism that we are not pursuing a *ceteris paribus* argument. Other factors may of course change, influencing the variables in which we are interested. We will however try to account for some of these factors.

Post-1968 growth rates have been, on average, higher than those experienced during the pre-1968 period. From 1960 to 1968 the growth rate was 3.9 per cent, while for the period 1968 to 1978 it reached 8.6.[53] Compared with the preceding period, this later period appears to have been rather successful. One should however be careful to interpret this as an indication that the restrictionist policies have contributed to an improvement in the rate of growth. Behind the high average for the period 1968–78 lie a few exceptional growth years, from 1969 to 1973. Growth rates are given in Table 6.4.

Table 6.4: Growth Rates of GDP and GDP per Capita

Annual growth, percent

	1960–68	1969	1970	1971	1972	1973	1974	1975
GDP	3.9	11.0	10.6	10.6	12.4	12.1	6.9	5.6
GDP per cap.	0.9	7.6	7.6	7.4	9.2	8.8	3.4	2.5
	1976	1977	1978	1979	1980	1981	1982	68–78
GDP	6.3	5.5	2.3	4.8	5.7	3.5	1.6	8.6
GDP per cap.	3.3	2.5	−0.5	2.0	2.7	0.6	−1.3	5.3

Source: United Nations (1982), p. 301, and Rubí (1984), p. 250.

Contrary to what is assumed by some observers, the high growth rates for the years 1969 to 1973 cannot be mainly attributed to the implementation of the new strategy. It would appear that the high rate of growth during these years is primarily attributable to three factors. First, in the second half of the 1960s, the Dominican Republic was emerging from a period of social tension culminating in the civil war of 1965. Balaguer had come to power and this reassured the business community of a period of stability. Balaguer's policy was highly anti-labour which may also have contributed to give industrialists confidence about the future. He promulgated an austerity law which explicitly aimed at keeping wages low by, for example, the imposition of serious restrictions on the organization of labour, wage negotiation, etc. These measures appear to have contributed to reduce real wages (see below).[54] Second, the Balaguer government implemented a heavy programme of public investment in building activity. Table 6.5 shows the high annual growth rates of construction activity during the years 1970 to 1973. The high growth rate of construction activity of course stimulated other economic sectors. Third, prices for the country's main export products rose substantially during these years. The rise in the price of sugar was extraordinary. The price of sugar rose from an index of 16 in 1969 to 146 in 1974.[55] The price of cocoa doubled during the same period, while the price of coffee increased by two-thirds.[56] When export prices and construction activities fell to more average levels, growth of GDP fell markedly. The increase in oil prices must also have contributed to the fall of the growth rate.

Table 6.5: Annual Growth Rates of Construction Activity

1969	1970	1971	1972	1973	1974	1975	1976
6.6	20.5	42.1	9.1	22.0	2.5	8.2	0.4

Source: United Nations (1982), p. 301.

The average growth rate for the period 1975 to 1982 was 4.4 per cent. This performance is not conspicuously better than that recorded for the 1960 to 1968 period. In view of the political turmoil that characterized these earlier years, the 1975 to 1982 performance can in fact be viewed as disappointing particularly if one considers the proclaimed ambitions of government regarding the new policy.

Agricultural Output

One of the alleged drawbacks of import substitution policies is the discrimination imposed on the agricultural sector. This is in a way a necessary consequence of the fact that one sector, industry, is favoured. Little, Scitovsky and Scott point to the fact that countries pursuing import substitution policies have experienced low agricultural growth.[57]

In the Dominican case the restrictive policy of the Instituto de Estabilización de Precios (INESPRE) with regards to food prices should have reinforced the discrimination imposed on the agricultural sector through the industrialization strategy.[58] According to a World Bank estimate, the internal terms of trade, agriculture vs. industry, fell from an index of 100 in 1969 to one of 63 in 1979.[59] Prices paid for inputs to agriculture have increased more than the prices of agricultural output between 1973 and 1979.[60]

We would thus expect a poor performance from the Dominican agricultural sector. In fact, as we showed in Chapter 4, the growth rate of the agricultural sector has during the last 15 years barely sufficed to keep *per capita* production constant, which is equivalent to a growth rate of about 3 per cent.[61] This is in line with agricultural development during earlier periods. As we also showed in Chapter 5 institutional factors, such as land ownership, are extremely important in explaining the difficulties of the agricultural sector. It is thus very difficult to ascertain to what extent slow agricultural output is attributable to industrialization policies as such.

Stagnating Exports

An import substitution policy will discriminate against exports. The discrimination operates via, for instance, the overvaluation of the exchange rate. The existence of import restrictions enables the exchange rate to be higher than under free trade. The exporter will thus receive less domestic currency for a given quantity of exports. It has often been alleged that exports and imports of developing countries are rather insensitive to exchange rate changes. Demand elasticities, for both exports and imports, are assumed to be low, hence the notion 'elasticity pessimism'.[62] Several Dominican observers argue that these elasticities are low for the Dominican Republic. But this has not been proved, and there is reason to assume that both imports and exports are in fact sensitive to changes in the exchange rate, since there is much evidence in general that this is the case. On the basis of the country studies Little, Scitovsky and Scott affirm that exports are responsive to exchange rate incentives/disincentives.[63] According to Bhagwati, regression analysis strongly suggests that exports of the countries under study are responsive to price changes. The evidence is destructive of 'elasticity pessimism'.[64]

There is no evident reason why Dominican exports (except sugar) should not conform with this general pattern. There is thus reason to assume that the discrimination of exports through the policies pursued has also affected the volume of exports. As we discussed above a dual exchange rate system has been in operation. The official rate has been at par with the US dollar. This is the rate at which exporters, until recently,[65] have had to convert all their export earnings to domestic currency. The parallel exchange rate has developed as indicated by Table 6.6.

Table 6.6: Price of the US dollar on the Parallel Market

1972	1.12
1973	1.13
1974	1.14
1975	1.18
1976	1.19
1977	1.22
1978	1.25
1979	1.22
1980	1.26
1981	1.29
1982	1.46
1983	1.60

Source: Figures from Banco Central, Departamento de Estudios Económicos (1984).

The increasing overvaluation of the official rate appears obvious. We cannot, however, simply interpret the parallel rate as the rate that would obtain under a unified exchange rate which was free to adjust. Exchange rate theory does not provide us with any simple tool with which to estimate the rate that would give external equilibrium.[66] Purchasing power parities (PPP) are usually seen as the best, albeit rough, indicator of the long run equilibrium of exchange rates, while short-term changes may be induced by for instance speculative capital movements.[67] In brief, the theory of PPP states (in its 'relative' interpretation) that changes in relative prices between countries indicate the necessary adjustment in the exchange rate.

Now the value of the *peso* is very much dependent on movements of prices for a few agricultural exports, whose weight in domestic and foreign price indices does not reflect their large impact on the exchange rate. This means that a calculation of PPP would not yield a very accurate estimate of the equilibrium rate. Nevertheless, keeping this shortcoming in mind, a calculation of PPP, pesos per US dollar, based on consumer price indices for the Dominican Republic and the United States, gives relative PPPs that are not too far from the parallel rate.[68]

What has then happened to the volume of Dominican exports? Table 6.7 indicates a very poor performance. The volume of total exports in 1982 was thus below the 1960 level. This poor performance is due to both a stagnation of traditional exports at the same time as manufacturing exports have risen too slowly and from too low a level to be able to compensate for the failure of traditional exports. Table 6.8 shows the growth of traditional exports, sugar, coffee, cocoa and tobacco.

Table 6.7: Volume Index of Total Dominican Exports (1980 = 100)

1955	60	67	70	71	72	73	74	75	76	77	78	79	80	81	82
82	106	92	109	127	139	141	145	124	134	139	119	139	100	114	102

Source: International Monetary Fund (1983), pp. 196–7.

It is difficult to ascertain to what extent the export volume of these products has suffered from the discrimination through the overvaluation of the exchange rate. As we argued in Chapters 4 and 5, sugar production is favoured in different ways and takes place

Table 6.8: Volume Index of Traditional Exports (1980 = 100)

	1955	60	67	70	71	72	73	74	75	76	77	78	79	80	81	82
Sugar	71	112	82	93	123	132	125	121	121	122	137	114	125	100	106	108
Coffee	124	149	113	133	128	134	180	158	128	198	102	124	197	100	137	173
Cocoa	96	111	102	147	115	137	99	113	93	105	109	119	107	100	116	164
Tobacco	60	70	92	90	119	149	144	194	146	155	92	171	195	100	180	52

Source: International Monetary Fund (1983), pp. 196–7.

under special institutional arrangements. Two-thirds of production is carried out by a state producer that seems rather unresponsive to price changes. In addition, the International Sugar Agreement, to which the Dominican Republic adheres, represents a constraint on exports. The volume of the other traditional crops ought to have suffered due to the overvaluation of the exchange rate. Although the poor performance of the last few years partly reflects the depressed state of world markets, it should be emphasized that over the last two decades Dominican exports have lagged far behind world trade. The Dominican share of world exports in 1982 was, in real terms, two-thirds lower than it had been in 1960. The Dominican share of exports from the Western hemisphere was in 1982 40 per cent of what it had been in 1960.[69]

The share of manufacturing exports in total exports has increased insignificantly, from 5–6 per cent in 1960–1 to around 8 per cent in 1980–1.[70] Most of the growth of manufactured exports has originated in Export Processing Zones (EPZ), where production has been concentrated on transforming imported raw materials or semi-processed products for reexport. The firms located in EPZs are mainly foreign and are those classified in category A and accordingly do not suffer from discrimination through the overvaluation of the exchange rate. The major products are: electrical and electronical components, metal products, tobacco and textiles. Non-EPZ manufacturing exports are mainly processed agricultural products. These have increased but remain of limited size.

Other policy instruments have also had a negative influence upon exports. CEDOPEX, whose main task was the promotion of non-traditional exports, has also been assigned the task of regulating domestic prices. In order to do so CEDOPEX has introduced export quotas and prohibitions for important manufactured exports such as fertilizer, cement and food products. Up to 1978, 65 product categories had been submitted to export control; exports of 27 product categories were prohibited while 38 were subject to export permits.[71] The argument behind these prohibitions was that domestic demand should be fulfilled before allowing exports in order to prevent internal price rises as a consequence of excess demand.[72] Producers will of course be hesitant to undertake the costs of venturing into foreign markets knowing that the authorities, by introducing export controls, may arbitrarily frustrate such efforts.

Employment and Income Distribution

According to Little, Scitovsky and Scott the pursuit of industrialization through import substitution in less developed countries has '. . . aggravated the problem of unemployment, and thus further contributed to inequalities in the distribution of income'.[73] An important objective of Dominican industrialization policies, as expressed in official publications, was the generation of employment in order to spread welfare to the masses. However, to say the least, the policies pursued have in this respect been unsuccessful. Data on employment and income distribution are scanty but the information available supports such an assertion.

Let us start with the employment situation. Estimates of overall unemployment indicate that the employment situation has not improved. According to an ILO study, unemployment in Santo Domingo was in 1973 estimated to be 20 per cent, while underemployment reached 60 per cent.[74] According to another study, from the Oficina Nacional de Estadística, the rate of unemployment in 1978 was 24.4 per cent. According to the same study, the rate of unemployment has remained almost at a standstill between 1970 and 1978, 23.6 and 24.4 per cent, respectively.[75] Thus despite fairly high growth rates, unemployment has not decreased.

The usual explanations of this pattern, which is also observed in other countries pursuing similar policies, are the following. The countries tend to import highly capital intensive manufacturing equipment which is designed and produced in rich countries with other factor supplies. High capital intensity is also encouraged by the importation of equipment at overvalued exchange rates and a credit policy of keeping interest rates on industrial loans low.[76] The Dominican Republic would appear to conform to this general picture.

The study by Little, Scitovsky and Scott affirms that industrialization policies have aggravated inequalities in the distribution of income. They argue for instance that '. . . the extra profits made in industry are not a net gain to the community'.[77] Little, Scitovsky and Scott emphasize the consequence of industrialization policies on sectoral (agriculture vs. industry) distribution. Internal terms of trade have been altered to the detriment of agriculture. The data presented above indicate a similar unfavourable development for the agricultural sector in the Dominican Republic.

Bhagwati discusses the relation between trade regimes, on the one hand, and the functional and size distribution of income, on the other. There is, however, little in the NBER project that is conclusive in this respect. On the functional distribution of income Bhagwati for instance argues that '. . . while it can strongly be related to foreign trade regimes in theoretical analysis (e.g. the familiar Stolper-Samuelson theorem), [it] does not appear to show anything like a strong and predictable relationship in the project studies.'[78]

It is also difficult to ascertain what has happened with the functional distribution of income in the Dominican Republic. There are, however, some indications that labour may have experienced a decline in its share of income. According to the Oficina Nacional de Planificación, real wages in industry fell by 24 per cent between 1969 and 1973.[79] According to the same authority real wages have fallen from an index of 100 in 1970 to 81 in 1981.[80] Minimum wages in the city of Santo Domingo fell by around 25 per cent between 1966 and 1978.[81] Balaguer's austerity laws and his control over labour undoubtedly contributed to this development.[82] From the above we know that profits have been very high. Consequently there is reason to suspect that a redistribution from labour to capital has taken place.

There is some evidence that the size distribution of income has become more unequal. An ILO study on the Dominican Republic showed that the size distribution had deteriorated between 1969 and 1973. For instance, the share of the poorest 20 per cent fell from 2.9 per cent of total income in 1969 to 1.4 per cent in 1973.[83] According to *Economía dominicana 1977* the deterioration had continued after 1973.[84] Different types of information presented above support the trends indicated by these studies. The combination of, on the one hand, stagnating *per capita* agricultural production, continued high levels of unemployment and falling real wages in the manufacturing sector and, on the other, high profits in import substituting industries, points towards a more unequal distribution of income.

Now, while it appears as if the distribution of income has become more unequal, it is difficult to prove that this is a consequence of the industrialization policies identified above. Population growth, a highly skewed distribution of land, unequal access to education, public infrastructure, etc., are underlying factors which strongly contribute to an extremely unequal distribution of income. Neither does the evidence in the NBER Project studies, according to Bhagwati, lead to any conclusion on the relationship between size distribution and trade regime.[85]

Appraisal of the Industrialization Policies

The officially proclaimed aim of promoting a continuous process of growth, less volatile and less subject to fluctuations on foreign markets, seems today far from fulfilled. It is not that the economy has not displayed growth. Growth rates have on average not been disappointing. But underlying these satisfactory average growth rates lie exceptionally high growth rates between 1969 and 1973, which can only in part be explained by the implementation of industrialization policies. The high rate of growth during this period can to a considerable extent be attributed to other factors: the price increase for the country's most important export products, heavy public investment in construction activity and a change in the political climate which made the business sector confident about the future after several turbulent years. After 1974 growth rates have been considerably lower and exhibit a clear downward trend.

The industrialization policies have had negative consequences for static efficiency. This is in line with the experience of other developing countries pursuing similar policies. The policies carried out have implied serious distortions. Industrial loans at negative real rates of interest and imports of capital goods at an overvalued exchange rate have led to an increase in the overall capital output ratio and to very high rates of capital intensity. Imports of intermediate goods and raw materials have by the same token been favoured at the expense of domestic inputs.

The system of industrial classification has generated inefficiency. Classification criteria have not always been very operative and some are unknown to applicants. Proximity to the authorities has become imperative, reflected perhaps in the increasing concentration of industry to Santo Domingo. Firms will dedicate substantial efforts in negotiations with the authorities. Instead of trying to increase competitiveness they may have put much energy into trying to convince the authorities of the necessity of granting or prolonging different kinds of benefits.

We have argued that the classification system may work as a barrier to entry. Firms classified will have a considerable cost advantage in relation to firms which are not classified. Classified firms will thus have a strong interest in preventing the classification of new firms. In the DDI, which has had to take decisions on classification and on the level of exemption to be allowed, the business representatives have been able to protect the interests of established firms.

Unequal access to credit may also work as a barrier to entry. Larger firms have had access to cheap official credit while non-classified firms have not had access to such credit. This will give larger firms a considerable cost advantage over smaller firms or potential entrants. The instruments used may thus have led to a strengthening of the position of large firms rather than a general stimulation of industrial activity. The high rate of return on investment recorded in import substituting industry supports such a presumption.

It was argued above that the influence of the industrial sector on government policy is an important factor in explaining why the industrialization policies, as identified below, have been pursued. 'Large business' thus constitutes a set of *strategic* decision makers in the Dominican industrialization process. 'Large business' has had an influence through the DDI, but has also had direct channels into government and the bureaucracy. If we account for the influence of the business sector, the consequence of policy for overall economic performance is not unexpected. The true aim of the policy has not been, as it seems, to achieve overall efficiency or to set the basis for a sound industrialization process, as argued in official publications, but rather to improve conditions for the influential business sector.

The balance of payments continues to be a serious problem for the Dominican economy. Current account deficits have been increasing. Although changes in terms of trade, such as the increase in oil prices, have undoubtedly contributed to this development, policy is also to be blamed. Government has maintained an overvalued exchange rate. The import substitution strategy has not reduced the importance of imports in the economy. For instance, the ratio of imports to GDP has increased from 0.19 in 1968 to 0.25 in 1980.[86] The heavy reliance of import substituting firms on imported capital goods and raw materials, has led to substantial increases in such imports. For the manufacturing sector, the share of imports in total supply increased between 1968 and 1977, indicating a small negative import substitution.[87] The share of imports in total supply has also increased for consumer goods such as processed food, the sector in which import substituting activities have been most in evidence.

We can thus argue that policies have provided disincentives for exports and have not decreased the economy's reliance on imports. The economy's vulnerability to changes in world market prices for traditional exports appears to have increased rather than decreased since the mid-1960s.

Concluding Remarks

In this chapter, the industrialization policies carried out since the mid-1960s have been shown not to have achieved the aims proclaimed by the authorities: to form the basis for a sound industrial development, to decrease unemployment and to improve the conditions of the Dominican masses. As we have argued, these official aims should not be taken too literally. The policies pursued have in reality reflected the interests of influential interest groups, such as the business sector, rather than the government's alleged concern for the poorest sections of Dominican society.

Many of the inefficiencies generated are in fact a consequence of the influence of strong groups on the decisions taken. The Industrial Incentives Law, for instance, has probably served to protect the interests of a number of established firms rather than to give *general* incentives for manufacturing activities. Although the emphasis on import substitution as such with its neglect of comparative advantage, has generated inefficiency, the arbitrariness and selectiveness resulting from the *instruments* used are perhaps at least as important in explaining the difficulties observed. This is an aspect to which we will return in the next chapter, where other policies, i.e. policies not directly related to the industrialization strategy, will also be discussed.

Notes

1. The OECD project is summarized in Little, Scitovsky and Scott (1970). Country studies: Lewis (1970), Hsing, Power and Sicat (1970), Bergsman (1970), King (1970), Bhagwati and Desai (1970). The NBER project is summarized in Bhagwati (1978) and Krueger (1978). Country studies: Krueger (1974), Leith (1975), Michaely (1975), Hansen and Nashashibi (1976), Baldwin (1976), Bhagwati and Srinivasan (1976), Behrman (1976), Frank, Kim and Westphal (1976), Diaz-Alejandro (1976).
2. Little, Scitovsky and Scott (1970).
3. Ibid., p. 2.
4. Ibid.
5. Cassá (1982), p. 287.
6. Ibid., p. 304. See also Moya Pons (1983), p. 70.
7. See for instance Cabral (1967) and Oficina Nacional de Planificación (1968).
8. Oficina Nacional de Planificación (1968).
9. Ibid., p..74.
10. Ibid., p. 75.
11. Wiarda and Kryzanek (1982), p. 65.
12. Secreteria de Estado de Industria y Comercio (1982), p. 3. The translation to English from Bell (1981), p. 349.
13. Vega (1973), p. 20.
14. Ibid.
15. Ibid., p. 26.
16. Calculated by de la Cuadra and presented in Moya Pons (1983), p. 125. While 'nominal' protection denotes the percentage by which the price of domestically produced goods can exceed what they would have had to be if there were no restrictions on imports, 'effective' rates of protection measure the percentage by which tariffs enable the value added to exceed what it would have been in the absence of tariffs. Since the second measure takes into account the protection of inputs it is usually more difficult to calculate accurately. In most cases 'effective' rates of protection will exceed 'nominal'. See, for instance, Little, Scitovsky and Scott (1970), pp. 169–74 and pp. 427–45.
17. Robischek and Sanson (1972).
18. See Chapter 7.
19. World Bank (1978a), p. 56.
20. Robishek and Sanson (1972), p. 308.
21. Ibid., p. 309.
22. Bhagwati (1978), p. 82.
23. Ibid.
24. Little, Scitovsky and Scott (1970), see for instance pp. 8–10.
25. See Bhagwati (1978), p. 83. See also Behrman (1976), pp. 286–7, where the limitations of this measure is discussed.
26. Oficina Nacional de Planificación (1980), p. 12.
27. Krueger (1982), p. 19.
28. Little, Scitovsky and Scott (1970), p. 208.
29. Since the end of the 1970s an increasing amount of imports have been transferred to the parallel market. See Chapter 7.

30. Aldo (1975), pp. 204–5.
31. Vega (1973), p. 2.
32. Ibid., the comparable figure for Venezuela was US $ 7,000 per employed.
33. Ibid. See also Aldo (1975), p. 205.
34. World Bank (1978b), p. 12.
35. Little, Scitovsky and Scott (1970), e.g. p. 87.
36. Bhagwati (1978), p. 113.
37. Ibid., p. 117.
38. The study, Centro Dominicano de Promoción de Exportaciones (1979), does unfortunately not tell us how 'capacity' is defined.
39. Little, Scitovsky and Scott (1970), pp. 93–9.
40. Ibid., pp. 95–7.
41. Food, beverage and tobacco manufacturing have made up 58.2 per cent of industrial growth between 1970 and 1980. Output of these sectors constituted 66 per cent of manufacturing production in the Dominican Republic in 1980. Chemical products made up 12 per cent, textiles and leather manufactures made up 5.3 per cent. See Oficina Nacional de Planificación (1983), p. 112.
42. Oficina Nacional de Planificación (1983), p. 116.
43. Secreteria de Estado de Industria y Comercio (1982), p. 7.
44. Vega (1973), p. 72.
45. According to information given to the author by officials at the Ministry of Industry.
46. Centro de Promoción de Exportaciones (1979), p. 76 and World Bank (1978a), p. 56.
47. Bain (1956), p. 144.
48. Oficina Nacional de Planificación (1983), p. 114.
49. Myint (1970).
50. World Bank (1978b), p. 10.
51. See Centro de Promoción de Exportaciones (1979), p. 52.
52. Bhagwati (1978), p. 160.
53. United Nations (1982), p. 301.
54. See Espinal (forthcoming), p. 20.
55. International Monetary Fund (1982), p. 171.
56. Ibid.
57. Little, Scitovsky and Scott (1970), pp. 6–7.
58. See, for instance, Moya Pons (1982c), pp. 48, 54–5 and 64.
59. World Bank (1981), p. 16. See also Quezada (1981), pp. 9–11.
60. Ibid.
61. See Chapter 5.
62. See, for instance, discussion on export pessimism in Little, Scitovsky and Scott (1970), p. 231.
63. Little, Scitovsky and Scott (1970), p. 324.
64. Bhagwati (1978), pp. 184–5. See also this study Chapter 7.
65. Some recent changes in exchange rate policies will briefly be discussed in Chapter 7.
66. On exchange rate determination see for instance Krueger (1983).
67. On purchasing power parities see for instance review article by Officer (1976). See also Krueger (1983), pp. 63–71.
68. Taking the differential rate of inflation between the Dominican Republic and the United States using 1968 as base year, gives 1.42 pesos per dollar in 1980, 1.40 in 1981 and 1.54 in 1982. The figures are slightly above the parallel rate presented in Table 6.6. However, the Dominican price index prior to 1977 referred to Santo Domingo only. This 'break' means that the price series are not completely comparable. Data from International Monetary Fund (1983), pp. 197 and 523.

69. Calculated with figures from International Monetary Fund (1983), pp. 74–5, and 80–1.
70. Oficina Nacional de Planificación (1983), p. 143.
71. World Bank (1978b), p. 36.
72. Ibid., see also p. v. For a discussion of this kind of policy in developing countries in general see Leff (1969).
73. Little, Scitovsky and Scott (1970), p. 8.
74. Oficina Internacional del Trabajo (1975), pp. 31–4.
75. Oficina Nacional de Estadística (1980a).
76. Little, Scitovsky and Scott (1970), pp. 86–7.
77. Ibid., p. 5.
78. Bhagwati (1978), p. 198.
79. Oficina Nacional de Planificación (1976), p. 226.
80. Figures presented in Colegio Dominicano de Economistas (1983), p. 10.
81. Figures from Oficina Nacional de Esdadística presented in Espinal (forthcoming).
82. See Espinal (forthcoming).
83. Oficina Nacional de Planificación (1974), p. 41.
84. Academia de las Ciencias en la República Dominicana (1978), pp. 142–4.
85. Bhagwati (1978), p. 200.
86. International Monetary Fund (1983), p. 197.
87. World Bank (1978b), p. 42.

7 IMPORT SUBSTITUTION VS EXPORT PROMOTION?
Industrial and Agricultural Policies for Development

In the preceding chapter, we made a critical assessment of import substitution policies pursued in the Dominican Republic since the second half of the 1960s. For instance, high capital output and capital labour ratios appear to have been a consequence of policies (credit at low rates of interest, capital imports at an overvalued exchange rate) which have promoted capital use. Unemployment has remained at very high levels. Growth of agricultural output has been lagging and there are indications that the distribution of income has become more unequal.[1]

However, we could not in any straightforward way establish a clear connection between, say, tariff policies and income distribution or agricultural growth. We should thus avoid a 'guilt by association' procedure, i.e. blame everything that has gone wrong on import substitution.[2] Although policies stimulating import substitution have been pursued, other factors may be at least as important in explaining some of the problems observed.

Accordingly in this chapter we will take up some 'loose ends' from the preceding chapter. First, it will be stressed that many government policies, other than those which can be labelled trade policies, have contributed to poor economic performance. In particular, a *set* of policies that discriminate against the rural sector are important in explaining the poor performance of the agricultural sector and the highly unequal distribution of income in the Dominican Republic. Trade policy is just *one* aspect of this discrimination.

Second, we will discuss the importance of agriculture in economic development and address the question of whether there are reasons to give industry special encouragement. Third, we will review the experience of some countries that have land tenure conditions which differ from those in the Dominican Republic, and which have had governments that have taken considerable interest in agricultural production. It will be stressed that under such conditions, 'proper' land tenure conditions and government commitment to agricultural development, it has been possible for the agricultural sector to develop even when tariffs have protected industry and when agriculture has been taxed.

Finally, we will examine the question of which policies could improve economic performance in the Dominican Republic. The experience of 'successful' countries shows that it is possible to achieve rapid industrial and agricultural growth and improvement in the distribution of income even when industry is given *some* protection provided that *other instruments* are used to improve the conditions of the rural sector. Accordingly it will be suggested that the Dominican Republic may maintain industrial protection in the form of tariffs, although these could be lowered. However, the exchange rate should be allowed to adjust to changes in demand and supply, credit policies should provide equal access to credits to agriculture and industry, pricing policy that discriminates against agriculture should be abolished and efforts to change land tenure conditions should be undertaken.

In the final chapter of this book, Chapter 8, we will discuss some of the political aspects of the changes in policies that are suggested in this chapter.

Anti-rural Bias in Government Policies

Discussing the rationale for the industrialization policies pursued in Chapter 6, it was argued that these were largely the result of the influence of the business sector. The influence of 'large business' has had two discriminating effects. First, 'large-scale' business has through the classification system, credit policies, etc., been favoured at the expense of traditional or small-scale industry. Second, industry in general has, by means of tariff and pricing policies, been favoured at the expense of the agricultural sector. The most salient factors in this bias against the rural sector are considered below.[3]

(1) Tariff Policy. The Dominican Republic has relied on high tariffs on manufactured goods for final consumption. Industrial protection is a way of 'taxing' agriculture: it raises the prices of manufactured goods relative to agricultural products in the home market.

(2) Exchange Rate Policy. The maintainance of an overvalued exchange rate affects the agricultural sector negatively. It dis-

courages agricultural exports since exporters will receive fewer units of domestic currency per unit of foreign exchange earned. Since food imports by the Price Stabilization Institute (INESPRE) have been carried out at the official exchange rate, agricultural imports have been overencouraged compared to a policy which would allow the exchange rate to adjust to changes in demand and supply.

(3) Price Policy. INESPRE was established in 1969. The outspoken object of this public institution is to keep prices low, which in practice means trying to keep prices below those which would clear a non-regulated market. There have been no such efforts to keep industrial prices at a low level. The policy of INESPRE appears to have turned relative prices against the agricultural sector.

(4) Credit Policy. While government has provided finance at low rates of interest to firms classified under the industrial incentives law (IIL) peasants have mainly had to rely on informal sources of credit at very high rates of interest.

(5) Deficient Rural Infrastructure. It is difficult to ascertain the extent of anti-rural bias in government spending. Government resources have been devoted to the construction of agricultural infrastructure. On the other hand, large sums have been spent on conspicuous buildings in the capital. For instance, according to Hans Illy, the political vision of the former president Balaguer was '. . . directed primarily towards ostentatious investments like large avenues and squares, urban housing projects, and, to a lesser extent, rural settlement projects.'[4]

Rural infrastructure is highly deficient; there is a widespread lack of roads, irrigation, electricity, etc. As mentioned in Chapter 6, there is a conspicuous difference in standards between rural and urban schooling. Statistics regarding access to health reveal the same discrepancy. According to, for instance, figures from 1964 there were 28.5 physicians per 10,000 inhabitants in Santo Domingo compared with 2.2 in the rest of the country.[5] All these factors indicate an anti-rural bias in government spending.

All agricultural producers have been lumped together into the 'rural sector'. But as was shown in Chapters 4 and 5, the very unequal pattern of land distribution implies that different operating units within the rural sector have highly different access to credit, infrastructure, etc. Large landowners do not generally suffer from the price policy carried out by INESPRE since they are concerned mainly with production for export. (However this has made them more vulnerable to the overvaluation of the currency.) Large landowners are usually resident in cities, and do accordingly have access to urban facilities as well as being close to politicians and the bureaucracy. In addition these *latifundistas* are often engaged in industry, and accordingly share common interests with the business sector at large. This leads us to a final aspect of government policy.

(6) Lack of Land Reform. The highly unequal distribution of land ownership is an important obstacle to rural development. This is even recognized in official publications. For instance, in the planning document from 1968, *Plataforma para el desarrollo economico y social de la República Dominicana 1968–1985*, in which the development strategy for the next decades was laid out, the importance of a land reform for both agricultural and industrial development was stressed.[6] However, little has been accomplished in this area.

The importance of land tenure conditions for development will be discussed below with reference to the experience of recent 'success stories' such as South Korea and Taiwan, but also to Japan, which illustrates the importance of 'proper' land tenure conditions.

This section has pointed to several factors that have affected the development of the agricultural sector. But while we can argue that this *set* of policies has had an adverse effect on agricultural production, it is more difficult to assess the relative importance or strength of different individual *elements* in the policy carried out. Let us reformulate this issue by posing the following question. What would have happened if industry and agriculture had had access to credit at equal conditions, if resources spent on conspicuous official buildings in the capital had been spent on rural infrastructure, if the government had changed land tenure conditions, while at the same time protecting industry with tariffs and import prohibitions? A definite answer to this question cannot be given, but there are reasons, as for instance will be shown by the discussion on South Korea and Taiwan, to assume that things would have gone much better. Thus we cannot in general terms blame everything that has gone wrong on 'import substitution'.

The adverse effects of policies that discriminate against the agricultural sector have not been confined to agricultural output and income distribution. The slow growth of agricultural output in the Dominican Republic has also affected the development of other sectors. This aspect will be dealt with in the next section, where we first discuss the general role of agriculture in development.

The Role of Agriculture in Dominican Development

There are several contributions that the agricultural sector can make in the process of economic development and there are many important interdependencies between agriculture and other sectors.[7] First, agriculture must provide food supplies for a growing population and raw materials for the industrial sector. Second, it can provide export receipts to finance capital goods imports. Third, in the development process, the agricultural sector must contribute capital and labour to non-agricultural sectors. Agriculture must also provide a market for manufactured products.[8] This final 'constraint' can only be avoided if industrialization is begun by exporting manufactures, which may well prove difficult.

What will then happen if the agricultural sector grows 'too slowly'? If the demand for food grows faster than food output the terms of trade will turn against the industrial sector, and this, in turn, will slow down industrialization, and/or lead to increased food imports which in turn will reduce the amount of exchange available for capital goods imports. If incomes in the agricultural sector grow slowly, so will demand for manufactured products. The market for industrial products will increase at a very slow rate since it is, in the words of Arthur Lewis, the '. . . affluent state of the farmers that enables them to be a market for industrial products'.[9]

As shown in Chapter 6, the increase in food production in the Dominican Republic has during the last decades merely sufficed to keep *per capita* output constant. Since GDP *per capita* has increased by 3.8 per cent per year between 1970 and 1982 the increase in demand for food must have outpaced the increase in output.[10] Since the government has tried to keep food prices artificially low through the activities of INESPRE, this discrepancy between demand and supply has not been allowed to affect fully the internal price of food. Agricultural imports have instead increased from about 83 million pesos in 1972 to 246 million in 1980 at 1980 constant prices.[11] If we exclude petroleum imports, agricultural imports accounted for 25 per cent of total imports in that year.[12]

A better performance of the domestic food sector would thus have made considerably more exchange available for capital goods imports. The slow growth of agricultural output combined with low output prices also means low rural incomes. An increase in domestic demand is of course crucial for the success of an import substitution strategy. After an initial 'easy phase' where an increase in domestic industrial output can substitute goods which were formerly imported, a continued industrial growth will depend on an increase of domestic demand. Dominican industrial production has been mainly geared to the domestic market. The slow growth of rural income must inevitably lead to a slowing down of industrial growth since as much as 56 per cent of the economically active population is engaged in agriculture.[13]

Agriculture vs Industry?

In our brief discussion of the effect of agricultural growth on economic development in the section above, we have not come further than to the rather obvious assertion that 'agriculture really matters'. The mere identification of factors which assign agriculture a central role is no guide to important issues such as whether scarce public resources should be allocated to agriculture or industry, or whether industry should be favoured at the expense of agriculture, or vice versa, by economic policies in general. We will try to address this question below.

A static, free trade, allocative optimum requires that the domestic marginal rate of transformation is equal to relative world market prices. At the margin, the return to investment in agriculture and industry will then be equal. Obviously this would be a situation where there is no pro-agriculture or pro-industry bias. Could a deviation or displacement from this static optimum lead to more rapid economic development? It has been argued above that Dominican policies have created a pro-industry bias. Are there theoretical arguments, or empirical evidence in general, that support such a bias in policy? This is the issue to be discussed next.

If prices are a correct reflection of scarcities, without monopolies or externalities, etc., there would be no reason to deviate from static efficiency. The question at issue is whether the price system provides the 'right' information for the economic actors. This is a topic on which much has been written. The balanced vs. unbalanced growth debate, for instance, was largely based on the presumption that market forces alone would not lead to an optimal allocation of investment. Balanced growth is the simultaneous expansion of several sectors of production, allowing for different sectoral income elasticities.[14] Since an investment in one sector will affect profitability in other sectors it will induce, in the words of Scitovsky, a 'dynamic external economy'.[15] The existing price system does not take account of these external economies and is consequently an inadequate guide to investment appraisal.

According to those advocating an unbalanced growth strategy resources should be concentrated in those sectors that exhibit the most rapid technological progress and forward and backward linkages.[16]

It is difficult to draw any clear-out conclusions from this debate. The debate, however, served as a point of departure for Hollis Chenery who, in his article from 1961, 'Comparative Advantage and Development Policy', states:

> The net effect of the discussion of dynamic interdependence and balanced vs. unbalanced growth is to destroy the presumption that perfect competition, even if it could be achieved, would lead to the optimal allocation of resources over time.[17]

According to Chenery there are reasons to give the industrial sector special encouragement since the market mechanism may discriminate against the manufacturing sector. It may do this since

> There is considerable evidence that external economies are more important in the industrial sector than in primary production because of internal economies of scale, training effect . . .[18]

These effects are not sufficiently reflected in the price system. The omission of these effects from investment calculation is therefore, according to Chenery, '. . . likely to bias resource allocation against manufacturing'.[19]

Similar thoughts are expressed by for instance Bela Balassa:

> Manufacturing activities provide social benefits in the form of the 'production' of skilled labour and technological change that are not fully captured in the entrepreneur's profit calculation. The existence of externalities in the manufacturing sector warrants the preferential treatment of this sector in developing countries.[20]

These quotations show that several distinguished economists have, on the grounds that industrialization provides external economies which are not reflected in the industrialist's profit calculation, argued in favour of *some* anti-rural bias in policies.[21]

Other arguments which have been put forth in favour of a pro-industry bias in economic policies are that there is a wage distortion between agriculture and industry and that savings are higher in the industrial sector than in agriculture.

However according to other trade analysts, most of these arguments do not appear to hold for a more rigorous theoretical scrutiny. Max Corden, reviewing the aforementioned arguments in favour of a pro-industry bias, finds very little support for them.[22] We will not dwell on Corden's detailed analysis here. However, *one* important argument is that 'learning potential' and 'external effects' may be as important outside as within the industrial sector. According to Corden the scope for learning in agriculture is enormous.[23]

What does the empirical evidence in this respect reveal? Historical experience shows that in developed countries, technological development in agriculture has been at least as rapid as in industry. For instance in the United States, total factor productivity has risen faster in agriculture than elsewhere.[24] According to Lewis, for example, the industrial revolution depended on a prior or simultaneous agricultural revolution.[25]

Thus there does not seem to be any clear reason why there should be less potential for learning in agriculture than in industry in developing countries. Nor is it clear why positive external economies should be more important in industry.

Hla Myint argues along similar lines. The infant industry argument for industrial protection is linked to the nineteenth-century economist Friedrich List, whom modern day advocates of protection often invoke. But according to Myint these protectionist writers '. . . have ignored [List's] injunction that an underdeveloped country with a backward agriculture should not adopt protection.'[26] In a poor country where both agriculture and industry may be considered as infant there is according to Myint no reason why industry should be protected.

From Chapter 6 we know that the state of agricultural technology in the Dominican Republic is still on the whole at a very rudimentary level. There is thus a huge potential for 'learning' in this sector. Accordingly it seems that there is no evident reason why the manufacturing sector should generate more 'external' effects, which would warrant the preferential treatment of this sector.

So far it has been argued that agriculture can play a very important role in overall economic development and that there does not seem to be any *a priori* argument for biasing policies in favour of industrialization. The experience of South East Asian countries like the 'latecomer' Japan and the 'late latecomers' South Korea and Taiwan, in fact show the importance of a simultaneous expansion of agriculture and industry. It also shows that land tenure conditions are very important for agricultural and thus for overall economic development. Agriculture can develop rapidly if suitable land conditons prevail even when it has been heavily taxed, as in the case of Japan, in order to provide resources for industrialization. Similarly the case of Taiwan shows that substantial protection does not necessarily impede the growth of the agricultural sector provided once again that suitable land tenure conditions prevail. We will briefly review the experience of Japan and Taiwan, and also refer to South Korea, since we believe several lessons can be drawn from the policies carried out in these countries, which can be contrasted with those carried out in the Dominican Republic.

The Agricultural Development of Japan and Taiwan

Two factors seem to be of particular relevance for the agricultural development of Taiwan and Japan.[27] First, the distribution of land holdings has been less unequal than in many other developing countries, the bulk of the land being cultivated by the bulk of the farmers. Second, political rulers have been very concerned with agricultural development. Figure 7.1 illustrates the difference in land holding conditions in Taiwan and Japan, on one hand, and the Dominican Republic, on the other.

Figure 7.1: Lorenze Curves of Agricultural Land Distribution for Japan, Taiwan and Dominican Republic.

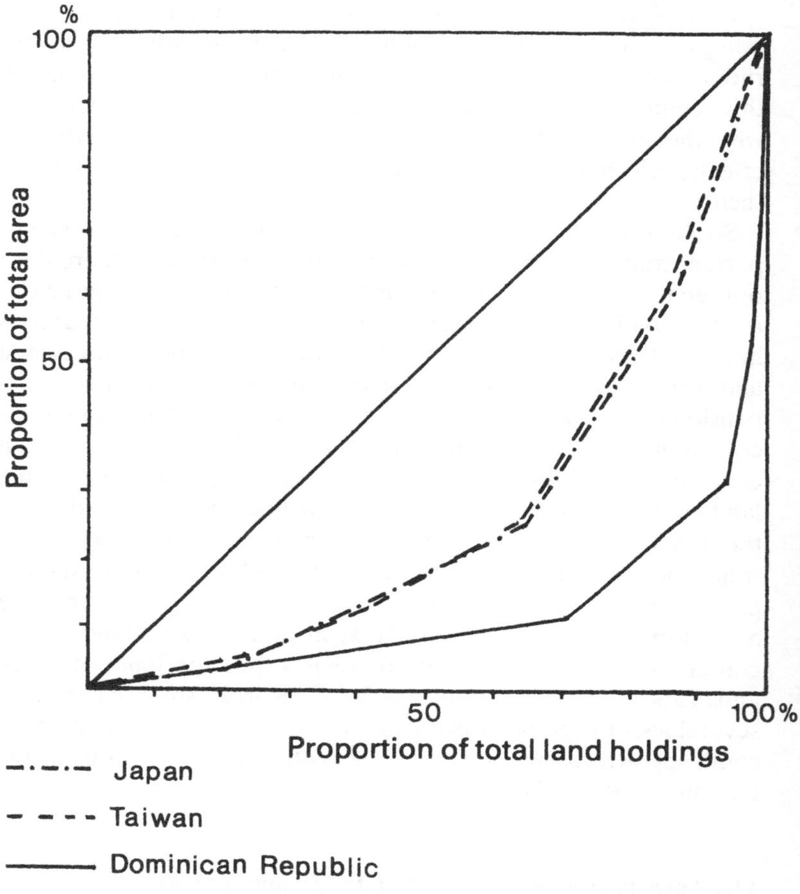

Sources: For Japan and Taiwan, Johnston and Kilby (1975), p. 16; for the Dominican Republic, Oficina Nacional de Estadística (1971).

Johnston and Kilby in their *Agriculture and Structural Transformation* emphasize the importance of land tenure conditions for the development of the agricultural sector and compare the uni-modal strategies of Japan and Taiwan with the bimodal[28] ones of Colombia and Brazil. The latter two countries have land ownership patterns similar to that of the Dominican Republic. They argue: 'The difference in size distribution not only indicates differences in the distribution of income in the traditional economy, but it has a profound effect on the pattern of agricultural modernization . . .'[29]

In both Japan and Taiwan agricultural output increased within the framework of a small-scale farming system. Widespread introduction of improved varieties and increased use of fertilizer were critical factors in the increase of farm productivity, and, it is important to stress that the bulk of the farmers were involved in this process of modernization. By contrast, in the Dominican Republic where a small number of farms control most of the land, the bulk of the farmers are outside the modernization process.

Government policies in Japan and Taiwan have shown a major concern for agricultural development. Under the Meji Restoration in Japan, government action facilitated the spread of new techniques, new varieties and the use of fertilizer. The government provided a substantial amount of infrastructure. These measures greatly increased farm output.[30] A land reform carried out after the Second World War also contributed to agricultural development.[31]

After Japan had seized Taiwan in 1895, the Japanese authorities were particularly interested in the agricultural development of the island. Mo-Huan Hsing argues:

> The first step that the Japanese took to develop the Taiwan economy was naturally to increase agricultural production. For this purpose, irrigation and flood-control systems were installed, chemical fertilizers were imported and applied, species and farming methods most suitable to local conditions were introduced, and to foster co-operation among them, farmers associations were established.[32]

After having carried out a land survey, a land reform was introduced, in which the rights of some 40,000 top-level landlords were abolished. It is interesting to make a comparison with the United States occupation of the Dominican Republic 1916–24. As may be recalled from Chapter 4, the measures introduced by the US military government in the area of land policy mainly served the interests of the American sugar plantations, which were able to expand their land holdings considerably. The US occupants did not take any interest in improving conditions for peasant farming.

The land reform carried out by Chiang Kai Shek around 1950 gave additional vigour to the agricultural development of Taiwan. Farmers' incentives increased and productivity improved after the implementation of the land reform.[33]

Although authorities have given considerable attention to agriculture in Japan and Taiwan, there does not seem to have been a pro-agricultural bias to policies in general. In fact land taxes have been used in both Japan and Taiwan to transfer resources to other sectors.[34] Policies in Taiwan after the Second World War implied that for agriculture the internal terms of trade deteriorated considerably.[35] Shirley Kuo, for instance, shows that a dramatic rise in the relative price of cotton textiles (import substitution industry) relative to rice (main agricultural product and export commodity) took place.[36] Despite this agriculture grew rapidly. For instance labour productivity doubled between 1946–50 and 1956–60.[37] Thus during this import substitution industrialization phase, agriculture continued to develop despite the fact that heavy protection, through tariffs and quotas, was given to industry. The change towards export orientation in Taiwan first appeared in the late 1950s. The role of tariffs is still important in the Taiwan economy.[38] In 1981, 19 per cent of government receipts still consisted of tariff revenues.[39]

It was argued in the preceding section that there is no straightforward theoretical argument for biasing policies in favour of industry. The experience summarized in this section shows that rapid growth may occur in agriculture even when industry is given preferential treatment in the form of protection, provided that government has a commitment to agricultural development. The discussion of policies in a two-sector model, industry vs. agriculture, may well be somewhat misleading. If the 'right' measures are used, both sectors can respond positively by using idle resources and/or by drawing resources from a third sector (services or whatever).[40]

Land Reform and Income Distribution

In Chapter 6 we presented data which indicated that income distribution in the Dominican Republic may have become more unequal after the reinforcement of protective measures in the late

1960s. However, we were unable to establish a clear-cut relationship between income distribution and protection.

Taiwan has not only experienced high growth rates for both industry and agriculture, as argued above, but also exhibits a fairly equal distribution of income. For instance, in 1974, the richest 20 per cent of the population in Taiwan earned 38.6 per cent of total income, while the poorest 20 per cent earned 8.8 per cent.[41] The corresponding figures for the Dominican Republic were, in 1973, 54.4 and 1.4 per cent, respectively.[42] Taiwan is usually considered one of the 'success cases' illustrating, according to for instance Anne Krueger, the superiority of export-oriented strategies.[43] But is the good performance in this respect (income distribution) mainly attributable to trade policies? There are two factors that indicate that trade policies may not be the main cause for the fairly equal distribution of income in Taiwan. First, it has proved difficult empirically to establish a clear cut connection between trade policy and income distribution in general. Second, the favourable distribution of land in Taiwan but also in South Korea, which is also considered to be a 'success case' with fairly equal distribution of income, appears to be a very important factor for reducing inequality in the distribution of income.

In his discussion of income distribution in the NBER volume, Bhagwati states that there does in fact not appear to be any 'strong and predictable relationship' between trade regime and distribution in the Project countries.[44]

In the Project study on Columbia, Carlos Díaz-Alejandro argues that import controls and the protective system in general do appear to reinforce inequality, regional disparities, and industrial concentration.[45] But Díaz-Alejandro goes on to argue that the dismantling of the protective system would not necessarily decrease inequality since: ' . . . the elimination of import controls would still leave a multitude of similar mechanisms through which the rich and powerful could take advantage of state power to buttress and further their position'.[46]

Díaz-Alejandro concludes:

> . . . focusing just on the protective system can give a misleading impression of the true sources of inequality, confusing a symptom for the cause of the disease, which, as noted by many Columbians, lies in the excessive economic and political power held by privileged minorities.[47]

The importance of land reforms for the favourable distribution of income in the 'success stories' South Korea and Taiwan is stressed by many observers. For instance, Little, Scitovsky and Scott argue that the favourable distribution of Taiwan is ' . . . undoubtedly the result of her thoroughgoing land reform in the 1950s'.[48] Distribution was markedly less unequal after the land reform than before.[49] Díaz-Alejandro argues along similar lines and also points to the importance for income distribution of the educational reform carried out in Taiwan.[50] From the start the government gave considerable attention to education, and, according to Shirley Kuo, equal opportunity for education was stressed by the authorities.[51]

In the case of South Korea, Charles Frank, Kwang Kim and Larry Westphal argue that the land reform completed in 1949 appears to have resulted in a ' . . . remarkably even division of land and income'.[52] South Korea has, according to Krueger, experienced satisfactory agricultural growth, although she does not refer to the impact of the land reform.[53]

The discussion in the preceding and the present sections shows two things. First, it indicates the importance of land tenure conditions and commitment to agriculture by the authorities, for the achievement of agricultural growth and a fairly equal distribution of income. Second, provided that such conditions are fulfilled, agriculture may develop, notwithstanding the taxation of the agricultural sector in order to provide resources for industrialization and despite that industry has been given substantial tariff and non-tariff protection (which is also a way of 'taxing' agriculture).

In the Dominican Republic, neither of these two conditons has been fulfilled. Land distribution is extremely skewed and Dominican governments have shown a disinterest in the agricultural sector (except for plantation sugar). This is probably more important in explaining low agricultural growth and unequal distribution than is industrial protection.

Import Substitution vs Export Promotion?

Consequently, it may be wrong to single out differences in trade policies as the main explanation of observed differences, in for instance income distribution, between countries. This however appears to be the approach of many neoclassical economists who take the experience of South Korea and Taiwan as proof of the superiority of export promotion strategies. Compare for instance Paul Streeten's assessment of 'orthodox economists' view of trade policy and the role of the state vs. market forces in development:

> Thus the success stories South Korea and Taiwan are used by orthodox economists to propagate export promotion as the key to equitable and rapid growth. And export promotion in turn is often identified with absence of government intervention and the free play of the market forces.[54]

We have already stressed the importance of land tenure conditions and government interest in agriculture for the successful agricultural growth and fairly equal distribution of income in countries like South Korea and Taiwan. However, Streeten points to two additional factors that blur the orthodox standpoint as expressed in the quotation. First, these countries promoted labour-intensive import substitution, as well as exports, and early import substitution led to subsequent exports, Streeten argues. Second, '. . . government intervention as well as the public sector played a very important role'.[55]

Both these factors are worth consideration. In fact countries now pursuing outward oriented policies have, with the exception of Hong Kong, all pursued import substitution policies for shorter or longer periods. Countries like South Korea, Singapore and Taiwan did adopt export oriented policies first after the completion of the first stage of import substitution (that is, the replacement of most non-durable consumer goods by domestic production).[56] Countries like Mexico and Brazil, which are also considered to have pursued fairly successful export oriented policies, pushed import substitution even further before changing policies.[57] This does not prove that prior import substitution is a necessary condition for an export promoting policy. On the other hand it cannot be proved that import substitution has been an obstacle for a subsequent export oriented strategy.

The observation made by Streeten that government intervention and the public sector has also played an important role in countries pursuing export promoting strategies is relevant. This point has also been made by several other observers. According to Bhagwati, export promotion may involve as much haphazard government intervention as import substitution.[58] According to the

World Bank, the role of government in those countries which are most successful exporters has been substantial[59] and according to Díaz-Alejandro: 'The example of South Korea suggests that export success is not simply a matter of following neoclassical textbook recipies.'[60]

Thus although theoretical considerations suggest that there does not appear to be any strong reason to deviate from free trade and *laissez faire*, a review of the successful countries show that these have indeed deviated and still deviate from free trade, and that government intervention has been substantial. The experience of today's developed countries also indicates that development is compatible with tariffs. However tariff levels in developed countries were usually considerably lower than in many developing countries today. A country like the United States relied heavily on tariffs, the nominal tariff in 1902 being as high as 73 per cent.[61] This is higher than the average level (69 per cent) of nominal tariffs in the Dominican Republic in 1971.[62] The experience of Italy shows, according to Díaz-Alejandro, that quantitative controls and *ad hoc* bureaucratic decisions may be compatible with and may survive economic development.[63]

The relation between trade policy and development does accordingly not appear to be as clear cut as some proponents of export promotion policies argue. Nevertheless it seems evident that many developing countries have pursued import substitution policies which leave much to be desired, while countries which in different ways have promoted exports appear to have had a more rapid growth of industrial production and exports, and have faced less balance of payments difficulties. What appears to be particularly important for the success of the latter countries in this respect is the question of exchange rate management. In fact, these countries have let the exchange rate more closely reflect the scarcity of foreign exchange. This appears to have been an important instrument in achieving a better allocation of resources.

This leads us to a final issue, before we turn to the question of policies in the Dominican Republic. To what extent must old policies be dismantled and new ones introduced to achieve a better performance of exports and balance of payments? Evidence shows that if the exchange rate is allowed to reflect more closely the scarcity of foreign exchange, exports may increase even though no effort to eliminate or drastically reduce industrial protection is carried out. According to Bhagwati, the experience from the

NBER Project Studies strongly suggests that exports from these countries are responsive to exchange rate incentives/disincentives.[64] In the volume on Columbia Díaz-Alejandro examines the responsiveness of non-traditional exports to changes in the exchange rate. He finds a significant connection between movements in the exchange rate and the development of minor exports, both agricultural and manufactured.[65] Columbian exports were able to increase without the extensive import control system being dismantled. The experience of Columbia may be of particular relevance for the Dominican Republic. The countries have a similar export structure, Columbia relying heavily on coffee and the Dominican Republic on sugar, and have fairly equal *per capita* incomes (US$ 1,237 for Columbia and US$ 1,211 for the Dominican Republic in 1980). Both have a strong need to increase minor exports. But while the former has implemented a policy package which led to the acceleration of such exports, the Dominican Republic has only recently tried to reduce the discrimination imposed on these exports (see below).

The fact that it has been possible to increase exports without dismantling the protective system is according to Díaz-Alejandro also proven by the experience of other successful countries:

> . . . a major point emerges from the successful cases: To reach rapid growth in exports it was *not* necessary to dismantle totally the paraphernalia of controls inherited from the stage of import substitution, nor to enter into an orthodox neoclassical decentralized world.[66]

According to Díaz-Alejandro, import liberalization efforts in many successful cases have been mainly limited to goods and services that do not compete with established domestic industry while not really reducing protection to genuinely import-competing industry.[67]

The policy proposal by Díaz-Alejandro is to *first* increase exports and *then* to liberalize imports. And: ' . . . this does not appear to be as difficult as many thought a few years ago'.[68] How can this be possible? In the traditional two-sector model in trade theory, incentives cannot be given to *both* import competing and export sectors. The competition for resources between the sectors implies that an expansion of export goods production must take place at the expense of import competing goods. However, if resources can be taken from *other* sectors or if there are underutilized resources 'correct' incentives can lead to the expansion of both sectors. Díaz-Alejandro argues that the trade and development problem of poor countries should be conceptualized in 'vent for surplus' or in three sector models:

> . . . . in which the competition of resources between the export and the import-competing sectors is mitigated by the existence of a home-good or subsistence sector that gradually yields resources to both (if the price is right).[69]

As shown above, a reorientation towards more openness can take place gradually with the introduction of measures that stimulate exports. As we have seen exchange rate management appears to be a crucial factor in this process. The exchange reform in 1958 was important for the subsequent development of the Taiwan economy.[70] In South Korea exchange rate policies have ' . . . aimed at maintaining the purchasing power parity of the won by adjusting for the effects of domestic and international price inflation'.[71]

Thus an important element in trade liberalization is the process of moving away from a disequilibrium to an equilibrium exchange rate at the same time as tariffs replace quotas.[72] By 'liberalized trade' regime, Krueger and Bhagwati in fact do not mean a complete absence of tariffs but a situation where incentives are more neutral between import substitution and exports, and where policies are such that an allocation *closer* to a (static) optimal resource allocation is achieved.[73]

New Directions for Dominican Policies

Trade policy is just *one* of the factors that affect economic development. This somewhat obvious argument, which is perhaps overshadowed by our concentration on trade policy, is brought out by the experience of several countries portrayed above. The good performance of the 'success cases' is not only attributable to trade policies, but also to suitable land tenure conditions, to government concern for agricultural development, etc. Nevertheless it is evident that trade policy really matters and it is difficult to refute the assertion that more liberal trade arrangements have contributed to an improvement in economic performance in various countries. Several lessons can be drawn from the above discussion.

First, the experience of countries such as South Korea and Taiwan give additional weight to our analysis in Chapters 4 and 5 where we, *inter alia*, discussed the negative consequences of a highly unequal distribution of land and the lack of government interest in peasant production in the Dominican Republic. These factors are very important in explaining stagnating agricultural production *per capita* and the highly unequal distribution of income. Second, the Dominican policy of maintaining an overvalued exchange rate has as it seems been a severe obstacle to the growth of non-traditional exports, which has contributed to the deterioration of the balance of payments. (A comparison can be made for instance with the positive development of such exports in Columbia after an exchange reform.) This was referred to already in Chapter 6 but the discussion in this chapter has underlined its importance. Third, it appears to be possible to increase exports without dismantling the protective system if proper policies, such as exchange rate incentives, are followed. Below we will try to convert these arguments into more concrete policy proposals, most of which will appear rather self-evident considering the preceding discussion.

Agriculture

The experience of the successful 'latecomer' Japan and the 'late latecomers' South Korea and Taiwan show the importance of achieving agricultural transformation before or at the same time as policies promoting industry are carried out. In contrast, the Dominican Republic has tried to industrialize without previously trying to promote agricultural development. As a result the demand for manufacturers has risen very slowly and an increasing amount of foreign exchange is used for food imports.

The interests of the peasant sector have traditionally been neglected by Dominican authorities.[74] The policies carried out since the late 1960s have put additional strain on this sector. While countries like Japan and Taiwan have given considerable attention to increasing production of food for domestic consumption by for instance keeping the price of rice above the world market level (Japan) in order to stimulate production, the interests of Dominican authorities have mainly been concerned with increasing sugar production for exports. The policy of 'price stabilization' has aimed at keeping food prices low. In order to do so INESPRE has tried to keep prices below their market clearing level. Excess demand at this price level has been replenished by imports, which INESPRE carried out using foreign exchange from the official market at the clearly overvalued one to one parity. Domestic food producers have undoubtedly been severely discriminated against as a result of the overvalued peso.

A policy package for improving conditions in the agricultural sector would have to include a complete revision of the present price policy. To keep food prices artificially low does perhaps help the situation of the urban poor in the short run, but it is not a viable long-run policy. On the other hand, government policy is highly concerned with the short run. A measure which immediately hits the welfare of large groups, while promising improvement in the long run, is extremely precarious. We will have more to say about this in Chapter 8.

Much more consideration ought to be given to rural infrastructure. Roads in rural areas are in a very poor state, and irrigation and sewerage is usually lacking. The conditions of rural education are deplorable. In a country like Taiwan much consideration has been given to education and to the importance of equal access to education, whereas Dominican governments have traditionally neglected education, particularly in rural areas. Conditions are still highly deficient. It is difficult to measure the contribution of education to development, but it appears evident that development cannot take place if the educational standard is not improved.

Rural credit is another important policy area. Access to credit has been very unequal in the Dominican Republic. While cheap credit has been available to industry (at least to 'large scale' industry, see below), the peasants have had to rely on informal sources of credits at rates of interest which can be extremely high. This is a serious distortion which heavily inflicts on the welfare of the peasants and on their opportunities to improve their methods of production by buying fertilizers, pesticides, extension services, etc. The improvement of access to credit for the peasants is an important task for the Dominican authorities.

The importance of land tenure conditions for agricultural development has been repeatedly stressed. We argued in Chapter 6 that the very unequal distribution of land was a determinant factor for the backward state of large segments of Dominican agriculture. Unequal distribution of land also implies unequal access to other inputs, such as credits. The experience of the 'success cases' demonstrates that a comparatively equal distribution of land has been an important factor in explaining the rapid technological transformation of agriculture in these countries and the fairly equal distribution of income. Land reform in South Korea and Taiwan during the 1950s contributed to agricultural development. Bruce Johnston and Peter Kilby point to the fact that the bulk of the farmers have been involved in the process of transforming a backward agriculture to a modern one. In contrast, the bulk of Dominican farmers are engaged in traditional agriculture characterized by the most rudimentary techniques. This shows the *potential*, that a land reform may have in terms of its contribution to both agricultural transformation and a more equal distribution of income. However, the success of a reform will depend on the particular setting in which it is implemented and the performance of the 'success cases' is not easily repeatable in other countries. Traditions, political conditions, power relations as well as the commitment by authorities to a reform are crucial factors. Moreover a redistribution of property rights in land may fail to achieve the change necessary to promote development if not accompanied by measures to provide credit and extension services.[75] Thus the failure to provide supervision and credit to new owners was according to Philip Raup the main reason for the disastrous consequences for production of the land reform in Bolivia in 1953.[76]

Industry

The different instruments used to promote industry have, as was argued in Chapter 6, had various adverse effects. For instance very high capital output and capital labour ratios have been recorded. This means that a large section of the manufacturing sector has adopted production methods that do not not appear to be compatible with the country's factor endowments. To enable a continuing growth of manufacturing, given such factor proportions, savings must increase at a very rapid rate. This has not occurred. Important factors in explaining the choice of capital intensive methods of production are credit policies and the exchange rate policy. Cheap credit to selected activities and capital imports at an overvalued exchange rate have stimulated capital use.

Official credit has mainly been geared towards firms classified according to the Industrial Incentives Law, while non-classified firms have had serious difficulties in obtaining credits of any kind. This indicates a serious distortion in the credit market, where the government favours the relatively modern sector at the expense of the traditional. This is not an unusual policy in developing countries, and, as argued by for instance Hla Myint, it may be a determinant factor in explaining the observed dualism within the manufacturing sector.[77] There does not appear to be any theoretical or empirical support for a credit policy that discriminates in favour of one sector of industry at the expense of the other.[78] Thus a credit reform should give all of the economic actors, within agriculture as well as within industry, equal access to credits. This would improve the allocation of resources and reduce dualism within and between the industrial and agricultural sectors.

Industrialization policies in the Dominican Republic have aimed at import substitution. After an initial 'easy phase', such strategies usually encounter serious difficulties. In the first stage of import substitution (replacement of light consumer goods), industrial production may rise more rapidly than domestic consumption since imports are replaced. When the first stage has reached saturation, the growth of industrial output will be constrained by the *increase* in domestic consumption of final goods. Some countries facing this situation have turned to the export of manufacture (South Korea, Taiwan) while some have moved to second-stage import substitution (Brazil, Mexico).

The Dominican import substitution strategy has run into increasing difficulties. Overall growth rates have decreased dramatically, as has industrial growth, after having experienced high growth rates between 1969 and 1974. The import substitution strategy has been based on the replacement of light manufactured goods while intermediate and capital goods have been imported. Moving into second stage import substitution would entail the replacement of imports of intermediate and capital goods and more sophisticated consumer durables, by domestic production. Venturing into second-stage import substitution would however not be advisable for such a small country as the Dominican Republic. Intermediate and capital goods tend to be highly capital intensive and subject to important economies of scale. Domestic demand would not be large enough to ensure an efficient plant size for intermediate and capital goods production. Consequently costs would be very high at lower levels of output. Embarking on second-stage import substitution would mean going into the production of commodities in which the country has less and less comparative advantage.

Consequently it would seem that a reorientation of industry towards foreign markets is inescapable. How could this then be done? As may be recalled from the discussion above, it has proved to be possible to increase exports without dismantling the protective system. Díaz-Alejandro argued that the least risky strategy was *first* to increase exports and *then* to liberalize imports.[79] Exchange rate policy is particularly important in this respect. All experience shows that the exchange rate 'matters', exports clearly responding to exchange rate incentives. An important element in a policy stimulating exports is thus to let the exchange rate adjust to changes in demand and supply.

As may be recalled from Chapter 6, the Dominican Republic has maintained a dual exchange rate system. The official rate has been at par with the US dollar since 1947, while the parallel rate has offered a constantly increasing premium on the dollar. Until a few years ago, exporters had to convert *all* their foreign exchange earnings at the official rate, which meant a clear loss for the exporter compared to what he would have achieved had the official rate been allowed to reflect the true scarcity of foreign exchange. Imports of capital and intermediate goods as well as some consumer goods were carried out at the official exchange rate, while other imports were only allowed using foreign exchange from the parallel market. In the late seventies, some changes were carried out. However the dual rate system was maintained and a series of *ad hoc* bureaucratic measures[80] were introduced due to the unwillingness to devalue the official exchange rate.[81] A unified exchange rate that could adjust to changes in demand and supply is an important instrument in the promotion of exports and in the generation of a better allocation of resources in general. This is not to say that the Dominican authorities should adopt a completely flexible exchange rate. A system with a crawling peg has proved successful in many countries.[82] According to Díaz-Alejandro such a system, with frequent and small exchange rate changes, may be more important in promoting export and GDP growth than any profound revision of protective systems.[83] This could also be a viable strategy for the Dominican Republic.

Concluding Remarks

In this chapter, we have discussed a set of factors which have had negative consequences for agricultural development and income distribution in the Dominican Republic: highly unequal distribution of land, price discrimination against agriculture, anti-rural bias in government expenditure. A brief review of some 'success cases' has shown that a fairly equal distribution of land together with government policies stimulating agricultural transformation and growth have been major factors in economic development. Rapid agricultural development in for instance Taiwan, stimulated industrialization by supplying cheap inputs to food processing industry, while a fairly equal distribution of expanding rural incomes has meant a high level of demand for manufactures. The experience of these countries also indicates that under such conditions it is possible to tax agriculture in order to provide resources for industrialization. Land taxes (absent in the Dominican Republic) have for instance been used in Japan and Taiwan. In addition to the provision of resources for other sectors, land taxes appear to have encouraged large landowners to increase land utilization. As is also shown by the experience of South Korea and Taiwan, it is possible to 'tax' agriculture by means of industrial tariff protection and nevertheless experience rapid agricultural growth.

This suggests that industrial protection may have little to do with the problems of the Dominican rural sector. A highly unequal distribution of land and anti-rural policies in general (credit policies, pricing policy, lack of rural infrastructure), are probably more important in explaining low agricultural growth and a markedly unequal distribution of income. To change land tenure conditions towards more equitable access to land, and to eliminate the anti-rural bias in, for example, credit and pricing policies would thus be desirable. A change in exchange rate policy would also constitute a reform which could improve the conditions of the rural sector.

The marked difference in economic performance between the Dominican Republic and some of the countries reviewed in this chapter appears to a considerable extent to be attributable to major differences in government policies. In earlier chapters, we have explicitly argued that a large part of Dominican economic problems have been caused by different rulers who, while pursuing personal goals, have induced different kinds of distortions and inefficiencies. In contrast, in several countries, the state appears to have carried out policies that have promoted overall development. To account for this difference in the behaviour of different states is difficult and is outside the scope of this study.[84] However, one explanation which in our opinion can be ruled out is that this difference can be attributed to differences in motivation or to 'cultural' factors between, say, Taiwan and the Dominican Republic. Rulers in South East Asia can be assumed to have been as interested in pursuing personal goals, in terms of power and income, as have rulers in less successful countries.

Notes

1. See Chapter 6.
2. The term is used by Díaz-Alejandro (1975), p. 115, who criticizes Little, Scitovsky and Scott (1970) and Díaz-Alejandro (1970) (*sic*!) for following such a 'guilt by association' procedure.
3. Points 1 to 4 have been substantiated in Chapter 6.
4. Illy (1978), p. 174.
5. Lipton (1976), p. 448.
6. Oficina Nacional de Planificación (1968), p. 75.
7. See for instance Dorner (1972), pp. 16–17, and Johnston and Mellor (1961).
8. It should be evident that these points may be in part mutually conflicting.
9. Lewis (1978), pp. 9–10.
10. Let p be the annual rate of population growth. If real *per capita* income rises by g per cent and the income elasticity of demand for food is n, demand will increase, at given prices, by D= p + ng (see Okhawa, 1956). In the Dominican Republic, population growth has been 3 per cent, while *per capita* income has increased by 3.8 per cent between 1970 and 1982. Assuming an income elasticity of 0.5, which should at least not be too high a guess (see for instance Johnston and Mellor, 1961), demand for food will increase by 4.9 per cent per year, compared with actual output growth of about 3 per cent.
11. Figure for 1972 from Oficina Nacional de Estadísdica recalculated using the price index from International Financial Statistics, figure for 1980 from Vicens (1982), p. 142.
12. Vicens (1982), p. 142.
13. FAO (1983), p. 64.
14. Nurkse (1961b), pp. 241–81.
15. Scitovsky (1954).
16. See for instance Hirschman (1958).
17. Chenery (1961), p. 22.
18. Ibid., p. 24.
19. Ibid., pp. 24–5.
20. Balassa (1978), p. 50.
21. Compare also the following quotation from Little, Scitovsky and Scott (1970), p. 349: '. . . it must be remembered that we accept that there should be some bias against agriculture, in the sense that industry would continue to be relatively favoured. In other words, agriculture must provide more resources for industrialization than it would under *laissez faire* policies.'
22. Corden (1974), Chapters 9 and 10.
23. Ibid., p. 268. Cf. also Livingstone (1968), p. 242. See also Baldwin (1969) for a criticism of the 'infant industry' argument for protection and Lipton (1976) for a criticism of the 'different saving propensities' argument for protection.
24. Lipton (1976), p. 105.
25. Lewis (1978), p. 8.

26. Myint (1969), p. 32.
27. This section draws on Johnston and Kilby (1975).
28. The term 'bimodal' strategy refers to a strategy whereby resources are concentrated within a subsector of large and capital intensive units, whereas a 'unimodal' strategy promotes wider diffusion of technical innovations adapted to the factor proportions of the sector as a whole. See for instance Johnston (1972).
29. Johnston and Kilby (1975), p. 17.
30. Ibid., p. 208.
31. Ibid., p. 219. See also Raup (1967).
32. Hsing, Power and Sicat (1971), 'Taiwan', p. 148.
33. Johnston and Kilby (1975), p. 244; Kuo (1983), p. 29.
34. Johnston and Kilby, pp. 213, 249.
35. Little, Scitovsky and Scott (1970), pp. 346–7.
36. Kuo (1983), p. 299.
37. Johnston and Kilby (1975), p. 246.
38. Kuo (1983), p. 300.
39. Ibid., p. 318.
40. See similar argument below by Díaz-Alejandro in connection with the discussion on import substitution vs export promotion.
41. Kuo (1983), p. 97.
42. See Chapter 5.
43. See for instance Krueger (1982), p. 5.
44. Bhagwati (1978), p. 198. See also the present study Chapter 5.
45. Díaz-Alejandro (1976), p. 239.
46. Ibid., p. 240.
47. Ibid.
48. Little, Scitovsky and Scott (1970), p. 45, see also p. 109.
49. Ibid.
50. Díaz-Alejandro (1975), p. 137.
51. Kuo (1983), p. 122.
52. Frank *et al.* (1975), pp. 224, 242.
53. Krueger (1978), p. 285.
54. Streeten (1983), p. 880.
55. Ibid., pp. 880–1. See also Streeten (1985).
56. Balassa (1978), p. 26.
57. Ibid.
58. Bhagwati (1978).
59. World Bank (1982), p. 17.
60. Díaz-Alejandro (1975), p. 121.
61. Little, Scitovsky and Scott (1970), p. 162.
62. See Chapter 5.
63. Díaz-Alejandro (1975), p. 128.
64. See Chapter 5.
65. Díaz-Alejandro (1976), pp. 66–7.
66. Díaz-Alejandro (1975), p. 133.
67. Ibid.
68. Ibid.
69. Ibid.
70. Kuo (1983), p. 298.
71. Frank *et al.* (1975), p. 119.
72. McKinnon (1979), p. 431.
73. Bhagwati (1978), p. 209; Krueger (1982), p. 9.
74. The behaviour of the Dominican state is discussed in Chapter 2.
75. Raup (1967).
76. Ibid., pp. 289–93.

77. Myint (1970).
78. Ibid.
79. Díaz-Alejandro (1975), pp. 133.
80. A main element in this policy was the reimbursement of foreign exchange to exporters who could use this exchange for whatever purpose they wished. They could for instance convert it to domestic currency on the parallel market or use it for imports. The exporter who had made a sale still had to deliver *all* his exchange earnings to the Central Bank, receiving one peso for one dollar. He then had to apply for reimbursement of a *share* of his foreign exchange receipts. The higher the share of domestic value added, the higher the share of receipts refunded. The increasing scarcity of foreign exchange at the official exchange rate forced the authorities to transfer an increasing amount of goods to the parallel market and from 1980, the official exchange for industrial inputs was subject to quotas for which only established producers were eligible. Quotas were drastically reduced after 1980 and by the end of 1984, all imports except fuel had been transferred to the parallel market. An analysis of these recent changes lies outside the scope of the present study.
81. In the beginning of 1985 the official rate was finally devalued with 200 per cent. Banco Nacional del Comercio Exterior (1985), p. 149.
82. Díaz-Alejandro (1975), pp. 134.
83. Ibid., see also Donges (1971).
84. According to Joel Bergsman (1979) the government of South Korea was strongly committed to economic growth, perhaps in large part to compete with the Korean Democratic Republic in the North.

8 CONCLUSION

In traditional economic theory the structure of production, income distribution, etc., is an outcome of the interplay of market forces. Institutions are taken more or less as given and when they enter the analysis, institutional factors are often introduced in an unsystematic and *ad hoc* manner. Now, market forces are extremely important, and throughout this work we have assumed that individual economic actors react (rationally) to market incentives, which means for instance that they are sensitive to price changes. But also the state reacts to price changes, and since government has a strong violence potential, its reaction is not limited to quantity adjustment in supply and demand (as the individual actor in the market model), but it can alter property rights and 'rules of the game' in order to maximize its own welfare function. The unlucky consequences of the behaviour of different Dominican rulers for some vital aspects of the Dominican economy will be summed up in this final chapter. The question whether continued democratic rule will lead to policies which improve the conditions of the majority of the Dominican population will also be briefly addressed.

The Dominican State and Economic Development

The preceding chapters show that Dominican governments have not conformed with the traditional picture of government behaviour in economic theory: that of a benevolent actor adopting policies that aim to improve social welfare. On the contrary, Dominican governments have carried out policies which have primarily aimed at increasing the wealth of those in power. There is nothing particularly 'Dominican' about this behaviour. Rulers can *generally* be expected to pursue personal goals and, as was argued in Chapter 2, the poorer a country the greater the likelihood that politics will take the form of an outright contest over the economic spoils of ruling. We used the term predatory state to describe the system where political power is used primarily to increase the welfare of the ruler. It was argued that many Third World countries fitted this description.

Since the ruler must be able to remain in power in order to increase his wealth, he must be sensitive to the wishes of important interest groups which could give their support to a competing ruler. Thus owners of sugar estates, *latifundistas*, the military, 'large business', etc., constitute groups which have been able to influence government decisions in the Dominican Republic. These groups' ability to increase their own share of national output emanates from the influence on those laws and rules which guide the economic life of the country. The outcome for overall development of this influence appears, on the whole, to be adverse.

The enforcement of property rights and rules which maximize the ruler's utility are according to North usually 'inefficient' in the sense that they lower national income: 'Even the most casual observation from history and the contemporary world would make clear that 'inefficient' property rights are the rule, not the exception.'[1] In this book we have tried to show that policies consistent with rulers' preferences have generally not promoted development. Let us here review some salient aspects and consequences of government behaviour limiting ourselves to the agricultural sector.

The State and International Trade

It has been shown that the Dominican state has not been committed to the promotion of general agricultural development. The state has enforced property rights in land and carried out other policies which have, if anything, retarded rural development. The state has neglected the construction of rural infrastructure such as roads, sewerage and irrigation. It has not taken much interest in improving production techniques, in educating peasants, etc. Two factors contribute to explain the rulers' lack of interest in expanding peasant production (it is of course assumed that peasants' welfare does not enter the rulers' utility functions).

First, an increase in peasant production will not lead to an increase in the ruler's wealth, since policies that would stimulate peasant production would take some time before they resulted in higher output. Moreover rulers have usually had an urgent need to gather income in order to pay those who support them; the military, political allies, etc. There have been other ways for increasing income more rapidly. Another important factor in explaining the weak link between peasant production and the ruler's wealth is that it is difficult to appropriate a surplus (however defined) from peasant production due to the very high transaction costs involved in such a procedure. In a rural sector where peasants, often producing for subsistence, are widely scattered, where communication is poor, tax collection for instance would probably entail very high costs.[2]

Second, peasants have never threatened the survival of the ruler (at least not until recently when government has been democratically elected). Peasants have never really organized to defend their interests. Different factors may account for this lack of organization by the peasants, but factors such as the state's large violence potential and the free rider problem go a long way towards an explanation. The state's superiority in the use of violence obviously makes it very expensive to oppose its rules. The free rider problem alludes to the fact that the individual peasant has little motivation to engage in (costly) activities which could provide the peasant sector with public 'goods' (public for the sector): better prices for agricultural products, land reform, etc. From Mancur Olson's writings, we know that in order for a large group, working for the common good, to be effective, individuals must receive exclusive benefits that are not available for outsiders. The peasants indeed constitute a *large* group and it is difficult to devise such individual benefits.

A better way for the ruler facing high transaction costs is to sell privileges to different actors. To enforce property rights in land and to adopt policies which suit the interests of a smaller group of actors, such as domestic and foreign sugar companies, may be the most profitable option for the ruler. This is also the option which maximizes the ruler's chance of remaining in power since these actors may also have the opportunity to choose another ruler, supporting for instance a rival *caudillo*. The expansion of the country's most important export sector, sugar, can be discussed in these terms. As may be recalled from Chapter 4, the interests of the rulers and the sugar sector were interlocking, and this sector has throughout this century been given special advantages. As was argued in that chapter the institutional set-up was changed in order to suit the interests of the sugar industry. Land laws leading to the concentration of land in a few hands and imports of labour for plantation work were promoted. This accords with North's framework of analysing the state and the behaviour of the ruler. According to North, institutional change will come from rulers rather than constituents since the former do not face the free rider problem, and: '. . . a change in the relative scarcity of land and labor which made labor scarcer would lead the ruler to innovate institutional changes to appropriate increased rents from labor.'[3] In the face of a labour shortage for plantation work the Dominican state took measures to increase the supply of labour through immigration. This was a policy which hurt the interest of the Dominican labour.

Another aspect of sugar plantation exports is worth reiterating here, namely the combination of the rulers' demand for foreign exchange and the existence of transaction costs. The ruler's demand for foreign exchange may derive from his and his group's desire to consume imported goods, to import military equipment and to place exchange in foreign banks. This set of motives describe the situation of Trujillo who as we have shown was heavily engaged in sugar production from the end of the 1940s. An alternative to plantations would be a smallholder system, but to gear small producers to production of export crops would entail heavy transaction costs. Transport costs as well as the costs of creating incentives to produce for exports may well be prohibitively high. The ruler may thus, in order to provide foreign exchange, enforce property rights that increase exports although such property rights may lead to a lowering of overall agricultural production. The enforcement of property rights in favour of plantation exports *may* have had this effect in the Dominican Republic. As shown in Chapter 5, Trujillo's enlargement of the sugar sector appears in part to have taken place at the expense of other agricultural production. Food production *per capita* decreased during the 1950s when the expansion of Trujillo's sugar activities took place.

A striking factor is that conditions have not drastically changed with the transition to democracy. Still the president must reward political supporters and show compliance towards important interest groups. Since the death of Trujillo the state has controlled his industries and much of his vast land holdings. These properties have served to enrich many persons who in different ways have been related to the regime. The military belong to those who have benefited in several ways. Among the Trujillo properties taken over by the Dominican state were his sugar estates, which, as may be recalled from Chapters 4 and 5, are now administrated by the state sugar council, CEA. Different official publications have for a long time repeatedly stressed the need to diversify out of sugar. Yet no such measures have been taken. As argued in Chapter 4, many persons have been able to make large individual benefits from the activities of CEA, despite CEA usually being a loss-making company. Employment with CEA has been a way of rewarding political allies and friends. Decision makers, within government and CEA, do not appear to have any strong incentives to diversify production.[4] Hence the continued reliance on sugar exports despite gloomy prospects on world markets. Still, and this is an interesting aspect of government policy, immigration of Haitian plantation labour is promoted.

There is thus a close link between government preferences and behaviour on the one hand, and trade structure on the other. Governments have stimulated plantation sugar, an activity with low transaction costs; output and income can easily be measured and taxed (if considered necessary) and (imported) labour can be strictly supervised. Peasant output, on the other hand, evades the interest of the state, it is difficult to measure, work cannot be supervised and taxation would involve exceedingly high administrative costs. These are outstanding factors in an explanation of an important feature of Dominican international trade: the combination of a high reliance of sugar exports (and with this a large share of Dominican land resources dedicated to cane) with substantial imports of primary foodstuffs.

Internal Factors vs 'Dependence'

In Chapter 1 it was argued that many Dominican economists and politicians blame much of Dominican economic problems on 'external' factors such as the 'unfair' international division of labour or the vagrancy of world market prices. Prices are said to be unfair and the need for a new international economic order is stressed. 'Dependence' is a usual word for this state of arts.

In this book we have stressed internal factors. Certainly avaricious foreigners have made full use of the opportunities given them by equally avaricious Dominican rulers' greed for wealth and power. But this does not imply that external factors are the culprits. As we have tried to show the enforcement of property rights in land and the adoption of policies in general have been consistent with the preferences of the Dominican rulers and important interest groups, of which *some* are foreign. That the Dominican Republic imports large quantities of food is not a consequence of 'dependence', as argued for instance by Lucas Vicens,[5] but is mainly due to the lack of interest for peasant production among the decision makers. Rulers' lack of interest for peasant production may in turn be explained, at least in part, by the high transaction costs involved in extracting a surplus from peasants widely scattered over a vast geographical area with poor communications. The discrimination of peasants by Dominican rulers is an important facet of Dominican underdevelopment.

This lack of interest in peasant production is not a thing which is limited to the Dominican Republic. The same pattern is clearly discernible in the Dominican Republic's poor neighbour, Haiti,[6] and anti-rural policies are the rule rather than the exception in poor countries, according to Michael Lipton.[7] The backward state of agriculture is perhaps the main problem in many developing countries. At least this is Arthur Lewis' argument in *The Evolution of the International Economic Order*. The best way of achieving a new international economic order is, according to Lewis, to make efforts to transform the backward agriculture: 'The way to create a new international order is to eliminate the 50 to 60 per cent of low productivity workers in food by transforming their productivity.'[8]

There is of course much that industrialized countries can do to improve the conditions for poor countries, in terms of tariff policy, aid, etc., but poor countries could themselves do much more if they adopted internal policies that were more suitable for development. As long as poor countries limit their efforts to a general complaint on the 'unfair' international division of labour things will not change.

Is Change Possible?

The rule of Joaquín Balaguer between 1966 and 1978 was characterized by severe repression, at least initially, and by extensive graft. A large number of individuals related to the Balaguer administration were able to make large fortunes. In 1978 Balaguer's Partido Reformista lost to the Partido Revolucionario

Dominicano (PRD) and Antonio Guzmán was elected President. The PRD maintained its primacy in the 1982 elections when Salvador Jorge Blanco became President. The PRD has traditionally supported thoroughgoing economic and social reforms. Can then continued democratic rule under a governing party which has 'popular' support be expected to lead to less parasitism and to the implementation of policies which improve economic performance and the lot of the Dominican masses?

Whether the misuse of public resources has diminished under the PRD in government is obviously difficult to assess. But it appears evident that persons related to the PRD governments have made large economic gains out of their political position. Parasitism in this form has thus not come to a halt.

Moreover, it might seem ironic that the PRD, who opposed the military and the economic 'elite' during the unrest of 1965, now have to rely on the same military force to maintain law and order when the urban poor violently protest against increasing food prices. It might seem equally ironic that the conservative opposition, Balaguer's Partido Reformista, accuses the PRD government of not taking the difficult agrarian situation and the need for land reform seriously. But these are in fact facets of a political situation where the space for government manoeuvre is extremely restricted. Both government and opposition transfer allegiance (and lip-service) from one group of society to another in order to remain in power (or to try to achieve power) and 'ideology' and the concern about overall performance appears to be of secondary importance. For instance, in order to try to defeat the Partido Reformista the PRD attracted groups which had formerly supported Balaguer. Guzmán thus received the backing of much of the middle and upper-middle class.[9]

We will not try here to evaluate the efforts and the results of the PRD administration in the vast area of economic policy. However we will attempt to show that even policy changes which, at least at first sight, do not appear to be very controversial or inflict upon the interests of important groups may be extremely difficult to carry out. Exchange rate policy is such a policy variable. It is then easy to imagine the insurmountable resistance that will meet changes that really threaten influential groups, such as tax reform and a change of agrarian structure.

We argued in Chapter 7 that a unified exchange rate which would be allowed to reflect more closely the scarcity of foreign exchange could contribute to a better overall economic performance. The present government has shown interest in increasing exports and some incentives have been given. However, to devalue is a highly controversial measure in the Dominican Republic. The exchange rate is a matter of focal interest for the political opposition and a part of the public. To defend the value of the peso is by some considered a moral issue for the nation. More important is perhaps that some important groups that are affected by the price increases that result from a devaluation try to resist such a measure. For instance, Santo Domingo taxi drivers protest violently whenever the price of petrol tends to rise. Thus even if the government considers devaluation to be an appropriate measure it finds it very difficult to carry it out. Through the transfer of more and more imports to the parallel market, a *de facto* devaluation has however been taking place during recent years.[10] By early 1985, all imports, except fuel, had been transferred to this parallel market.[11] This policy has then taken place, it appears, more as a consequence of urgent necessity, official exchange becoming increasingly scarce, than as a consequence of 'efficiency' considerations. The failure to undertake the necessary adjustment of the exchange rate in due time has undoubtedly been harmful for the Dominican economy. As a result of the *de facto* devaluation, and several other measures undertaken by the government, a series of strikes and demonstrations took place which forced the administration to lower the price of several types of goods, mainly basic foodstuffs.[11] This is one illustration of the difficulties which meet the government if it tries to redirect its policies. Carlos Díaz-Alejandro has noted that 'efficient' policies are typically not carried out in countries with democratic regimes:

> Indeed it is disconcerting that neoclassical liberal policies are more often than not pursued by LDC regimes with notoriously illiberal politics, while democratic LDC governments typically provide a good share of horror efficiency stories.[12]

Another case in point is the tax system, which as argued above is to a large extent based on taxes on foreign trade, and then mainly tariffs. However, to change the tax structure is also extremely difficult. A few years ago the government proposed the introduction of a quite moderate tax on urban property. The proposal was rejected by parliament using evasive arguments. According to the former chairman of the Chamber of Deputies, Hatuey de Camps, a recent increase in import duties was in response to the wishes of the entrepreneurial sector, which was firmly opposed to an increase in the value added tax originally proposed by government.[13] De Camps argues that at the decision making levels within the government and the bureaucracy there are individuals or groups that are closely related to the entrepreneurial sector.

Concerning agriculture the PRD governments have increased spending on rural infrastructure but the assistance to peasants is still highly deficient. The discriminatory price policy carried out by INESPRE has not come to an end. Many observers have drawn attention to the negative consequences of the agriculture price policy.[14] However, it is very difficult for the government to carry out changes in food prices. The political opposition is continually blaming the government for the 'high' prices. The government has normally reacted by introducing further regulations. The importance of food prices in the maintenance of social order was expressed by former president Guzmán as follows:

> . . . if we want to preserve social peace, so necessary for the development of entrepreneurial activity, if we want to avoid convulsions . . . if we believe in social justice . . . we must accept and support the programs carried out by INESPRE.[15]

When the prices of some basic foodstuffs were raised at the end of April 1984, riots broke out and dozens of people were killed.[16] This event, as well as those in the beginning of 1985 referred to above, clearly illustrates the constraint on government in this respect.

Despite its earlier commitments to reforms, when in government, PRD has given a low priority to land reform. Wiarda and Kryzanek have argued that the Guzmán government entered office with a renewed pledge to redress the inequalities of land ownership.[17] However, the traditional landowning elite, which had withdrawn its support from Balaguer in response to his land reform proposals, obviously considered the PRD sufficiently moderate in this respect since it appears to have transferred its support to this party. In fact the PRD had criticized Balaguer's land reform proposals apparently in order to attract other more moderate groups to the party.[18] President Guzmán and his closest friends were themselves large landowners and very little occurred in this area. The present PRD administration, under Salvador Jorge Blanco, has not given the work on land reform more vigour. Neither has it tried to reorient public investment, credit policies, etc., towards the peasant sector, despite the fact that the government is well aware of the problems caused by the skewed distribution of land, the deficient rural infrastructure, the lack of rural credit, lack of technical assistance to peasants, etc.[19]

Thus although the government is aware of the inappropriateness of much of present policies it will not try to enforce changes which threaten its survival. This is of course a highly rational behaviour for individuals who want to remain in power but does not lead to measures suitable to promote economic development.

Concluding Remarks

While traditional economic modelling is based on the assumption of voluntary action by individuals facing different options, the present analysis has highlighted the importance of force, or violence, in economic development. The state enforces property rights and rules since it has a strong advantage in violence potential. Now, it is true that individuals make voluntary choices within the institutional set-up. But this institutional set-up specifies the structure of incentives which guide economic actors. This set-up has not been the most appropriate for generating development in the Dominican context. This is why we have given a lot of consideration to the behaviour of the Dominican state, without, however, disregarding that within the limits posed by the state, individuals have reacted (rationally) facing different alternatives. However, the rulers also behave rationally and since they have access to a large violence potential, they have been able to enforce rules which, while detrimental to economic development, have served to increase the wealth and security of the rulers themselves.

One aspect of Dominican underdevelopment to which we have given particular attention is the rural problem. The majority of the economically active population is still engaged in agriculture, with a backward technology, employing few modern inputs such as fertilizer and pesticides. The majority of this rural population live on very small plots, barely sufficient for subsistence, and many do not have land at all.

Landless peasants have to practise a slash and burn agriculture which increases erosion which is alarming for decision makers. The other side of the coin is the control, by a few large landowners, of the bulk of the cultivable land. Much of the land controlled by these large landowners is left idle, and what is used is cultivated very extensively.

The discussion in the present book does unfortunately not allow us to hope that this situation will really change in the foreseeable future.

Notes

1. North (1981), p. 28.
2. See Chapters 2 and 3.
3. North (1981), p. 32.
4. See Chapters 3 and 4.
5. Vicens (1982), pp. 161–6.
6. Lundahl (1979), Epilogue.
7. Lipton (1976). Byres (1979) and Currie (1979) criticize Lipton's argument that there is an urban bias.
8. Lewis (1978), p. 37.
9. Bell (1981), pp. 361–70.
10. See Chapter 7.
11. Banco Nacional de Comercio Exterior (1985), pp. 149 and 375.
12. Díaz-Alejandro (1975), p. 56.
13. See Moya Pons (1983), pp. 56–7.
14. See for instance Despradel (1981), p. 64.
15. Quoted in Vicens (1982), p. 172, translation from Spanish by the present author.
16. See *Latin America Political Report* (1984), pp. 8–9.
17. Wiarda and Kryzanek (1982), p. 56.
18. See for instance Dore y Cabral (1981).
19. That the government is aware of these shortcomings can be seen for instance by the speech by Encarnación Oviedo, Undersecretary of Agriculture, in Moya Pons (1983), pp. 13–28.

BIBLIOGRAPHY

Academia de las Ciencias en la República Dominicana (1977), *Economía Dominicana 1976*, Santo Domingo

—— (1978), *Economía Dominicana 1977*, Santo Domingo

Aldo, A. (1975), 'Desarrollo industrial y promoción de exportaciones en la República Dominicana', *Revista de economía Latinoamericana*, Vol. 11

Alemán, J. L. (1982), *27 Ensayos sobre economía y sociedad dominicanas*, Santo Domingo

Andersson, C., Heikensten, L. and de Vylder, S. (eds) (1984), *Bistånd i kris. En bok om svensk u-landspolitik*, Stockholm

Andreski, S. (1966), *Parasitism and Subversion. The Case of Latin America*, London

Anti-Slavery Society For the Protection of Human Rights (1979), *Migrant Workers in the Dominican Republic*, Report for 1979 to the United National Working Group of Experts on Slavery

Atkins, P. G. (1981), *Arms and Politics in the Dominican Republic*, Boulder, Colorado

Bain, J. S. (1956), *Barriers to New Competition*, Cambridge, Mass.

Balassa, B. (1978), 'Export Incentives and Export Performance in Developing Countries: A Comparative Analysis', *Weltwirtschaftliches Archiv*, Vol. 114

Baldwin, R. E. (1963), 'Export Technology and Development from a Subsistence Level', *Economic Journal*, Vol. 72

—— (1969), 'The Case against Infant Industry Protection', *Journal of Political Economy*, Vol. 77

—— (1976), *Foreign Trade Regimes and Economic Development: The Philippines*, New York

Ball, R. (1962), 'Capital Imports and Economic Development: Paradoxy or Orthodoxy?', *Kyklos*, Vol. 15

Banco Central de la República Dominicana (1961), *Boletín Mensual*, Diciembre, Santo Domingo

—— (1966), *Cuentas Nacionales de la República Dominicana, Producto Bruto Nacional 1950–1966*, Noviembre, Santo Domingo

—— (1980), *Estudio del mercado de divisas propias, 1976–1980*, Mimeo, Santo Domingo

—— (1985), *Boletín Mensual*, Enero, Santo Domingo

Banco Nacional de Comercio Exterior (1985), *Comercio Exterior*, Vol. 35, Mexico

Barraclough, S. and Domike, A. (1966), 'Agrarian Structure in Seven Latin American Countries', *Land Economics*, Vol. 42

Beckford, G. (1972), *Persistent Poverty*, London

Behrman, J. R. (1976), *Foreign Trade Regimes and Economic Development: Chile*, New York

Bell, I. (1981), *The Dominican Republic*, London

Bergsman, J. (1970), *Brazil: Industrialization and Trade Policies*, London

—— (1979), 'Growth and Equity in Semi-Industrialized Countries', *World Bank Staff Working Paper*, No. 351

Bhagwati, J. N. (1978), *Foreign Trade Regimes and Economic Development: Anatomy and Consequences of Exchange Control Regimes*, New York

—— (1982), 'Directly Unproductive, Profit-Seeking (DUP) Activities', *Journal of Political Economy*, Vol. 90

—— *et al.* (eds) (1971), *Trade, Balance of Payments and Growth*, Amsterdam
—— and Desai, P. (1970), *India: Planning for Industrialization and Trade Policies since 1951*, London
—— and Srinivasan, T. (1976), *Foreign Trade Regimes and Economic Development: India*, New York
Blomström, M. and Hettne, B. (1981), *Beroende och Underutveckling*, Borås
Boin, J. and Serulle, R. (1981), *El proceso de desarrollo del capitalismo en la República Dominicana*, Santo Domingo
Bookers Agricultural and Technical Services Limited (1975), *Dominican Republic. Study on the Rehabilitation and Expansion of the Sugar Industry*, London
Bosch, J. (1959), *Trujillo. Causas de una dictadura sin ejemplo*, Lima
—— (1965), *The Unfinished Experiment*, New York
Boserup, M. (1978), 'Uligheten mellem verdens lande' in P. N. Rasmussen (ed.) (1978)
Byres, T. J. (1979), 'Of Neo-Populist Pipe Dreams: Daedalus in the Third World and the Myth of Urban Bias', *Journal of Peasant Studies*, Vol. 6
Cabral, M. J. (1967), *Trayectoria de la economia dominicana 1950–1966*, Universidad Autónoma de Santo Domingo, Santo Domingo
Calder, B. J. (1981), 'The Dominican Turn Towards Sugar', *Caribbean Review*, Vol. 10
—— (1984), *The Impact of Intervention. The Dominican Republic During the U.S. Occupation of 1916–1924*, Austin, Texas
Cassá, R. (1980), *Historia social y economica de la República Dominicana Tomo II*, Santo Domingo
—— (1982), *Capitalismo y dictadura*, Santo Domingo
Centro Dominicano de Promición de Exportaciones (1979), *Estudio de actualización de la oferta exportable industrial de la República Dominicana. Documento I*, Santo Domingo
Centro de Estudios de la Realidad Dominicana (1978), *CERESD 11*, Universidad Autónoma de Santo Domingo, Santo Domingo
Chacholiadis, M. (1978), *International Trade Theory and Policy*, Tokyo
Chenery, H. B. (1961), 'Comparative Advantage and Development Policy', *American Economic Review*, Vol. 51
—— Elkington, H. and Sims, S. (1970), 'A Uniform Analysis of Development Patterns', *Economic Development Report No 148*, Project for Quantitative Research in Economic Development, Cambridge, Harvard Center for International Affairs
—— and Taylor, L. J. (1968), 'Development Patterns: Among Countries and Over Time', *Review of Economics and Statistics*, Vol. 50
Clausner, M. (1973), *Rural Santo Domingo: Settled, Unsettled and Resettled*, Philadelphia
Colegio Dominicano de Economistas (1983), *Posición del CODECO sobre la ley 299, de incentivo y protección industrial y el proyecto de ley 18 que la modifica*, mimeo, Santo Domingo
Connolly, M. B. and McDermott, J. H. (eds) (1985), *The Economics of the Caribbean Basin*, New York
Corden, W. M. (1974), *Trade Policy and Economic Welfare*, Oxford
Cordero (1959), *Analisis de la Era de Trujillo*, Universidad Autónoma de Santo Domingo, Santo Domingo
Corten, A. *et al.* (1976), *Azucar y politica en la República Dominicana*, Santo Domingo
Crassweller, R. (1966), *Trujillo: The Life and Times of a Caribbean Dictator*, New York
Currie, L. (1979), 'Is There an Urban Bias? Critique of Michael Lipton's *Why Poor People Stay Poor*', *Journal of Economic Studies*, Vol. 6

Deardorff, A. V. (1984), 'Testing Trade Theories and Predicting Trade Flows' in Jones, R. W. and Kenen, P. B. (eds) (1984)

Del Castillo, *et al.* (1974), *La Gulf+Western en la República Dominicana*, Santo Domingo

Del Villar, B. (1979), *Hacia donde va el cambio?*, Santo Domingo

Despradel, C. (1981), *Trayectoria de un pensamiento economico*, Santo Domingo

Díaz, A. (1976), 'The Role of Haitian Braceros in Dominican Sugar Production', *Latin American Perspectives*, Vol. 3

Díaz-Alejandro, C. (1970), *Essays on the Economic History of the Argentine Republic*, New Haven

—— (1975), 'Trade Policies and Economic Development' in Kenen, P. (ed.) (1975)

—— (1976), *Foreign Trade Regimes and Economic Development: Colombia*, New York

DiPalma, G. and Whitehead, L. (eds) (forthcoming), *The Central American Impasse*, London

Dominican Customs Receivership (1919), *Report 1918*, Washington

—— (1923), *Report 1922*, Washington

Donges, J. B. (1971), *Brazil's Trotting Peg: A New Approach to Greater Exchange Rate Flexibility in Less Developed Countries*, Washington, American Enterprise Institute

Dore y Cabral, C. (1979), *Problemas de la estructura agraria dominicana*, Santo Domingo

—— (1981), *Reforma agraria y luchas sociales en la República Dominicana 1966–78*, Santo Domingo

Dorner, P. (1972), *Land Reform and Economic Development*, Harmondsworth

Duvál Perez, M. (1977), *Leyes agrarias en la República Dominicana,* Universidad Autonoma de Santo Domingo, Santo Domingo

ECLA (1983a), *Statistical Yearbook for Latin America 1981*

—— (1983b), *Economic Survey of Latin America 1981*

—— (1984), *Notas sobre la economía y el desarrollo de America Latina*, No. 387/388, Jan.

Emery, R. F. (1967), 'The Relation of Exports and Economic Growth', *Kyklos*, Vol. 20

Enzenberger, H. M. (1967), 'Porträtt av en landsfader', *Ord och Bild*, Årgång 76

Espinal, R. (forthcoming), 'Democratic Transition in the Dominican Republic' in DiPalma, G. and Whitehead, L. (eds) (forthcoming)

Estrella, J. (1971), *La moneda, la banca y las finanzas publicas el la República Dominicana*, 2 vols., Santiago de los Caballeros

Evertsz, F. (1978), *Azucar y dependencia en la República Dominicana*, Santo Domingo

Ferrán, F. I. (1976), *Tabaco y sociedad*, Santo Domingo

Findlay, R. (1970), *Trade and Specialization*, London

—— (1984), 'Growth and Development in Trade Models' in Jones, R. W. and Kenen, P. B. (eds.) (1984)

Fishlow, A. (1976), *Foreign Trade Regimes and Economic Development: Brazil*, New York

Food and Agriculture Organisation (1983), *Production Yearbook 1981*, Vol. 35

Franco, F. (1967), *República Dominicana, clases, crisis y comandos*, Santo Domingo

Frank, C. R., Kim, K. S. and Westphal, L. E. (1975), *Foreign Trade Regimes and Economic Development: South Korea*, New York

Galindez, J. de (1962), *La Era de Trujillo*, Buenos Aires

Garcia, E. (1982), *El sector externo Domincano — sus principales problemas y medidas adoptadas por su solución*, Santo Domingo

Geertz, C. (1970), *Agricultural Involution. The Progress of Ecological Change in Indonesia*, Berkeley
Gomez, L. (1981), *Economía politica e investigación social*, Santo Domingo
Gordon, A. (1983), *Plantation Agriculture and Society: Ambiguities in Indonesia's Development Process*, Paper presented at the Arne Ryde Symposium, Lund
Graber, E. (1978), *Strategy, Policies and Programs for Economic Growth and Social Progress in the Dominican Republic: With Reference to Rural Development*, Iowa State University
Griffin, K. (1969), *Underdevelopment in Spanish America*, London
—— (1974), *The Political Economy of Agrarian Change*, London
Grubel, H. (1977), *International Economics*, Homewood, Ill.
Guerra y Sanchez, R. (1964), *Sugar and Society in the Caribbean*, London
Guiliani Cury, H. (1980), *Reflexiones acerca de la economía Dominicana*, Santo Domingo
Haberler, G. (1959), *International Trade and Economic Development*, National Bank of Egypt Fiftieth Anniversary Commemoration Lecture, Cairo
Hagelberg, G. (1974), *The Caribbean Sugar Industries: Constraints and Opportunities*, Yale University
Hansen, B. and Nashashibi, K. (1976), *Foreign Trade Regimes and Economic Development: Egypt*, New York
Hansson, G. (1984), 'Världshandelns utveckling och tredje världen' in Andersson, C., Heikensten, L. and de Vylder, S. (eds) (1984)
Haring, J. E. (1963), 'Dynamic Trade Theory and Growth in Poor Countries', *Kyklos*, Vol. 16
Herman, H. (1981), *Recursos*, Santo Domingo
Hernandez, F. M. (1973), *La inmigración haitiana*, Santo Domingo
Hicks, J. (1983), 'Structural Unemployment and Economic Growth: A "Labor Theory of Value" Model' in Mueller D. (ed.) (1983)
Higgins, B. (1959), *Economic Development. Principles, Problems, and Policies*, 2nd edn, London
Hirschman, A. O. (1958), *The Strategy of Economic Development*, New Haven
Hoetink, H. (1965), 'Materiales para el estudio de la República Dominicana en la segunda mitad del siglo XIX', *Caribbean Studies*, Vol. 5
Hoy (1983), 22 April
Hsing, M. H., Power, J. and Sicat, G. (1970), *Taiwan and the Philippines: Industrialization and Trade Policies*, London
Hultman, C. (1967), 'Exports and Economic Growth: A Survey', *Land Economics*, Vol. 43
Huntington, S. P. (1968), *Political Order in Changing Societies*, New Haven and London
Hymer, S. and Resnick, S. (1971), 'International Trade and Uneven Development' in Bhagwati, J. N. *et al.* (eds.) (1971)
Illy, H. F. (1978), 'Social Control Instead of Social change: The Administration of Land Reform in the Dominican Republic', *Verfassung und Recht in Übersee*, Vol. 11
—— (ed.) (1983), *Politics, Public Administration and Rural Development in the Caribbean*, München
Instituto Azucarero Dominicano (1982), *INAZUCAR*, no. 33
Instituto de Capacitación Tributaria (1982), *Tributación*, Vol. 32, Oct.-Nov.
—— (1983), *Tributación*, Vol. 33, Enero-Marzo
International Monetary Fund (1982), *International Financial Statistics Yearbook 1982*, Washington
—— (1983), *International Financial Statistics Yearbook 1983*, Washington
Johnson, H. G. (1953), 'Equilibrium Growth in an International Economy', *Canadian Journal of Economics and Political Sciences*, Vol. 19

Johnston, B. F. (1972), 'Criteria for the Design of Agricultural Development Strategies', *Food Research Institute Studies in Agricultural Economics, Trade, and Development*, Vol. 11

—— and Kilby, P. (1975), *Agriculture and Structural Transformation*, London

—— and Mellor, J. W. (1961), 'The Role of Agriculture in Economic Development', *American Economic Review*, Vol. 51

—— and Southwork, H. M. (eds) (1967), *Agricultural Development and Economic Growth*, Ithaka, NY

Jones, R. W. and Kenen, P. B. (eds) (1984), *Handbook of International Economics*, Amsterdam

—— and Neary, P. (1984), 'The Positive Theory of International Trade' in Jones, R. W. and Kenen, P. B. (eds) (1984)

Kenen, P. B. (ed.) (1975), *International Trade and Finance*, London

Kindleberger, C. P. (1951), 'Group Behavior and International Trade' *Journal of Political Economy*, Vol. 59

King, T. (1970), *Mexico: Industrialization and Trade Policies since 1940*, London

Kleiman, E. (1976), 'Trade and the Decline of Colonialism', *Economic Journal*, Vol. 86

Knight, M. (1928), *The Americans in Santo Domingo*, New York

Krueger, A. O. (1974), *Foreign Trade Regimes and Economic Development: Turkey*, New York

—— (1978), *Foreign Trade Regimes and Economic Development: Liberalization Attempts and Consequences*, New York

—— (1982), 'Comparative Advantage and Development Policy: Twenty Years Later', Mimeo, *Industrial Institute for Economic and Social Research*, Stockholm

—— (1983), *Exchange Rate Determination*, Cambridge

Kuo, S. W. (1983), *The Taiwan Economy in Transition*, Boulder, Colorado

Kuznets, S. (1966), *Modern Economic Growth. Rate, Structure, and Spread*, New Haven

La industria azucarera en marcha (1955), Santo Domingo

Lall, S. (1975), 'Is "Dependence" a Useful Concept in Analyzing Underdevelopment?', *World Development*, Vol. 3

Lasswell, H. P. and Kaplan, A. (1950), *Power and Society*, New Haven

Latin America Political Report (1984), May, London

Latorre, E. (1973), 'CEA-Dominican State Sugar Corporation', *Sugar Journal*, Vol. 36

Lee, J. K. (1971), 'Exports and Propensity to Save in LDCs', *Economic Journal*, Vol. 81

Leff, N. (1969), 'The "Exportable Surplus" Approach to Foreign Trade in Underdeveloped Countries', *Economic Development and Cultural Change*, Vol. 17

Leith, J. C. (1975), *Foreign Trade Regimes and Economic Development: Ghana*, New York

Levin, J. (1960), *The Export Economies*, Cambridge, Mass.

Lewis, S. R. (1970), *Pakistan: Industrialization and Trade Policies*, London

Lewis, W. A. (1955), *The Theory of Economic Growth*, London

—— (1978), *The Evolution of the International Economic Order*, Princeton, New Jersey

Lipton, M. (1976), *Why Poor People Stay Poor*, London

Listin Diario (1984), 13 Junio

Little, I., Scitovsky, T. and Scott, M. (1970), *Industry and Trade in Some Developing Countries*, London

Livingstone, I. (1968), 'Agriculture versus Industry in Economic Development', *Journal of Modern African Studies*, Vol. 6

Logan, R. W. (1968), *Haiti and the Dominican Republic*, London

Lundahl, M. (1979), *Peasants and Poverty: A Study of Haiti*, London

—— (1983), *The Haitian Economy. Man, Land and Markets*, London
—— (1984a), 'Defense and Distribution: Agricultural Policy in Haiti during the Reign of Jean-Jacques Dessalines 1804–1806', *Scandinavian Economic History Review*, Vol. 32
—— (1984b), 'Jord och fattigdom i Latinamerika', *Ekonomisk Debatt*, Vol. 12
—— (1985), 'Government and Inefficiency in the Haitian Economy: The Nineteenth-Century Legacy' in Connolly, M. B. and McDermott, J. (eds) (1985)
—— and Vargas, R. (1983), 'Haitian Migration to the Dominican Republic' in Lundahl, M. (1983)
Maizels, A. (1968), *Exports and Economic Growth of Developing Countries*, Cambridge
Martin, J. B. (1966), *Overtaken by Events*, New York
Massell, B. (1964), 'Exports, Capital Imports and Economic Growth', *Kyklos*, Vol. 17
McKinnon, R. I. (1979), 'Foreign Trade Regimes and Economic Development: A Review Article', *Journal of International Economics*, Vol. 9
Meier, G. M. (1968), *The International Economics of Development*, London
—— (ed.) (1976), *Leading Issues in Economic Development*, New York
Michaely, M. (1975), *Foreign Trade Regimes and Economic Development: Israel*, New York
—— (1977), 'Exports and Growth: An Empirical Investigation', *Journal of Development Economics*, Vol. 4
Moya Pons, F. (1980), *Manual de historia dominicana*, Santiago de los Caballeros
Moya Pons, F. (ed.) (1982a), *FORUM 1. Los problemas del sector externo en la economía Dominicana*, Santo Domingo
—— (1982b), *FORUM 2. Los problemas de la institucionalización y preservación de la democracia en la República Dominicana*, Santo Domingo
—— (1982c), *FORUM 3. Los problemas del sector rural en la República Dominicana*, Santo Domingo
—— (1982d), *FORUM 4. Los déficits del sector publico*, Santo Domingo
—— (1982e), *FORUM 5. Los Grandes problemas nacionales*, Santo Domingo
—— (1982f), *FORUM 6. Implicaciones de la nueva politica economica*, Santo Domingo
—— (1983), *FORUM 7. Régimen de incentivos el la economia Dominicana*, Santo Domingo
Mueller, D. (1979), *Public Choice*, London
—— (ed.) (1983), *Political Economy of Growth*, London
Munguia, G. (1975), *A Transitional Stage in the Agricultural Sector: The case of the Dominican Republic*, PhD thesis, Fordham University
Munro, D. G. (1964), *Intervention and Dollar Diplomacy in the Caribbean 1900–1921*, Westport, Connecticut
Muto, P. (1974), 'La economia de exportación de la República Dominicana 1900–1930', *Eme-Eme*, Vol. 3
—— (1976), *The Illusory Promise: the Dominican Republic and the Process of Economic Development, 1900–1930*, PhD thesis, University of Washington
Myint, H. (1958), 'The "Classical Theory" of International Trade and the Underdeveloped Countries', *Economic Journal*, Vol. 68
—— (1964), *The Economics of the Developing Countries*, London
—— (1969), 'International Trade and the Developing Countries' in Samuelson (ed.) (1969)
—— (1970), 'Dualism and the Internal Integration of the Underdeveloped Economies', *Banca Nazionale del Lavoro Quarterly Review*, Vol. 23
Myrdal, G. (1957), *Economic Theory and Under-Developed Regions*, London
—— (1968), *Asian Drama. An Inquiry into the Poverty of Nations*, New York

—— (1977), 'Lysande utsikter för ekonomisk forskning', *Ekonomisk Debatt*, Vol. 56

North, D. G. (1981), *Structure and Change in Economic History*, Toronto

Nurkse, R. (1953), *Problems of Capital Formation in Underdeveloped Countries*, Oxford

—— (1961a), *Equilibrium and Growth in the World Economy: Economic Essays by Ragnar Nurkse*, Haberler G. (ed.), London

—— (1961b), 'Balanced and Unbalanced growth' in Nurkse (1961a)

Officer, L. (1976), 'The Purchasing Power Parity Theory of Exchange Rates: A Review Article', *IMF Staff Papers*, Vol. 23

Oficina Internacional del Trabajo (1975), *Generación de empleo productivo y crecimiento economico. El caso de la República Dominicana*, Geneva

Oficina Nacional de Estadística (1971), *6to Censo nacional agropecuario*, Santo Domingo

—— (1980a), *Informativo Estadístico*, No. 14, Febrero

—— (1980b), *República Dominicana en Cifras*, Santo Domingo

—— (1982), *Boletín trimestral de estadísdica*, Santo Domingo

Oficina Nacional de Planificación (1965), *Bases para el desarrollo nacional*, Santo Domingo

—— (1968), *Plataforma para el desarrollo economico y social de la República Dominicana 1968–1895*, Santo Domingo

—— (1974), *Plandes 19. Bases para formular una politica de empleo en la República Dominicana*, Santo Domingo

—— (1976), *Plandes 26. Posibilidades del desarrollo economico-social de la República Dominicana*, Santo Domingo

—— (1980), *Plan trienal de inversiones publicas 1980–1982*, Santo Domingo

—— (1981), *Participación de la mano de obra haitiana en el mercado laboral: los casos de la caña y el cafe*, Santo Domingo

—— (1983), *Lineamientos de politica economica y programa de inversiones publicas 1983–1986*, Santo Domingo

Okhawa, K. (1956), 'Economic Growth and Agriculture', *Annals of the Hitotsubashi Academy*, Vol. 7

Olson, M. (1965), *The Logic of Collective Action*, Cambridge, Mass.

—— (1982), *The Rise and Fall of Nations: Economic Growth. Stagflation and Social Rigidities*, New Haven

—— (1983), 'The Political Economy of Comparative Growth Rates' in Mueller (1983)

Ornes, G. E. (1958), *Trujillo, Little Caesar of the Caribbean*, New York

Palmer, E. (1976), *Land Use and Landscape Change Along the Dominican-Haitian Borderlands*. PhD thesis, University of Florida

Prebish, R. (1950), *The Economic Development of Latin America and its Principal Problems*, United Nations, Economic Commission for Latin America, New York

Quezada, N. (1981), *Endogenous Agricultural Price and Trade Policy in the Dominican Republic*, PhD thesis, Purdue University

Rafael, F. (1973), 'Alternativas de politica industrial el la República Dominicana', *Trimestre economico*, Vol. 40

Rasmussen, P. N. (ed.) (1978), *Om ökonomisk väkst*, Köpenhamn

Raup, P. (1967), 'Land Reform and Agricultural Development' in Johnston, B. F. and Southwork, H. M. (eds) (1967)

Robishek, W. E. and Sanson, C. E. (1972), 'The Balance of Payment Performance of Latin America and the Caribbean 1966–70', *IMF Staff Papers*, Vol. 19

Rostow, W. W. (1971), *The Stages of Economic Growth*, 2nd edn, Cambridge

Rubí, G. (1984), 'República Dominicana: Alcances y limitaciones del crecimiento', *Comercio Exterior*, Vol. 40

Salter, W. E. G. (1969), *Productivity and Technical Change*, London
Samuelson, P. A. (ed.) (1969), *International Economic Relations*, London
Schori, P. (1981), *I orkanens öga*, Stockholm
Schumpeter, J. A. (1976), *Capitalism, Socialism and Democracy*, 5th edn, London
Scitovsky, T. (1954). 'Two Concepts of External Economies', *Journal of Political Economy*, Vol. 77
—— (1971), *Welfare and Competition*, revised edn, London
Secretaria de Estado de Agricultura (1982/3), *Plan de Desarrollo Agropecuario*, Santo Domingo
Secretaria de Estado de Industria y Comercio (1982), *Ley num. 299 sobre incentivo y protección industrial*, Santo Domingo
Senauer, B. (1982), *An Analysis of Foodgrain Price and Trade Policy in the Dominican Republic*, Mimeo, University of Minnesota
Sharpe, K. E. (1977), *Peasant Politics. Struggle in a Dominican Village*, Baltimore and London
Södersten, B. (1980), *International Economics*, 2nd edn, London
Spitzer, D. (1972), *A Contemporary Political and Socioeconomic History of Haiti and the Dominican Republic*, PhD thesis, University of Michigan
Stern, R. (1973), *The Balance of Payments*, London
Streeten, P. (1983), 'Development Dichotomies', *World Development*, Vol. 11
—— (1985), 'A Problem to Every Solution', *Finance and Development*, Vol. 22
Tamames, R. (1968), *La República Dominicana y la integración económica de America Latina*, Buenos Aires
Taylor, C. and Hudson, M. (1975), *World Handbook of Political and Social Indicators*, London
Thomas, H. (1971), *Cuba. The Pursuit of Freedom*, New York
Tullock, G. (1974), *The Social Dilemma*, Blacksburg, Virginia
United Nations (1982), *Yearbook of National Accounts 1980*, Vol. 2
—— (1983), *Yearbook of National Accounts 1981*, Vol. 2
United Nations, Economic Affairs Department (1949), *Relative Prices of Exports and Imports of Under-developed Countries*, New York
US Department of Agriculture (1963), *The Dominican Republic. Agriculture and Trade*, Washington
—— (1972), *Agriculture and Trade of the Dominican Republic*, Washington
Vargas, R. (1981), 'Unemployment, Underemployment and Labor Imports in the Dominican Republic: A Sketch of some Problems', *Ibero Americana*, Vol. 10
Vega, B. (1966), *La República Dominicana ante el proceso de integración economica latinoamericana*, Santo Domingo
—— (1973), *Evaluación de la politica de industrialización de la República Dominicana*, Santo Domingo
—— (1978), *Estudio de las implicaciones de la incorporación de la República Dominicana a la comunidad del Caribe*, Santo Domingo
—— (1982), *Comentarios sabatinos 1981–1982*, Santo Domingo
Veras, R. (1981), 'Cuantos haitianos hay aqui?', *Ahora*, No. 942
Vicens, L. (1982), *Crisis Economica*, Santo Domingo
Voivodas, C. (1973), 'Exports, Foreign Capital Inflow and Economic Growth', *Journal of International Economics*, Vol. 3
—— (1974), 'Exports, Foreign Capital Inflow and South Korean Growth', *Economic Development and Cultural Change*, Vol. 22
Volmar, G. (1971), *Impact of the Foreign Sector on the Domestic Economic Activity of the Dominican Republic From 1950 to 1967*, PhD thesis, Columbia University
Wiarda, H. (1968), *Dictatorship and Development*, Gainesville
—— (1969), *The Dominican Republic. Nation in Transition*, London
—— (1975), *Dictatorship, Development and Disintegration*, 3 Vols., Ann Arbor, Michigan

—— and Kryzanek, M. (1982), *The Dominican Republic. A Caribbean Crucible*, Colorado

World Bank (1978a), *The Dominican Republic. Its Main Economic Development Problems*, Washington

—— (1978b), *Economic Memorandum on the Dominican Republic*, Washington

—— (1981), *Economic Memorandum on the Dominican Republic*, Washington

—— (1982), *Trade and Employment Policies for Industrial Development*, Washington

Yotopolous, P. and Nugent, J. (1978), *Economics of Development: An Empirical Investigation*, New York

INDEX